MW00612796

BOARD N'STONES

Acknowledgements

My wholehearted thanks go to Iku for her assistance, since without her the translation of this outstanding book would not have been possible.

August 2020, Gunnar Dickfeld

The English version of this book is based on the German translation, with occasional reference to the Japanese original. Many thanks to Max for his great help!

October 2020, Peter Gebert

YAMADA SHINJI

HOW TO PLAY GO THE **AI WAY**!

Explained with illustrative diagrams

BOARD N'STONES

『誰でもカンタン！図解で分かる囲碁AI流の打ち方』
DARE DEMO KANTAN!
ZUKAI DE WAKARU IGO AI-RYU NO UCHIKATA
by Shinji Yamada

Original Japanese edition published by Mynavi Publishing Corporation
This English language edition is published by arrangement with
Mynavi Publishing Corporation, Tokyo c/o Tuttle-Mori Agency, Inc., Tokyo

The German National Library lists this publication in the Deutsche National-bibliografie; detailed bibliographic data are available in the Internet at https://dnb.dnb.de.

ISBN 978-3-940563-78-1

Cover design: Lars Decker
Translation: Peter Gebert
Print: Books on Demand GmbH, Norderstedt

The Diagrams in this book were created with
SmartGo™: http://www.smartgo.com

Foreword

This book is intended for amateurs in go who would like to learn and employ the modern AI style. As a distinguishing feature, the "Illustrated Series" („*zukai shirīzu*") shows the explanations directly in the go diagrams, making them easier to understand.

I believe that many people find the AI style confusing because there are so many tactics far away from traditional thinking, such as the early 3-3 invasion. It was like that in the professional go world at first, too. But as there were many pro players eagerly studying the AI style, it became popular among go players much faster than expected. Today it is applied by players almost as a matter of course.

In the beginning I also was very confused myself. But I encountered many studies of the AI style being carried out all over the world, and also game records, and I tried to understand them. I wrote this book with a lot of enthusiasm and I hope that this way everybody can profit from the insights of my studies.

I am very happy to be able to witness this important turning point towards a new era, one in which an AI can defeat humans in the game of go. Engaging with the AI style has given me joy like I have never felt before in go. I hope this kind of joy will be conveyed and passed on through the book.

Why don't you take the transition from the Heisei era to the Reiwa era as an occasion to meet the challenge of a new kind of go? As the author, I hope this book will help you.

One day in October 2019, Yamada Shinji

Contents

Game 1

The first game is an encounter between two strong talents, from China and Korea respectively.
Lian Xiao 9p is a gifted Chinese player who often takes part in international tournaments. Park Yeonghun 9p has already won the Fujitsu Cup twice.

(1 – 19)

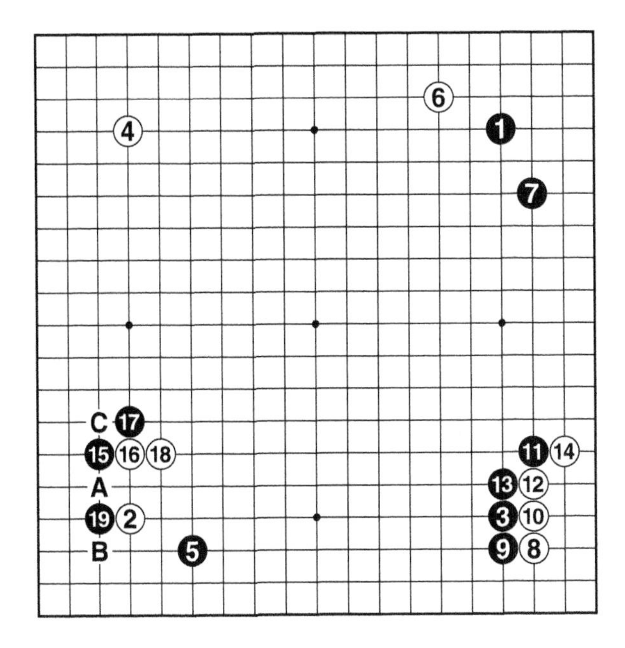

White to play

After the kakari at 5 in the lower left, White played tenuki. In the lower right we see a typical AI joseki. There is a particular way of AI play after Black 19 that you should really know.

Where is White going to continue: At A, B, or C?

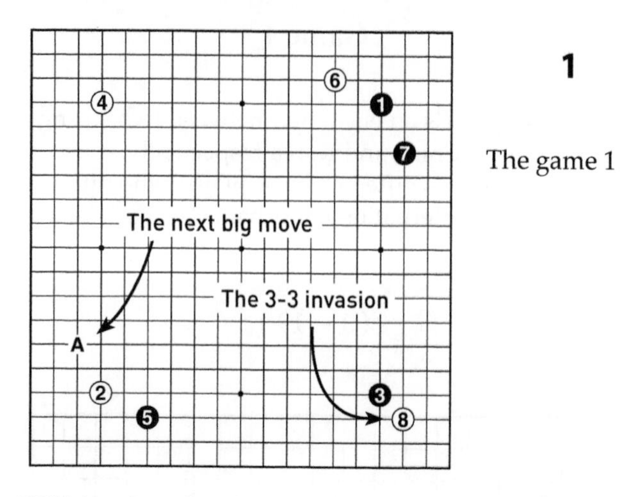

1

The game 1

If White played at A, it would be mirror go. Instead, White opts for the 3-3 invasion with 8. This is the AI style. And indeed there are many situations in which the kakari at 5 is ignored. The meaning of the kakari at 6 will become clear later.

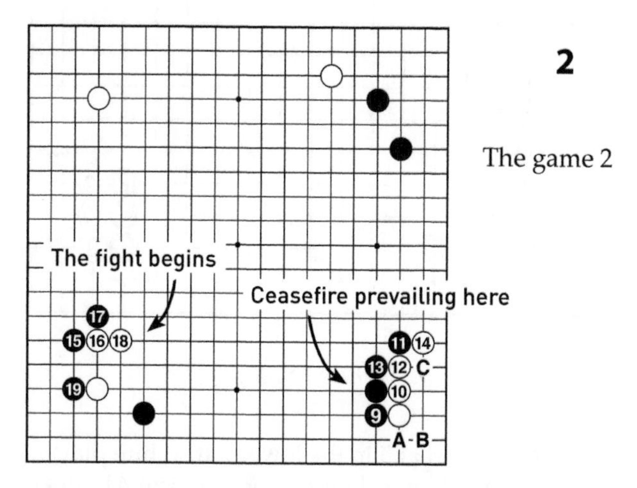

2

The game 2

After White 14, there are variations for Black that begin with A to C. But here he attacks with 15. This double kakari is generally regarded as very big, which is why White would usually not allow it. The AI, however, is not really afraid of this double attack.

3

A Joseki.
A little better for Black

Good for Black
The empty triangle is bad shape
Here's a cutting point

Pushing in with 1 is not AI style. It is an old joseki that has almost disappeared from pro games. Its advantage is that it is so simple, which is why it is often chosen by amateurs.

4

White comes under attack

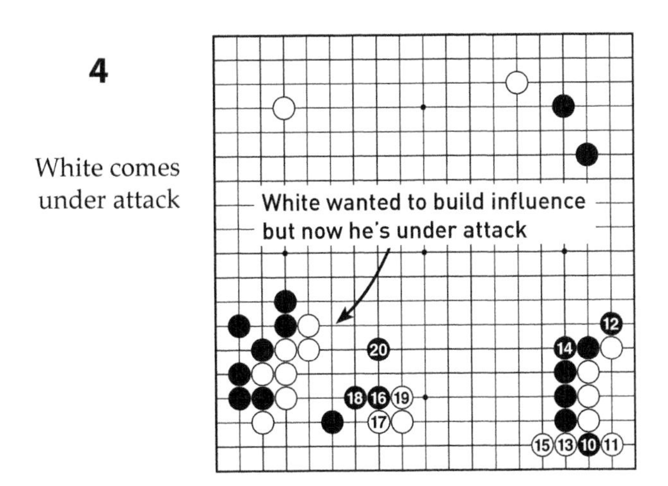

The continuation at the lower edge is an example of Black intending to take sente with 16. After the jump to 20, his aim is to attack White's group on the left. Black will be happy with this development.

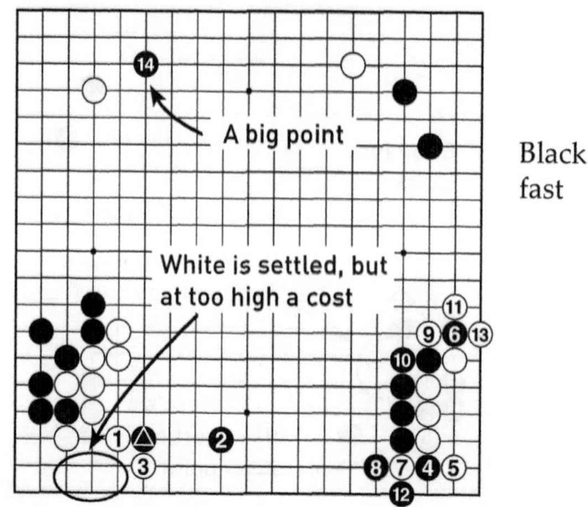

5

Black develops fast

If White continues in the lower left with the kosumi at 1, Black gratefully goes for the sequence of 2 to 9. The marked stone is not important for Black. White 1 and 3 are slow moves. The development up to 14 is good enough for Black.

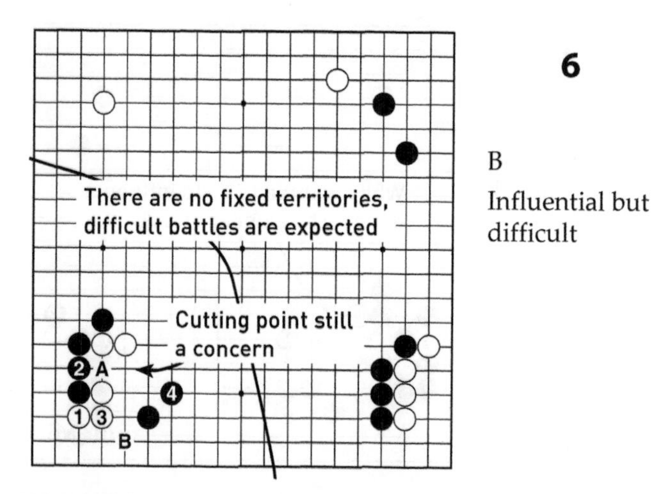

6

B

Influential but difficult

White 1 is a strong technique which has led to new variations. Even if Black now pushes through at A, White can live with B. So White – rather than defending against A – takes sente here.

7

Black engages in the fight

White A next is difficult to play

Black is going to fight

A

The wall is facing White

Among all the different options for both sides, it seems that this one may be worth considering. Black's influence in the lower right offers good assistance in the battle. For White, by contrast, it's a fight without any support.

8

Favourable for Black

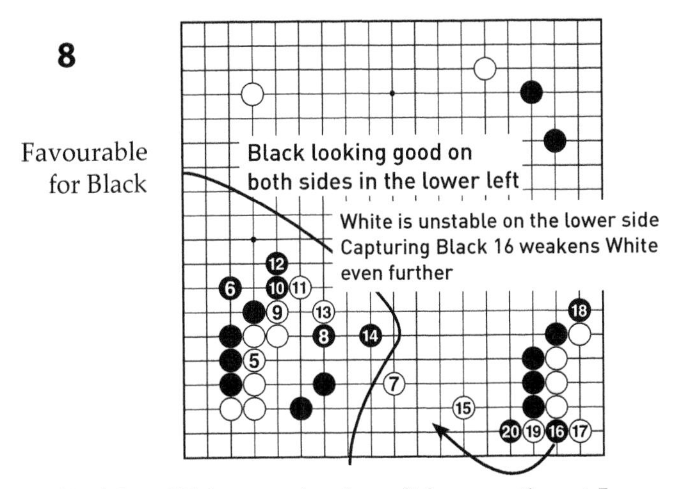

If after all of that, White opts for the solid connection at 5, the continuation up to 15 can be expected. Now Black has a good position on this side. And on the lower right, Black surrounds the corner with 16 – the overall result is good for Black.

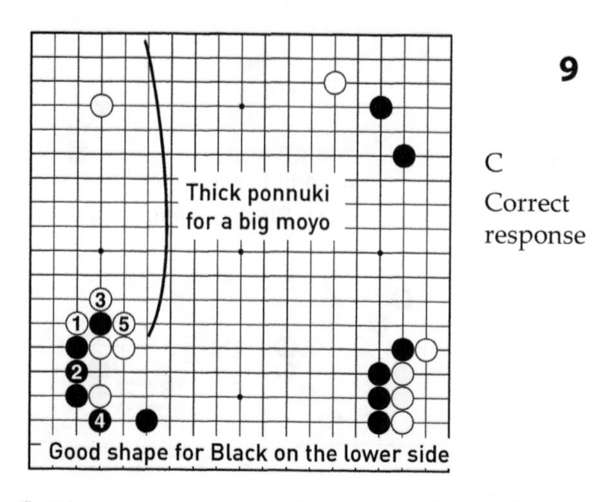

9

C
Correct response

Cutting at 1 is a remarkable move. AI considers the continuation up to 5 to be a little better for White. It is important to make sure that Black's stone can indeed be captured in a ladder with 3.

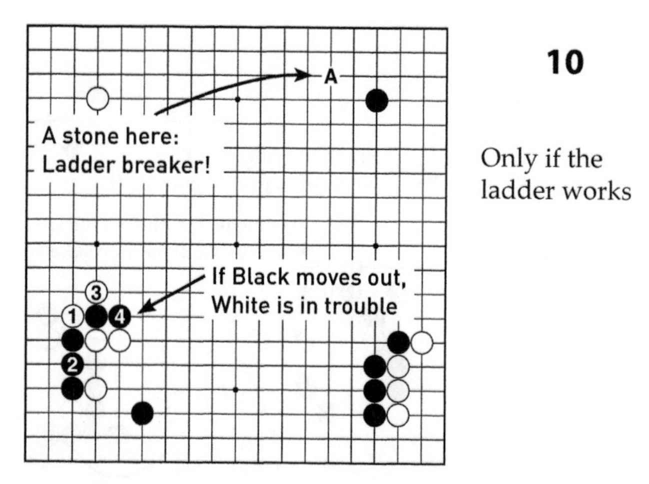

10

Only if the ladder works

An absolutely necessary condition is the ladder after White 3. If it doesn't work for White, Black escapes, and the outcome would be disastrous. This means that an earlier kakari at A is necessary for having the option of this joseki in the lower left.

11

Big corner

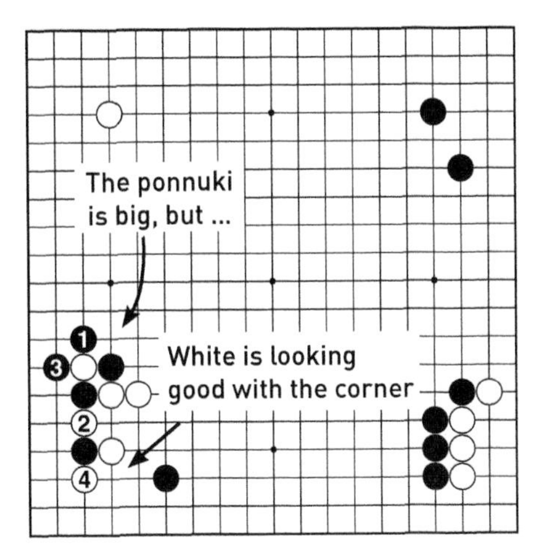

Black plays 1. In case White now extends at 3, then Black at 2 is strong. Instead, White 2 and 4 capture the corner. The shape with a captured stone is good and White is satisfied.

12

Breaking through is not good

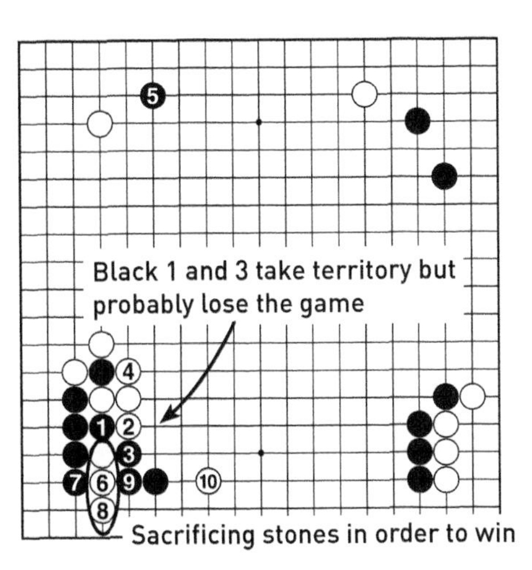

A continuation with 1 instead of Black 4 in diagram 9 is a greedy way of playing. White will sacrifice the corner by first extending with 6 and 8 and then attacking from the outside with 10.

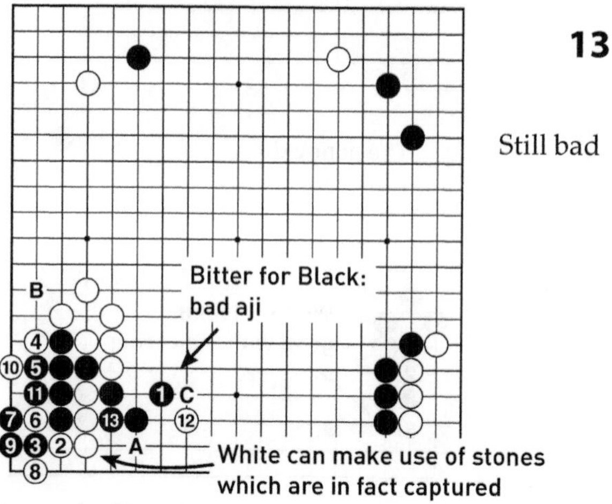

13

Still bad

Instead of 9 in the previous diagram, should Black opt for a big move such as 1, then White 2 to 6 are a strong technique for creating aji. Black cannot play at A instead of 13, because it will make White B sente. White answers Black 13 by pressing at C.

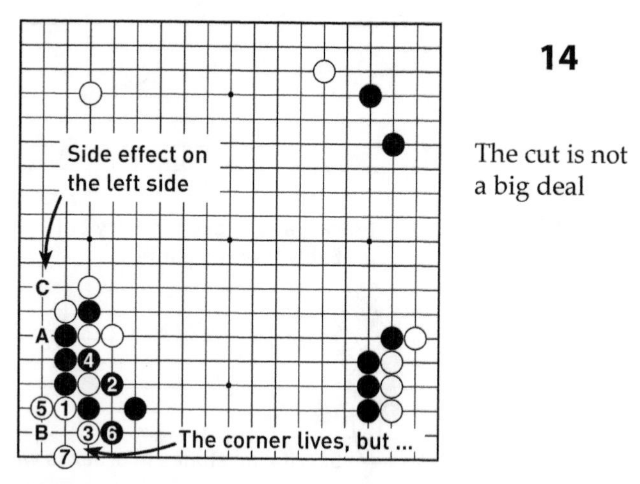

14

The cut is not a big deal

If White cuts after diagram 9, Black plays atari with 2. If White answers at 4, Black plays 5. While White can live in the corner with 3, after 7 there is the danger of a move at A to kill the corner with B, so that Black can jump to C. Playing like this, White hasn't achieved much.

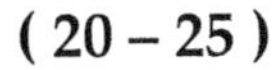

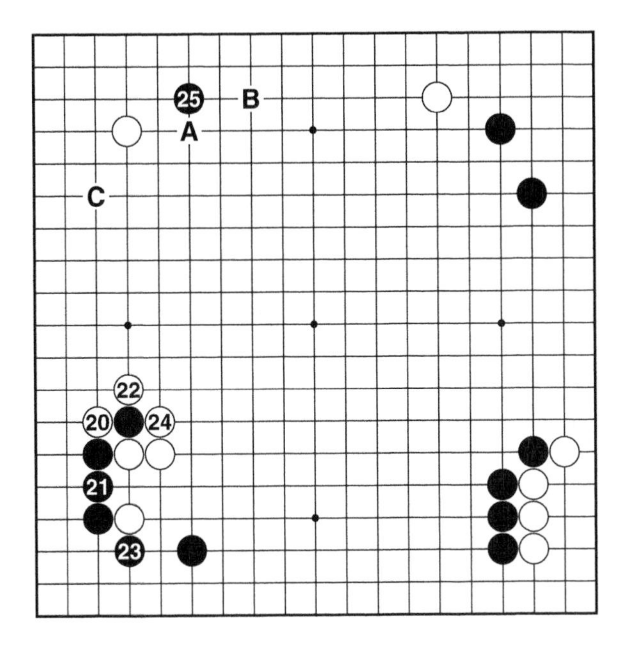

White to play

The figure shows the game position after Black 25. A, B, and C are available to choose from. Don't they all look like classical moves ...? Moves that pro players have identified and rejected as too "soft" can now be freshly evaluated with AI.

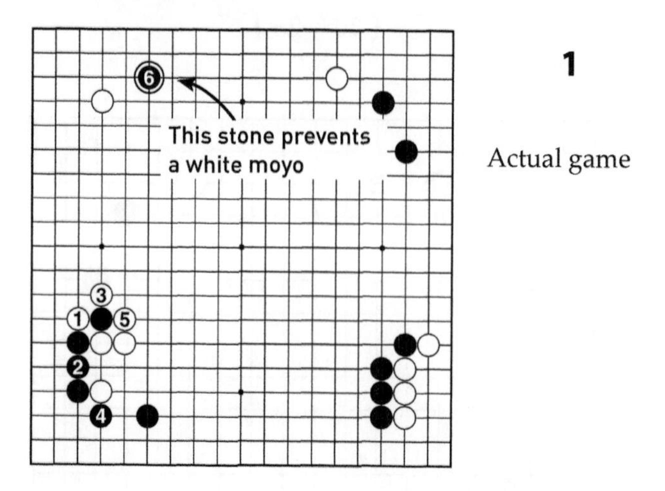

1

Actual game

Once again, this is the solution to the first problem. The kakari at 6 is a good point for Black, because if White would take this point, a huge moyo for White would develop in the upper left.

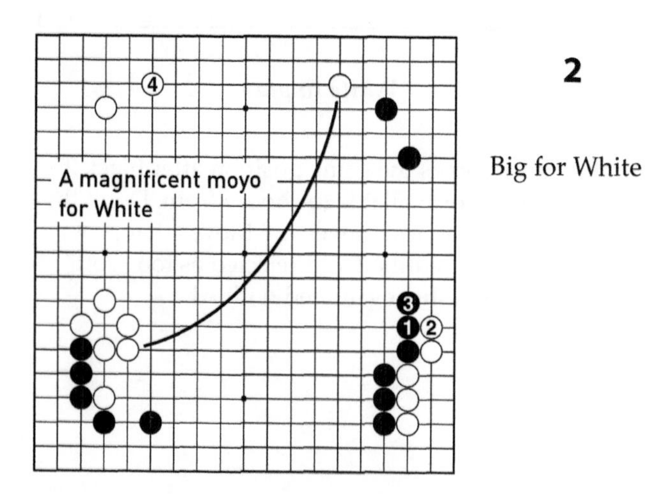

2

Big for White

With a white stone added at 4, the kakari in the upper right, the shimari in the upper left and the ponnuki work together beautifully. A moyo is taking shape. White is not unhappy with this development.

3

B

Concern about the 3-3 invasion

Excellent move in order to devalue the left side

Making use of the thickness is difficult

If White chooses the pincer at 1, Black jumps to 3-3. This is painful for White. White 3 is a standard move, but now Black 10 ends up in a perfect position, as this stone devalues White's thickness. After this, it will be difficult for White to develop a suitable strategy.

4

White's strategy is easy to see through

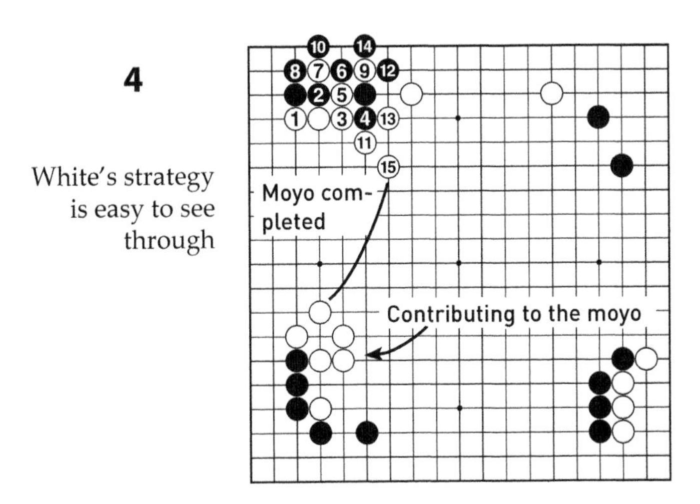

If White wants to make use of the lower group's thickness, he plays at 1. Whether this is a better position than in the previous diagram is hard to say. But it is clear what White wants to accomplish. Now a wide moyo emerges on the left.

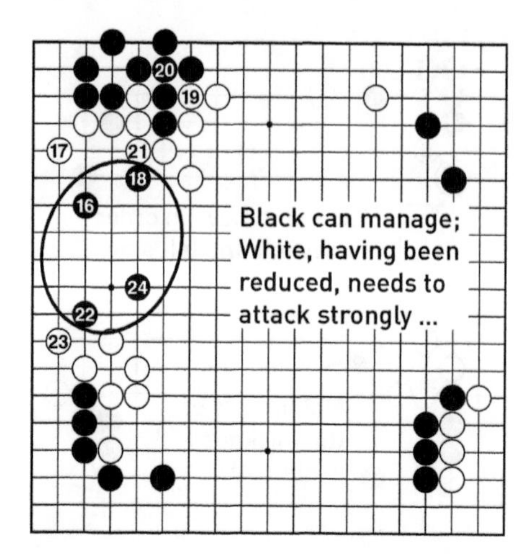

5

White might be weakened

White's position is very wide, and so it offers points of attack. If Black invades with 16, White needs to defend at 21. After Black 24, White must find a strong attack, or will be weakened. While this is a seemingly solid moyo, it is not easily defended against this invasion.

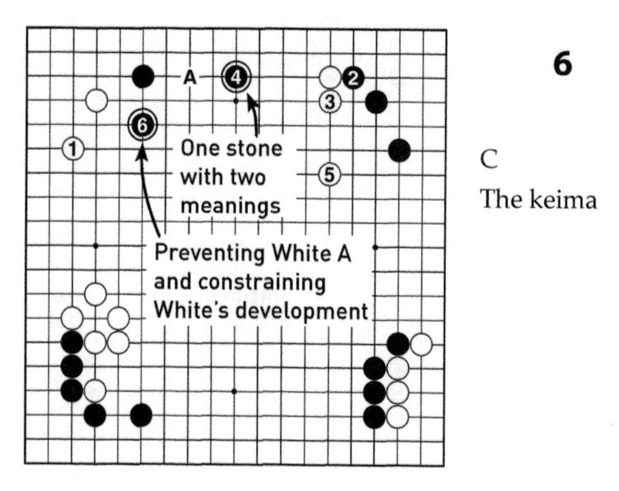

6

C

The keima

The keima at 1 is a normal move, but the kick at 2 and the pincer at 4 form a strong combination. If White now jumps to 5, Black 6 forestalls a White invasion at A. This is a solid development for Black.

7

The hane is perfect

Still active

Almost dead

Playing tenuki after the kick cannot be considered, as Black can make good shape with the hane at 2. This way, Black is not dissatisfied. Now the shapes in the upper left and the right are similar, but the marked stone is very weak.

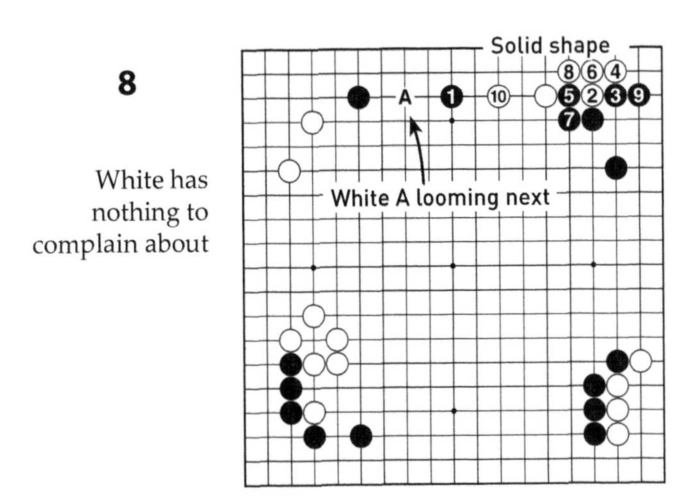

8

White has nothing to complain about

If Black plays 1 here instead of 2 in diagram 6, the continuation White 2 to 10 can be expected. In this case, White would not be dissatisfied. Compared to diagram 6, Black's way of playing is a little tepid.

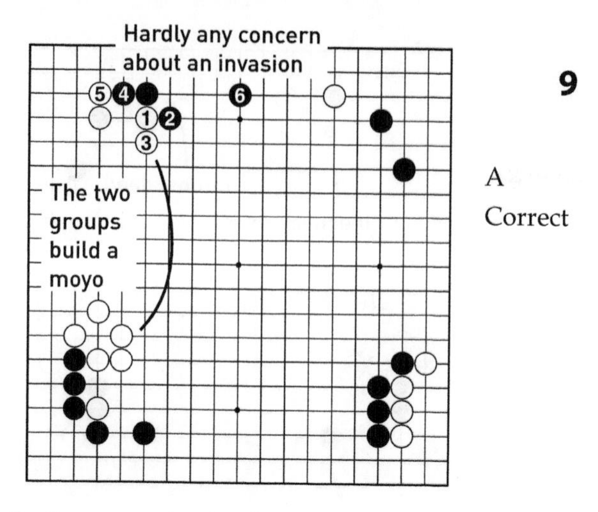

9

A
Correct

In the game, the familiar attach-and-extend joseki was played. Until now it has generally been known as a joseki for handicap games, as it was considered safe, if a little unfavourable. AI however regards it as a strong joseki.

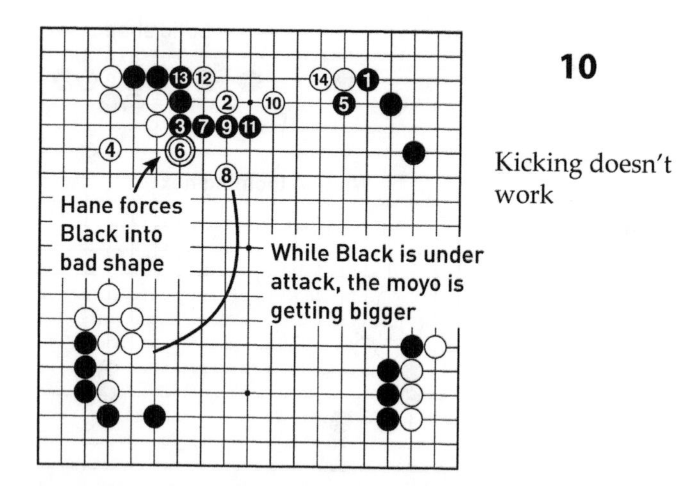

10

Kicking doesn't work

After Black 1 instead of 6 in the previous diagram, White plays tenuki and responds with the pincer at 2. Black boldly plays 5, but now the hane at 6 is strong and the attack up to 14 is a success for White.

11

Tenuki in the upper left, continuing in the upper right

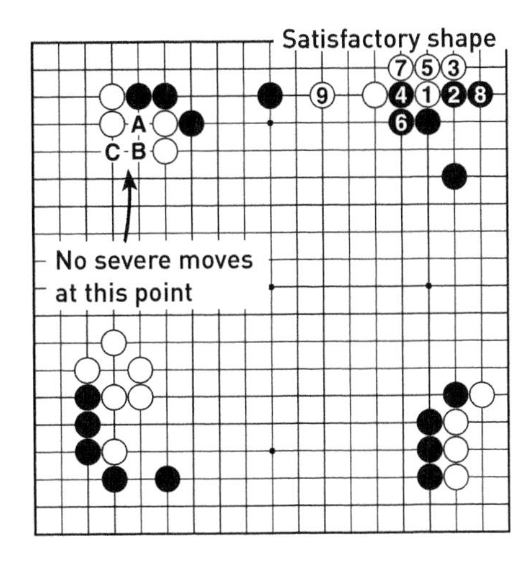

After diagram 9, White puts down the stones at 1 and 3. Black 4 and 6 are normal here. White plays at 9 and gets a satisfactory position. If Black pushes at A, White blocks at B. White need not fear the cut at C, as he will calmly sacrifice two stones.

12

Strong counter-attack against the invasion

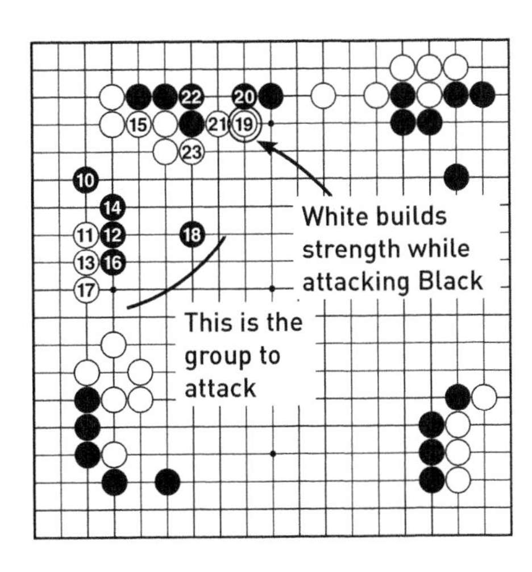

White counters the invasion of Black 10 with 11. As more of Black's stones are added, White needs to connect at 15. White 19 is a good move, as White can make good shape in the continuation up to 21 while attacking Black at the same time.

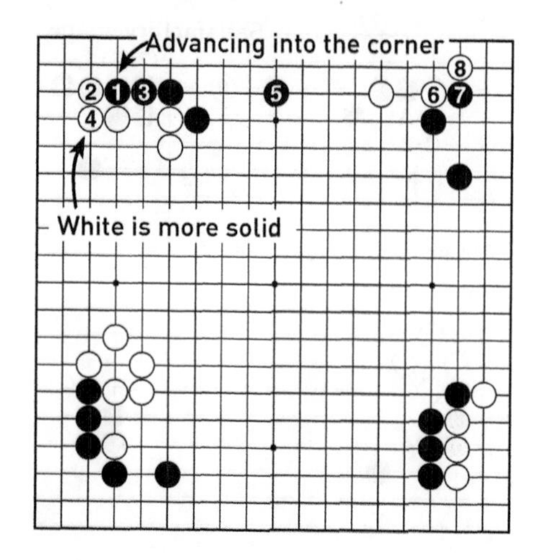

13

Alternative for Black

Instead of 4 in diagram 9, 1 is a strong alternative for Black. If White answers at 2, then Black has advanced one step further into the corner. Conversely, penetrating into the left side is now more risky. So there are both pros and cons.

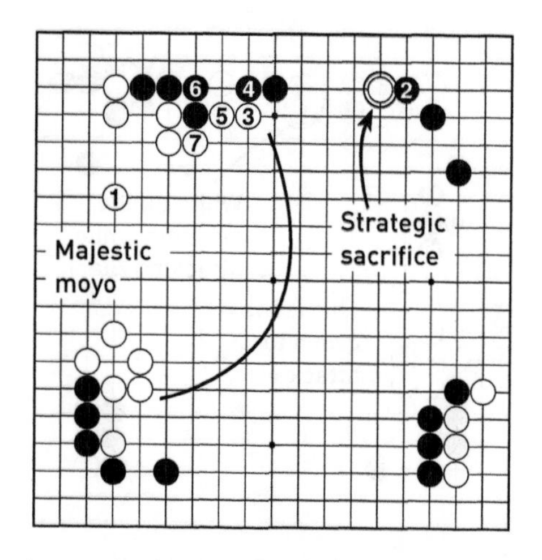

14

Another way for White

As an alternative to White 1 in diagram 11, this White 1 may also be considered. After the kick at 2, White continues to develop his wall. The corner in the upper right is treated lightly. This is another option for proceeding in the game.

15

The game 1

The expected invasion

Attack against White, a simple but effective move

Big move

In the game, Black extended at 1 after the marked stone. This move is hard to find. But this is the move the AI recommends here. It aims at attacking White's stones with 9.

16

The game 2

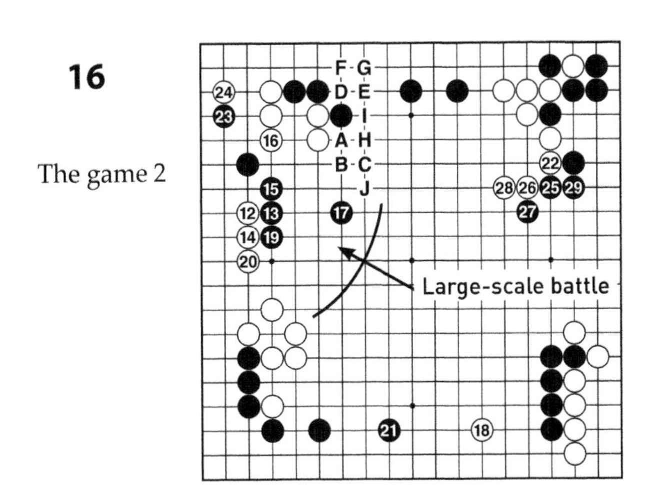

White's answer at 12 is natural, initiating the fight. White responds to Black 17 with tenuki, as White can counter Black A with the sequence of B to J. Instead of White 26, a move at C would also be effective, although it seems a bit trivial.

The game

Moves after 81 omitted.

Black wins by resignation in the middle game.

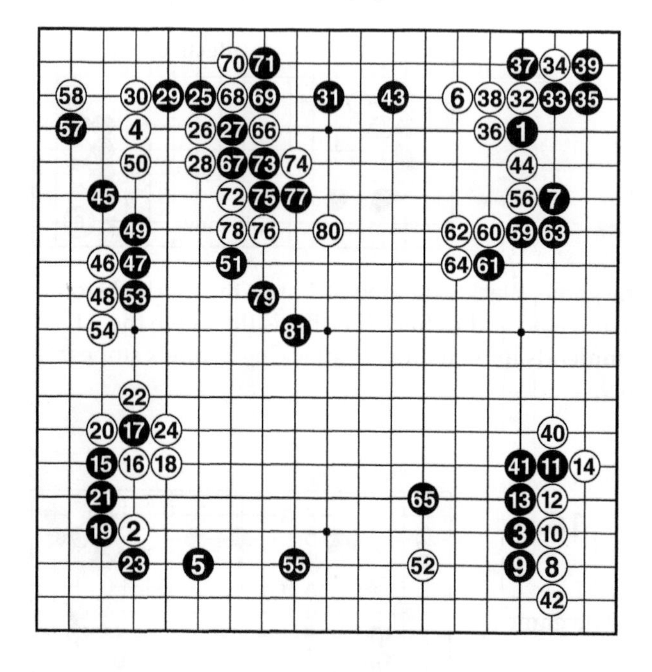

In the second game, two Chinese top players clash in the semi-final of the Bailing Cup: Ke Jie 9p vs Chen Yaoye 9p.

Game 2

This is a spectacular game displaying ambitious techniques, in particular by White in the upper right corner.

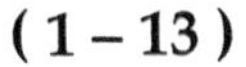

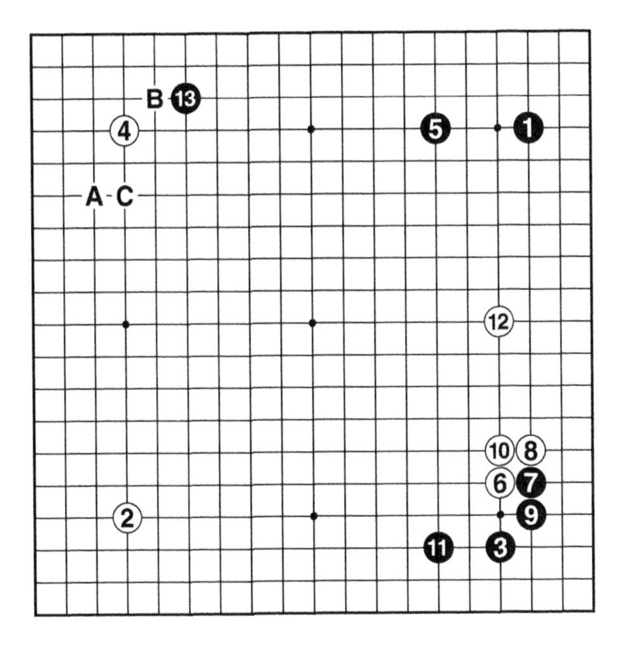

White to play

In his answer to Black 13, White employed the AI style. The move looks bad, however this game will help demonstrate why AI often plays these kinds of moves.

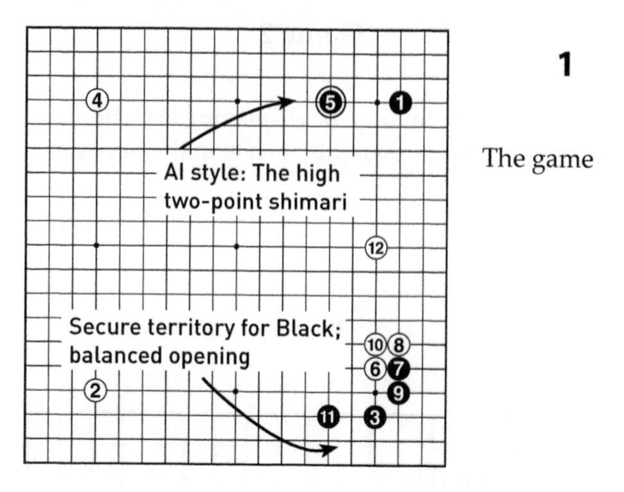

1

The game

The large high shimari is a frequent choice by AI. As a response to the 3-4 point in the lower right, it is common to play the low kakari. In this position, however, the high kakari of 6 is a typical move. The development up to 12 is often seen these days.

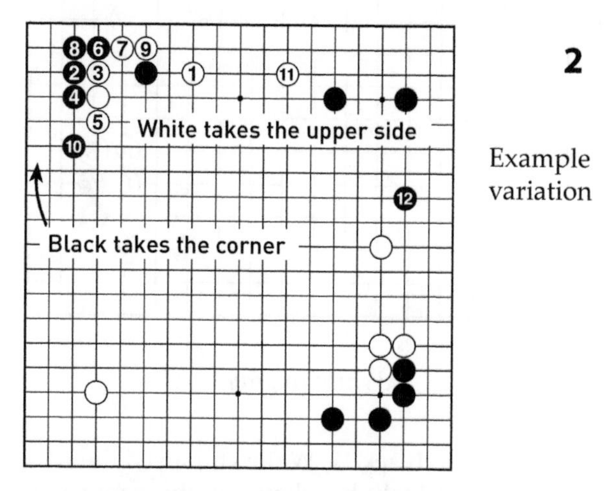

2

Example variation

White can answer the kakari in the upper left with the pincer at 1. The sequence up to 12 shows a possible continuation. All of the options in the initial diagram are excellent moves, their evaluations do not differ dramatically. The AI favours the move that White played in the game.

3

A
Keima

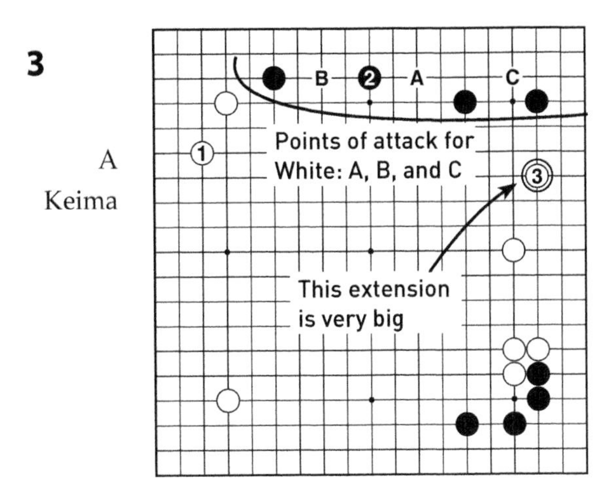

The keima at 1 is the most common response. If Black now plays 2, White gets to make the big extension to 3. There is nothing to complain about in this development.

4

Attach and hane

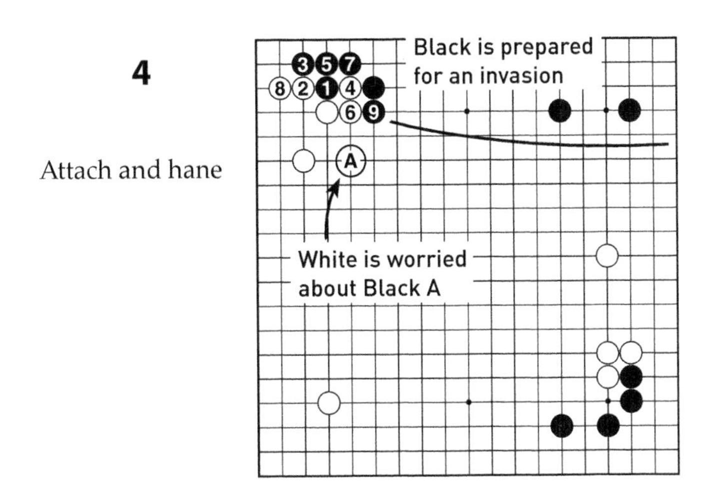

Among all the AI moves, Black 1 and 3 here are very easy to understand, and are also easily implemented by amateur players. Their purpose is to develop the upper side by approaching White. The next point for Black is A.

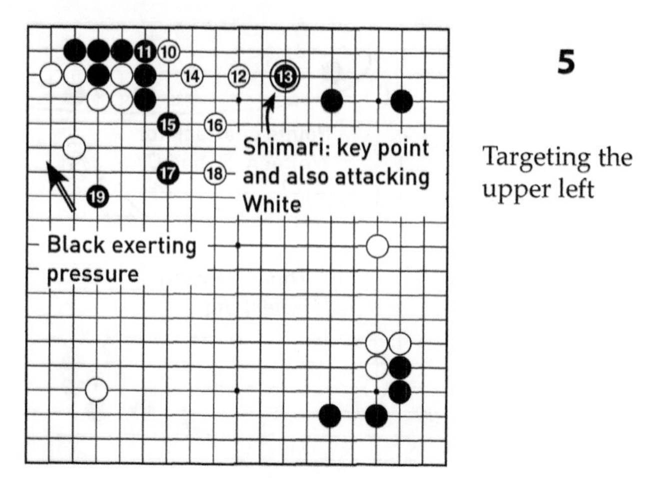

5

Targeting the upper left

If White invades on the upper side, the development up to 19 may be considered. Black accomplishes enough if he can apply pressure to White in the upper left. If White jumps to 13 instead of 12, then Black will strike at 12 himself of course.

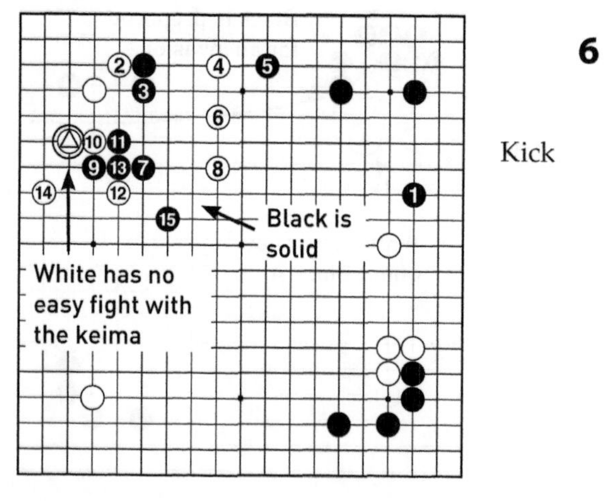

6

Kick

In the case of the keima, the kick at 2 isn't such a strong move for White, once Black has taken the big point of 1. After White 2 and 4, Black 5 to 15 are a common tactic for a counterattack.

7

C

One-point jump

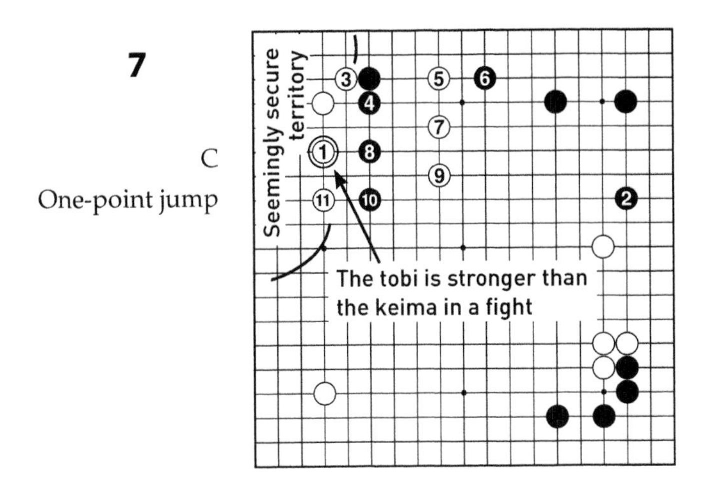

The tobi, i.e. the one-point jump, is a common move, albeit much less common than the keima. It offers the advantage that White can fight more vigorously after kicking at 3, in case Black plays tenuki with 2.

8

Peep from the outside

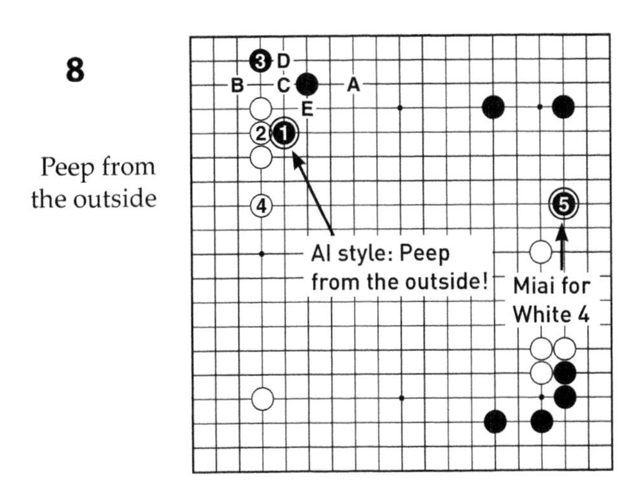

The AI's recommendation after the tobi is to immediately play the peep from the outside at 1. This prevents the sequence of White A to E. Additionally, White B would be inappropriate after Black's slide into the corner with 3. Shown here is one possible variation. In the game, White opted for moves that take secure territory.

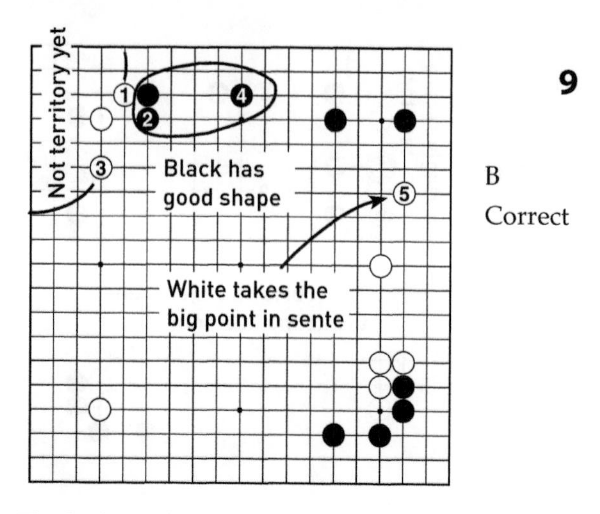

9

B

Correct

The kick used to be regarded as bad, since Black is making good shape and it leaves some weakness in the corner. An aspect in White's favour is that he can take sente after 4 in order to conquer the big point at 5.

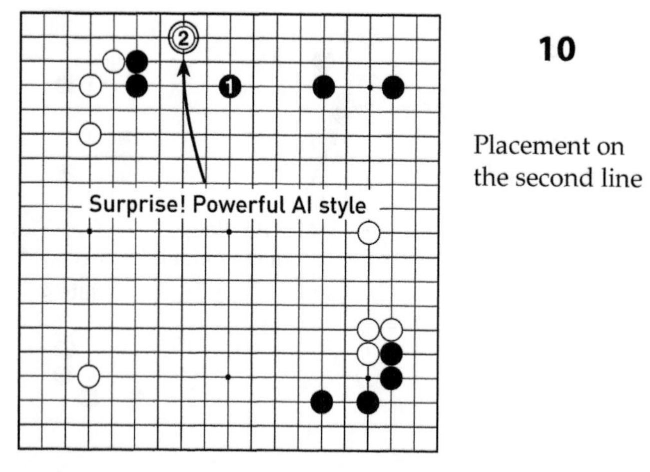

10

Placement on the second line

If Black plays the high extension to 1, White immediately responds with the placement at 2. It is difficult to see how Black should handle this move. I was very surprised when I first saw this move. It concerns not only the corner, it's a strong move on a global scale.

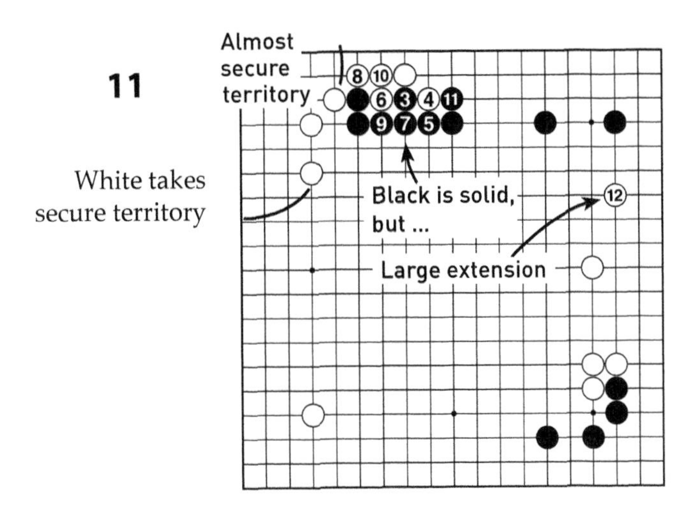

Black 3 is a normal, safe response. If the moves up to Black 11 follow, then White will take sente and conquer the big point of 12.

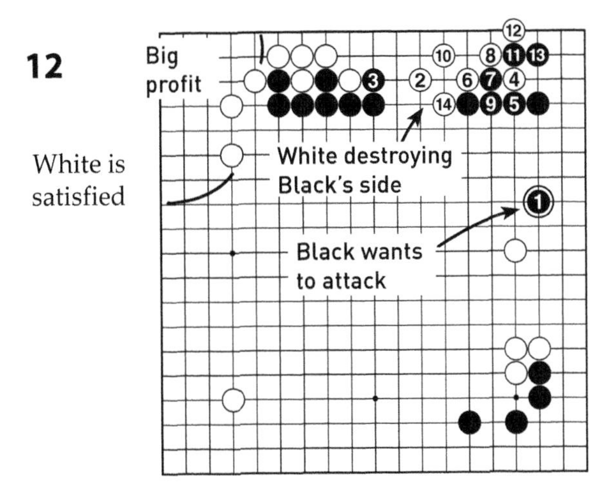

If Black attacks White's position on the right with 1, then White 2 and 4 are a strong combination that lays waste to Black's moyo. This is just one variation, but here Black lets White have secure territory too easily. For White this is a satisfactory development.

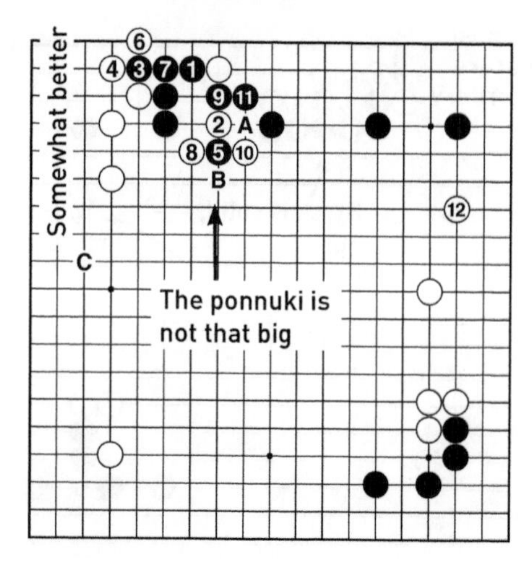

13

Example variation

Instead of Black 3 in diagram 11, the sequence from the kick at 1 up to 11 is a possible variation. Having reduced the upper side to some extent, White turns towards 12. White 11 instead of 10 would be dangerous, as Black separates at A. Next, White cedes the upper side to Black with B and takes the left side for himself with C.

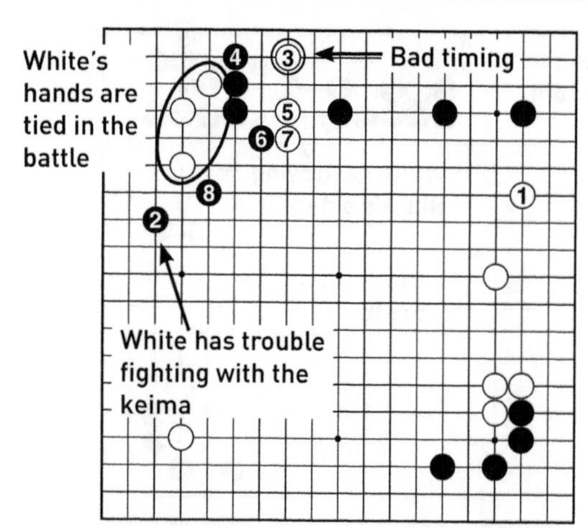

14

Meaning of the early placement

If White made the placement of 3 only after Black played 2, then Black would stand up with 4. After Black has surrounded the corner with 8, White faces a difficult time ahead.

(14 – 19)

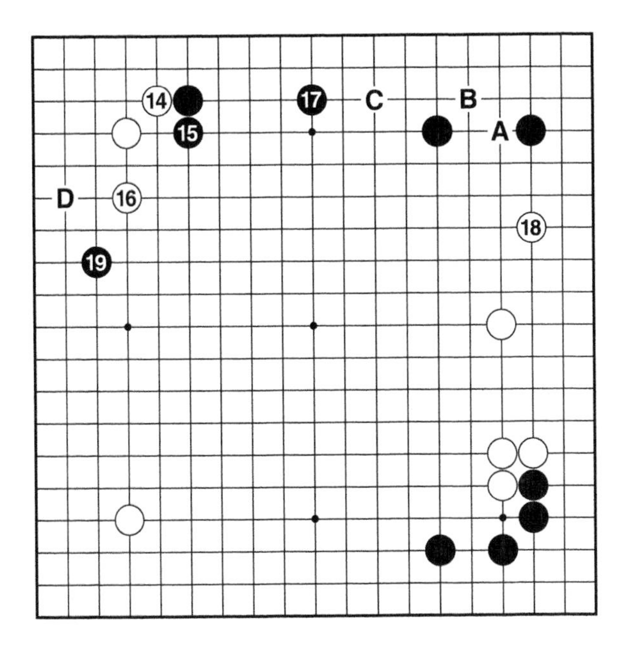

White to play

In the game, Black attacked with the pincer at 19, putting pressure on White's corner. How did White answer?

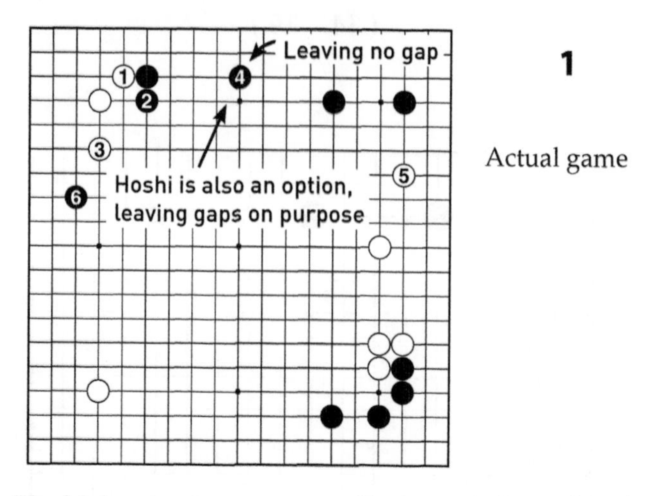

1

Actual game

The high extension seems to offer better balance, but there are numerous players who are afraid of the placement on the second line and therefore play low. In addition, Black's position is safe. There is the drawback, however, that White can reduce the upper side more easily, Black's position being so low.

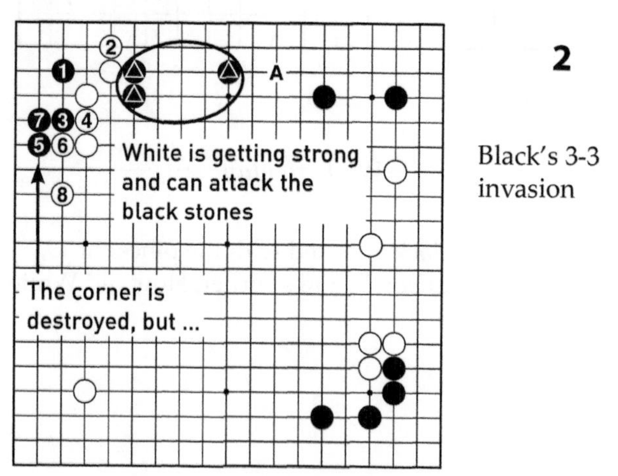

2

Black's 3-3 invasion

If Black jumps into the corner, White can let him live small there. After that, an attack at A is a serious threat that allows White to bring the strength of his stones into play. Therefore the invasion at 3-3 seems premature.

3

D

Passive

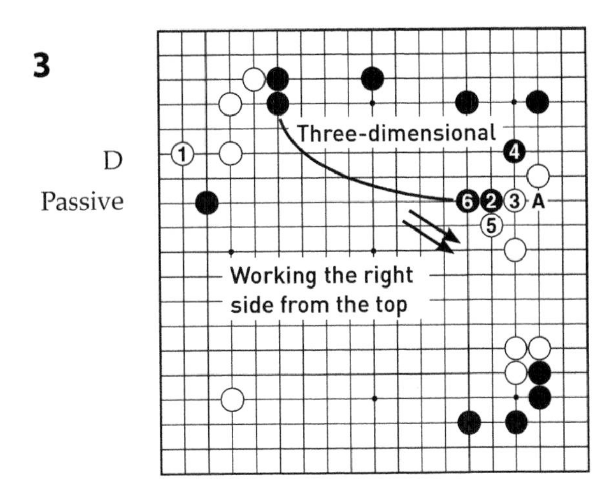

White 1 is a normal but somewhat passive way of playing. Black plays 2 with the intention of attacking the right side while at the same time developing the upper side.

4

Resisting with the kosumi

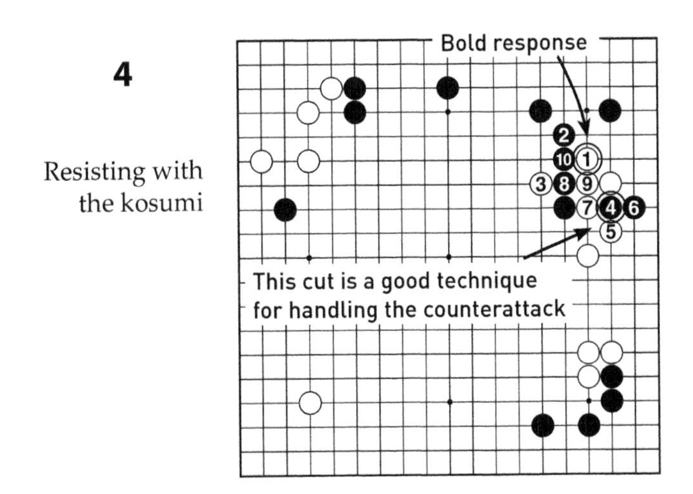

The kosumi of 1 is a bold response. Black takes the opportunity to secure the corner with 2 and to consolidate his position. If White continues with 3, Black attaches at 4. After 5, Black firmly cuts with 8 and 10. This result is good for Black.

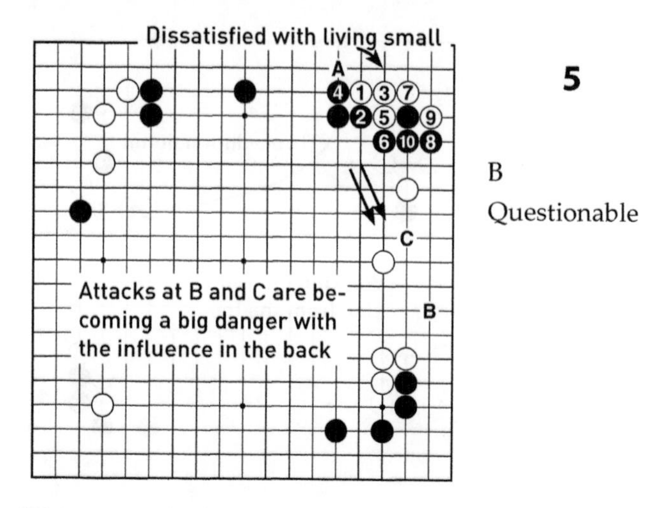

5

B

Questionable

White can ruin the corner with the invasion at 1, but at this stage in the game it is questionable to strengthen Black in this way. White lives after a move at A, but the damage done to the right side is immense.

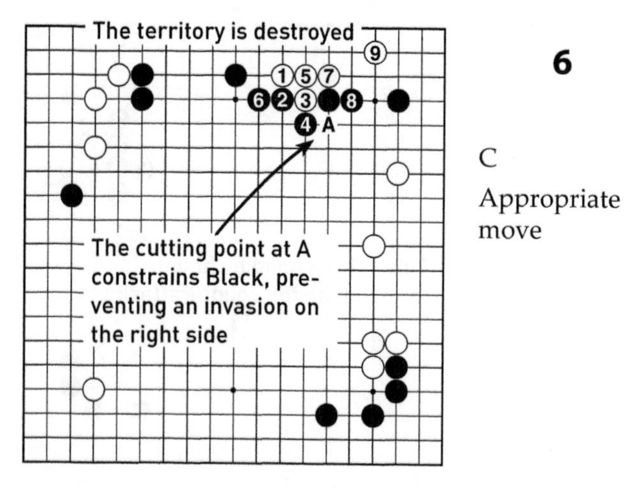

6

C

Appropriate move

The invasion at 1 is a good move for penetrating into the upper side. After 2 to 9, the side is destroyed and White is satisfied. Even though White's life is similarly vague, the position in this diagram is clearly preferable to the previous one.

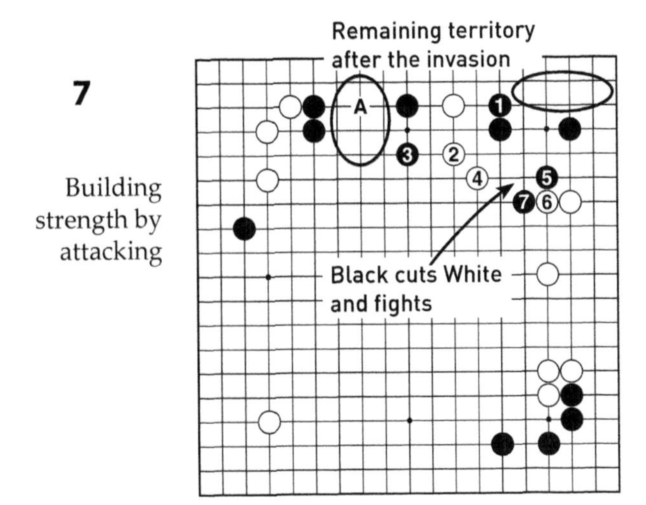

It seems better for Black to push White out into the centre with 1. After White 2, Black attacks with 3. This way Black is also taking care of the weak point at A. After White 4, Black will play 5 and 7 and fight.

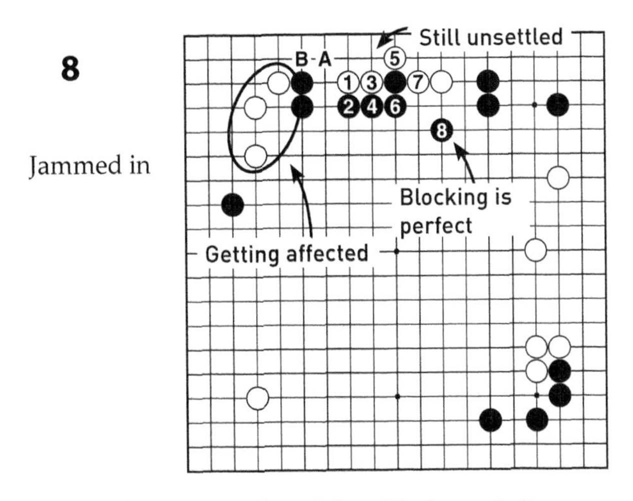

White would like to invade at 1, but Black needn't worry. With the moves up to 8 he can build strength, and if White exchanges A for B, the top left corner will get affected.

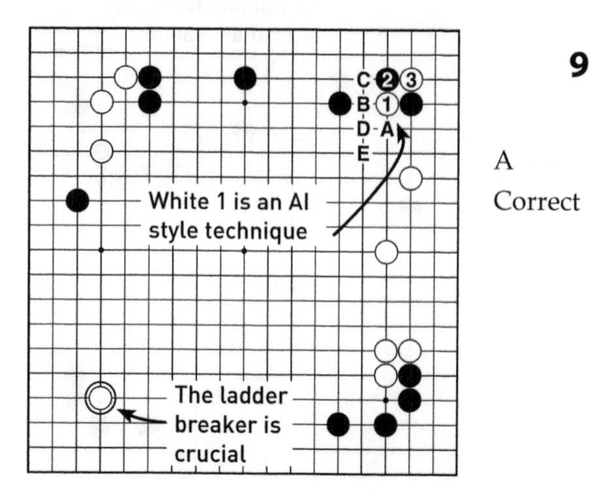

9

A
Correct

White cuts with 1 and 3. No matter how Black responds, White comes out well. At first glance, this seems impetuous, but when Black plays A to E, the result is a ladder that is good for White.

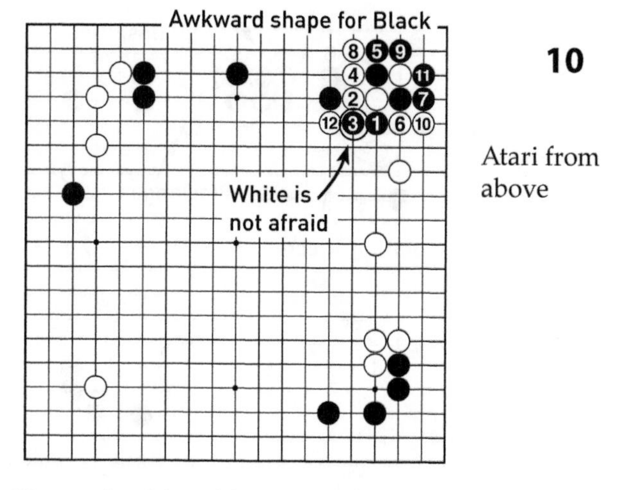

10

Atari from above

The ataris of 1 and 3 are confident moves, but White can make sabaki. After the kikashis at 8 and 10, White cuts at 12.

11

Good enough for White

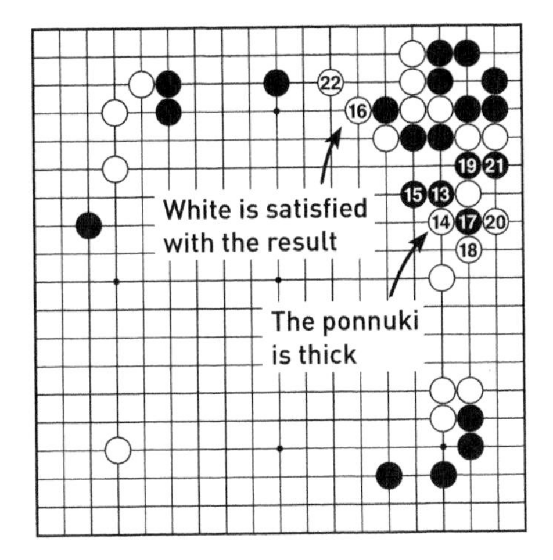

If Black fights with 13, White sacrifices two stones after the cut at 17. The result after White 22 is good for White: The upper side has been broken up and the right side clearly strengthened.

12

Simple and straightforward way of playing for White

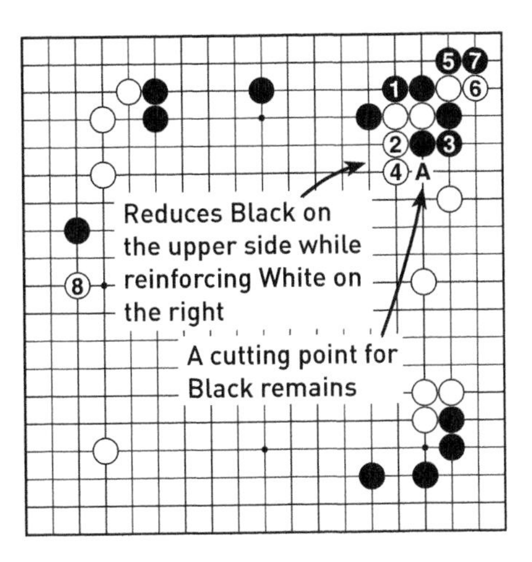

If Black plays the atari at 1 from below, he must defend with 3. Extending at 4 is a straightforward way of playing. Black's position at the top is somewhat reduced, and White strengthens the right side. In the game White extended at 5 instead, getting an even better result.

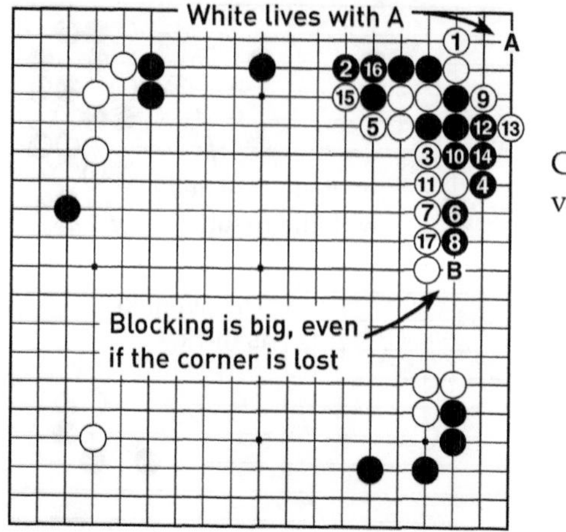

13

Complicated variation

In the game, White continued with 1 and 3. At this point it may be considered that Black will not take the corner and attaches at 4 instead. White ignores this move and responds at 5. This is a difficult fight; the chosen continuation up to 17 is playable for White.

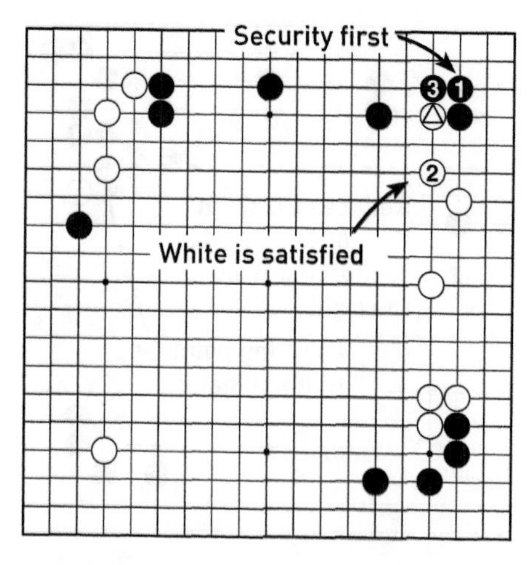

14

Reasonable response for Black

If White attaches with the marked stone, Black 1 is a reasonable way of playing, and White jumps to 2. White's position seems a little better, but Black has chosen a safe variation that aims for a long game.

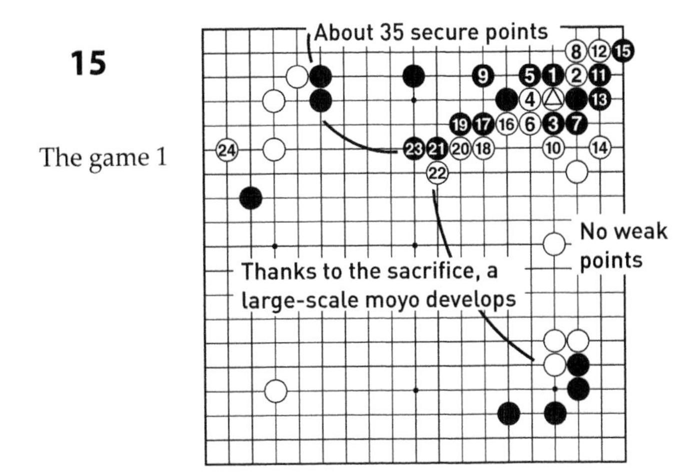

15

The game 1

After the attachment △, Black played 1 and the sequence up to 23 followed. The figure illustrates White's strategy of sacrificing the corner in order to strengthen his position. White is satisfied. He takes sente and defends the still-open corner with 24.

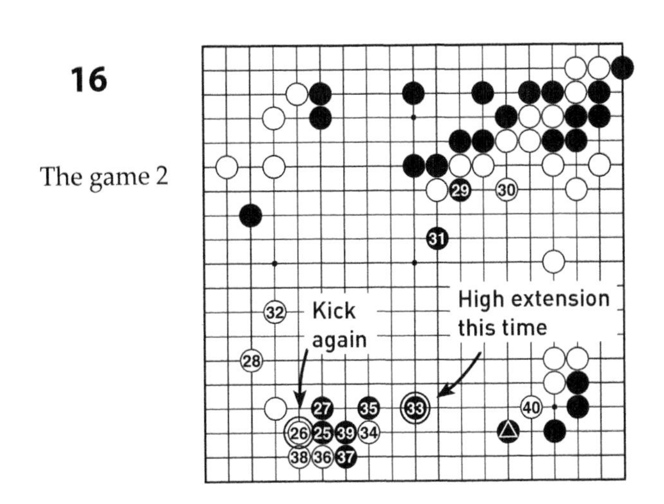

16

The game 2

With 26, White chose the kick again. Black judged the threat of an invasion to be small and therefore picked the high extension, as its position is in better balance with the marked stone than the low one's. White played the hane-and-connect and eventually took sente for 40.

The game

Moves after 91 omitted.
Black wins by 1.5 points.

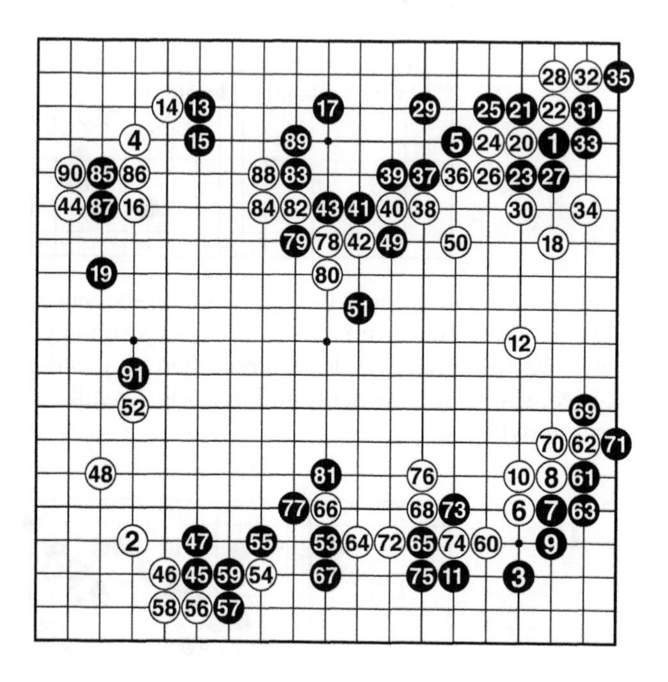

The next game is an encounter between Iyama Yuta 9p and Shibano Toramaru 9p in the Meijin League. At this time, Iyama holds seven big titles, while Shibano is an emerging 19-year-old whose remarkable results attract attention. When this book is published, I'm sure Shibano will already have won the Meijin.*

* (And indeed: On 7 Oct 2019, Shibano won the 44th Meijin, 4–1.)

Game 3

In the upper left corner, a popular variation of an AI joseki was played. If you're not familiar with it, you're well advised to have a look.

(1 – 10)

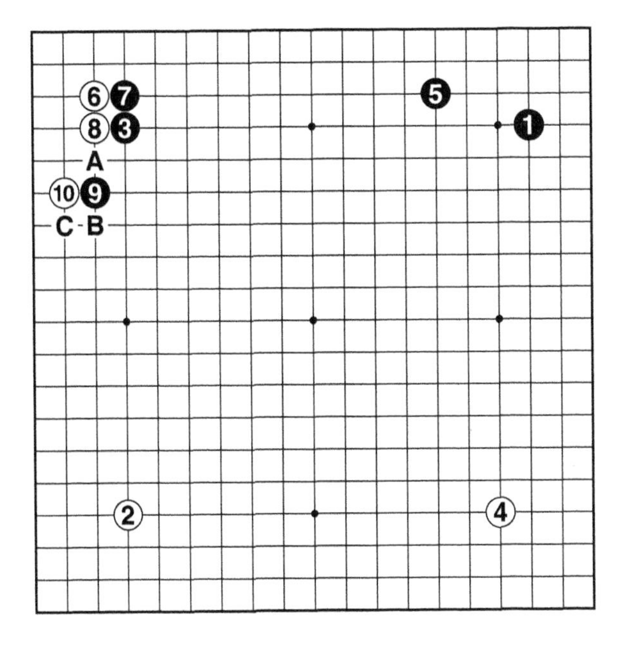

Black to play

After Black 9, a move at A is the most common response for White. There is a subtle difference, however, if White first attaches at 10.

In the game, Black tried not to play to White's expectations and went for a complicated variation.

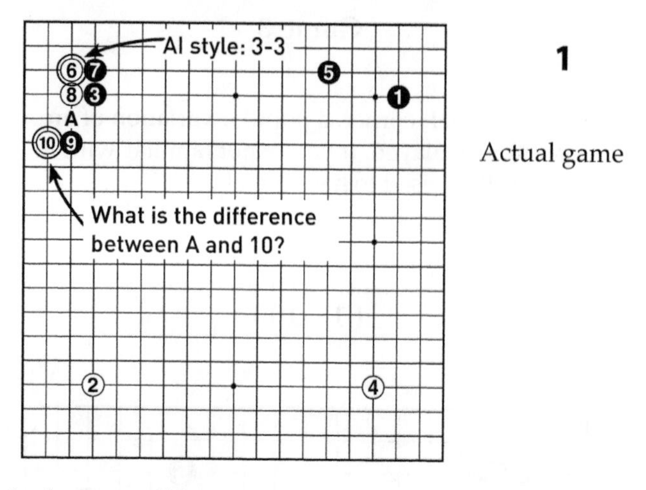

1

Actual game

In the game, White invaded at 3-3, and the sequence up to 10 was played. The 3-3 joseki have been studied extensively – with the help of AI – and as a result, many new variations have emerged over the last few years. The one that was chosen here is one of these modern developments.

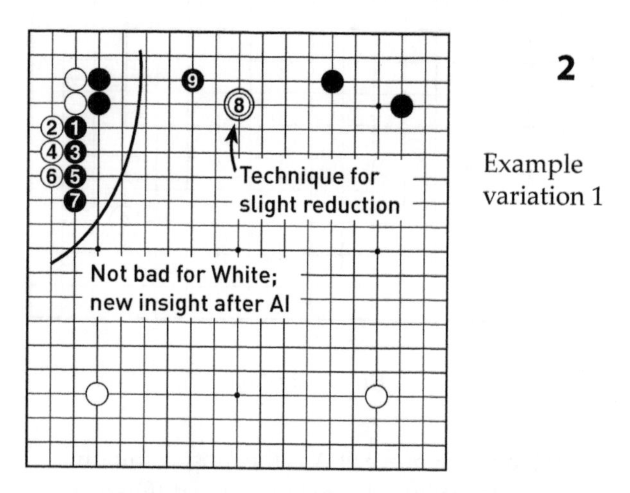

2

Example variation 1

The seasoned joseki with Black 1 and 3 is no longer seen in the world of pros. The AI regards the position after 7 as somewhat unsatisfactory for Black. Up until a few years ago this result would have been seen as bad for White.

3

Example variation 2

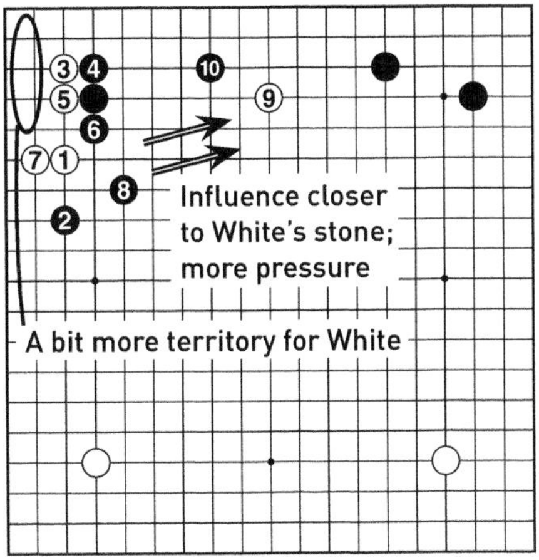

People are still reluctant to play the 3-3 invasion, thinking they are bound to play the sequence in example diagram 1, and not liking the result for White. Let's compare the previous position with a similar standard joseki.

The joseki in example variation 2 is considered somewhat unfavourable for Black if Black doesn't have a stone at 9. The AI's estimate of the position is also that White has a bit of an advantage. But AI also says that White has a somewhat bigger advantage with the joseki in example variation 1.

When you hear that Black's position here is a little better than the normal joseki, can you appreciate that the 3-3 invasion has gained in importance?

There will be further explanation of the 3-3 invasion below, however there are many complicated variations. That's why it is important to be aware of them – you cannot simply invade at 3-3 and not be sensitive to the fact that White can be comfortable with the result of the moderate shape in the last diagram.

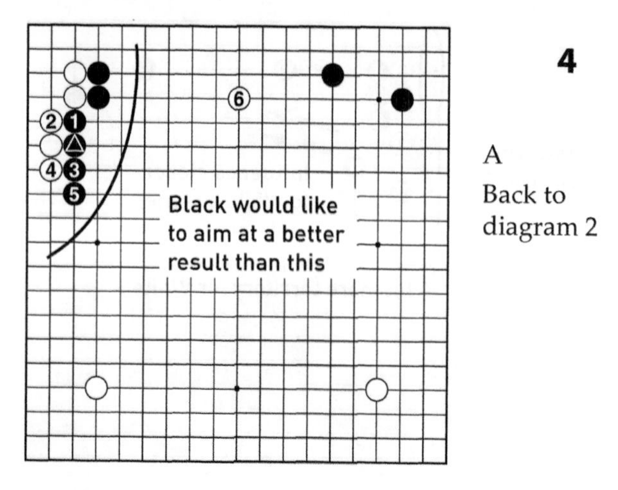

4

A

Back to diagram 2

With A, Black reverts to diagram 2. If you're happy with this, feel free to play Black 1. However, if you already have the marked stone in place, you might like to aim for a better result.

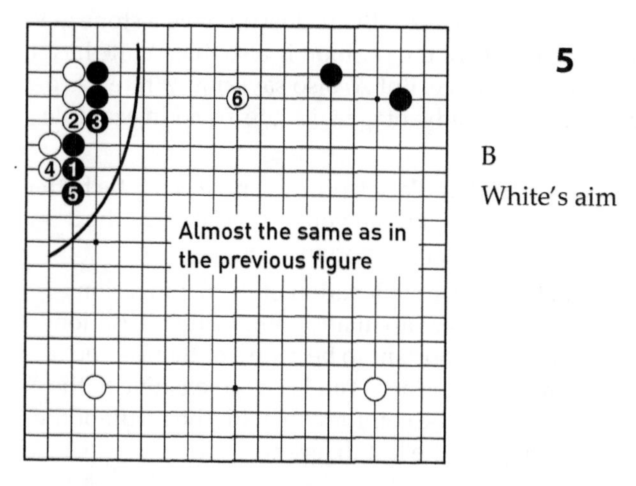

5

B

White's aim

Extending at 1 is normal, but the result is exactly what White wants. The reason for this is shown in the next diagram.

6

Better way for Black

B A C D

This is mainstream

Extending is unnecessary

After White 1, Black 2, and White 3 are played, Black does not need to extend but can play tenuki with 4, or attack the corner in the upper left with A to C. There exist only few examples where D was played. In the previous diagram Black was forced to play at D.

7

Tenuki is unsafe

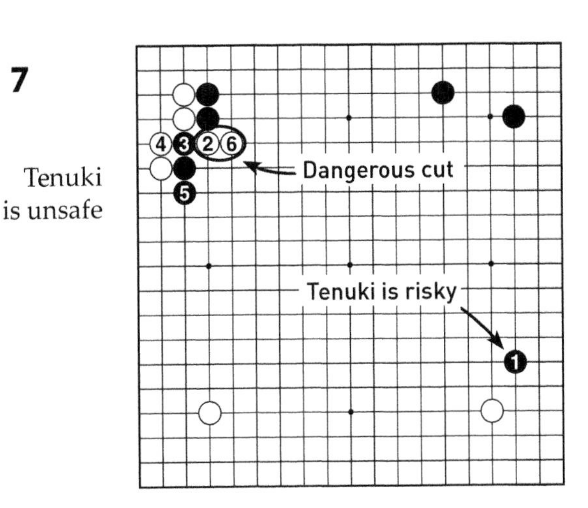

Playing tenuki and allowing White 2 is questionable. After White extends at 6, Black is facing problems. So rather than at 1, he will instead play in the upper left corner.

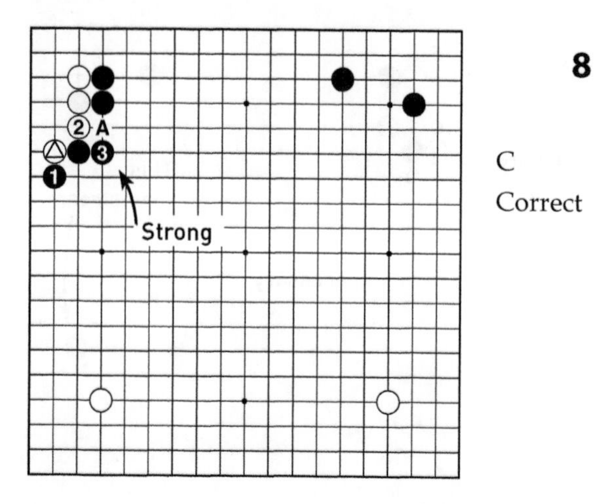

8

C
Correct

Blocking at 1 is a severe move that causes White to regret having played the marked stone. Before, Black would almost always have played at A after White 2. The new variations are explained in the following diagrams.

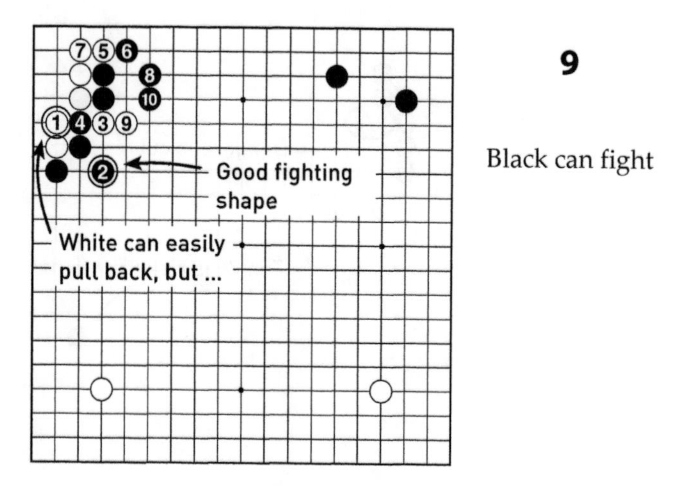

9

Black can fight

If White 1, then Black 2, and White will run out at 3. But this is not a bad fight for Black.

10

If White cuts on the outside

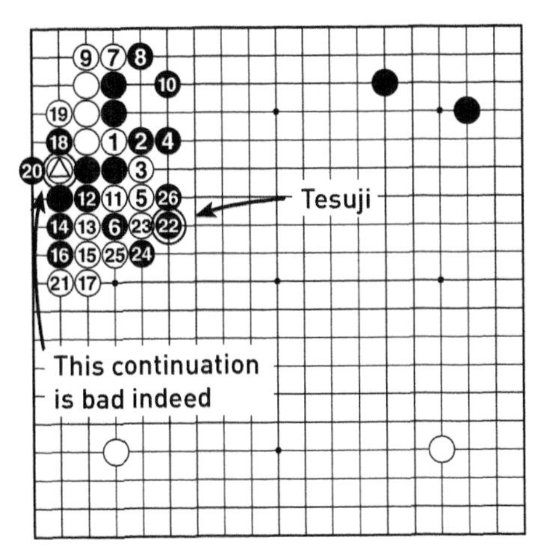

As a continuation of diagram 8, White might cut on the outside at 3 after 1 and Black 2. But this clearly turns the marked stone into a bad move. This is why the cut is hardly playable for White. Further on in this continuation, Black 22 is a strong tesuji.

11

Not playable without hane

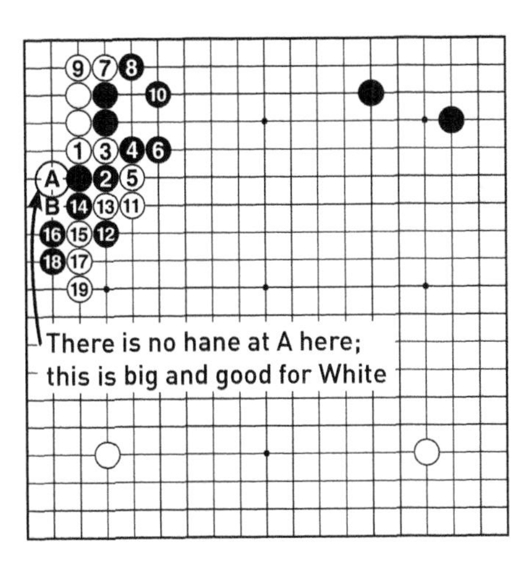

After White 1, it is not easy for Black to play at 2 like in the previous diagram, because White comes out well here. Usually, Black doesn't play at 2 if White hasn't exchanged A for Black B beforehand.

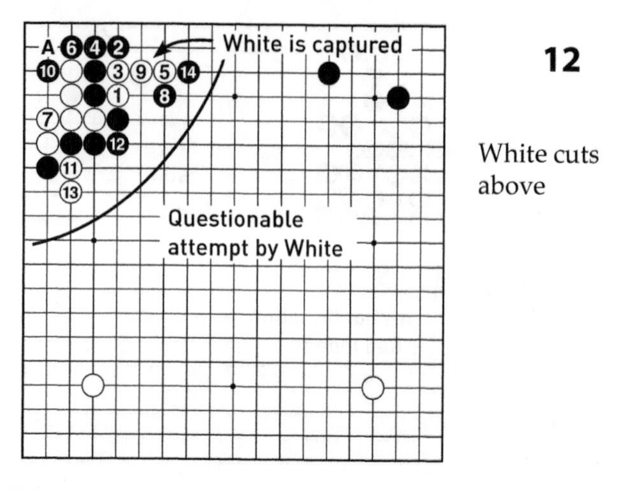

12

White cuts above

White should cut above at 1 instead of at 3 in diagram 10. Black boldly responds at 2. The atari at 3 is vulgar play and good for Black. The development up to 14 is also good for Black. After 6, if White blocks at A, Black plays at 7.

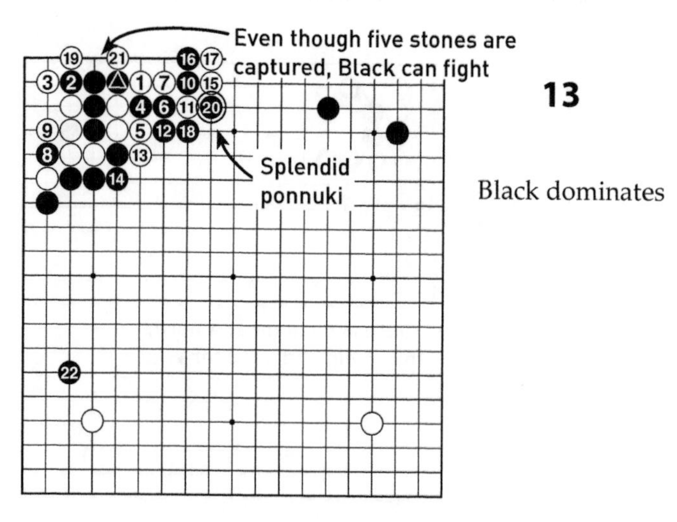

13

Black dominates

Blocking at 1 is too dangerous. As White has a stone in the lower right, the ladder is favourable for him. For Black this is uncomfortable and not easy to play. But he plays the way shown here, sacrificing the marked stone for influence, which gains him the upper hand in future events.

(11 – 20)

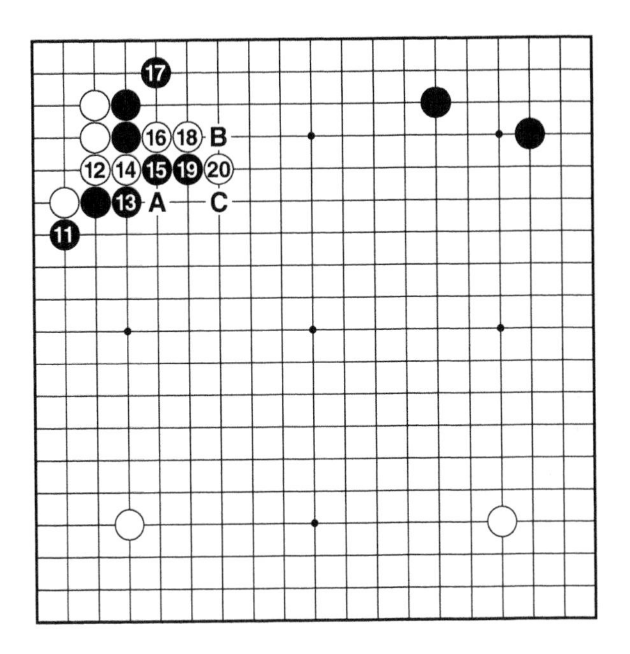

Black to play

Against White's plan, Black played at 11, the start of a complicated joseki. After the hane at 20, Black can respond in a way that leads to a very complicated game. Personally, I think the continuation chosen in the actual game is easier to understand.

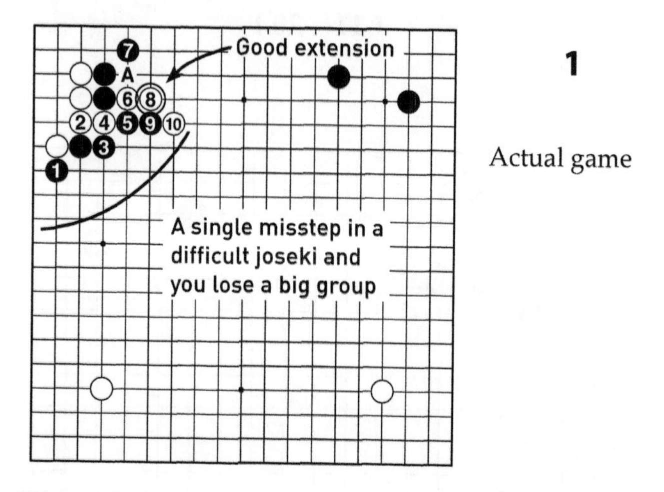

1

Actual game

White 8 is the appropriate move, whereas A comes to nothing. If you haven't made yourself familiar with this shape beforehand, you run the risk of losing a big group here.

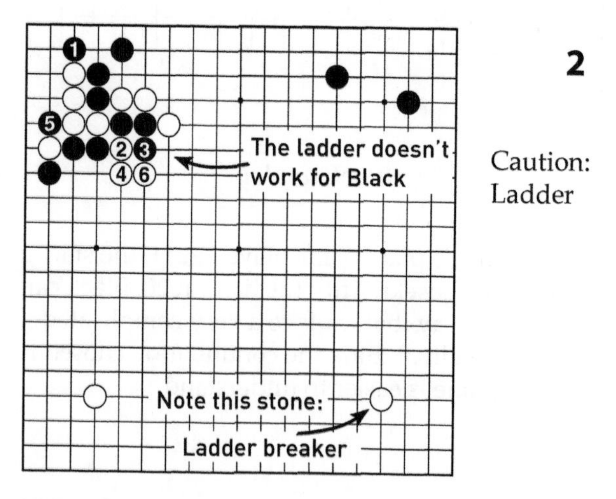

2

Caution: Ladder

If Black goes into the corner with 1, you need to check for the ladder after White 2 to 6. This ladder is also vital for White, because if there is a Black stone in the lower right, it'll be just as dangerous for White. This variation is risky if the ladder doesn't work.

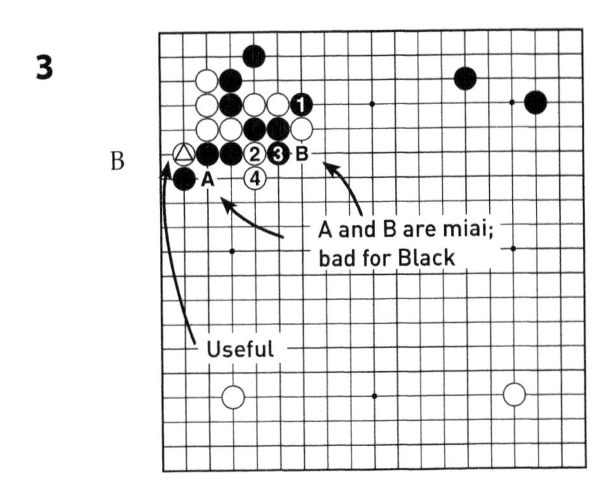

Cutting at 1 doesn't work, as White cuts with 2 and 4 and either threatens to capture two stones, or to play the ladder at B. The hane (marked stone), even though it's not good in general, gives White an important edge in this case.

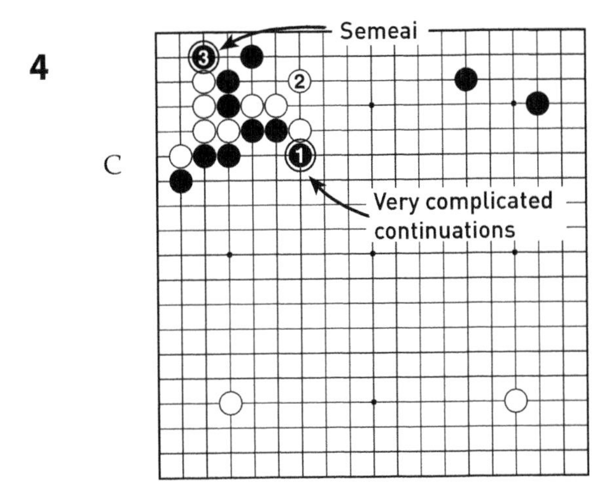

The hane at 1 leads to a very complicated variation. The way of playing from here depends on the whole-board situation. That's why it's hard to say what moves would be normal. In the diagrams that follow we will see what the continuations might look like.

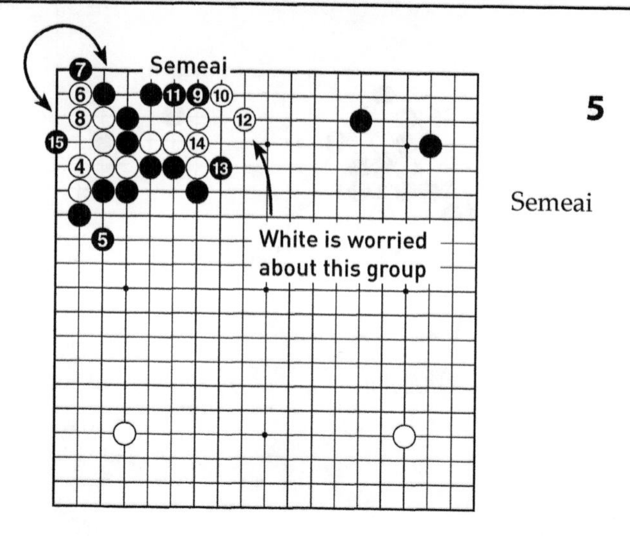

5

Semeai

The upper side is fought over. Depending on the situation, either party might give it up though. The surprising thing is that even 9 and 11 are played, stones you really wouldn't want to sacrifice. Nevertheless Black will sometimes throw them away again.

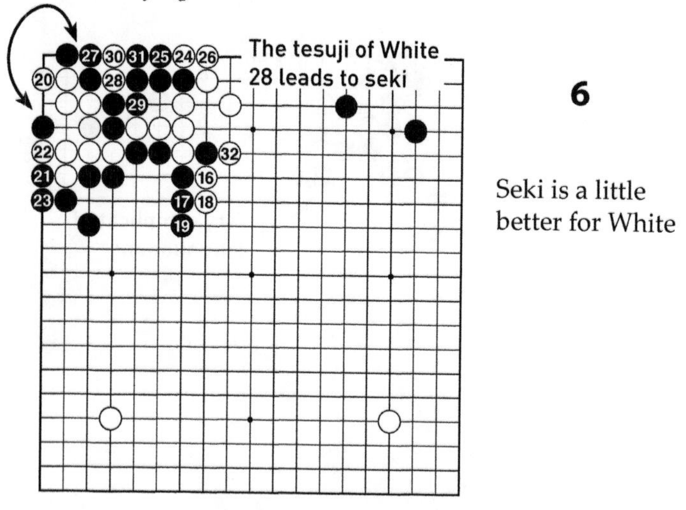

6

Seki is a little better for White

White 28 is a tesuji and leads to seki. This means that White gets sente. White is not unhappy with the result up to 32. Apart from this diagram there are also other moves for both sides with very complicated variations.

7

Example from a game

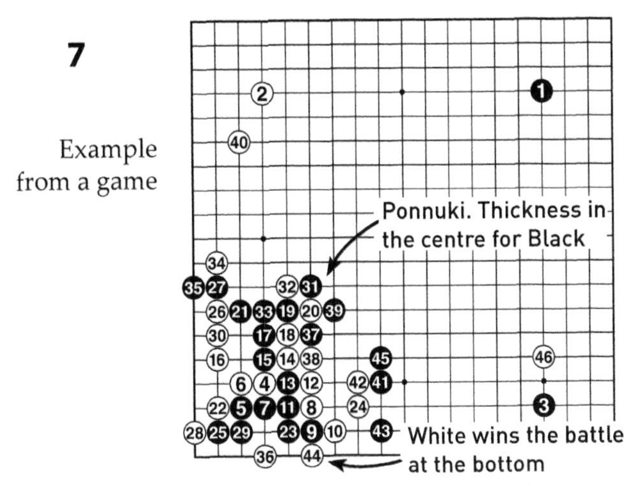

A similar division occured in the game between Ke Jie 9p (W) and Xu Jiayang 8p (B) in the semi-final of the 8th Qisheng. Black gives up the lower side, getting thickness in the centre in return.

8

A Correct

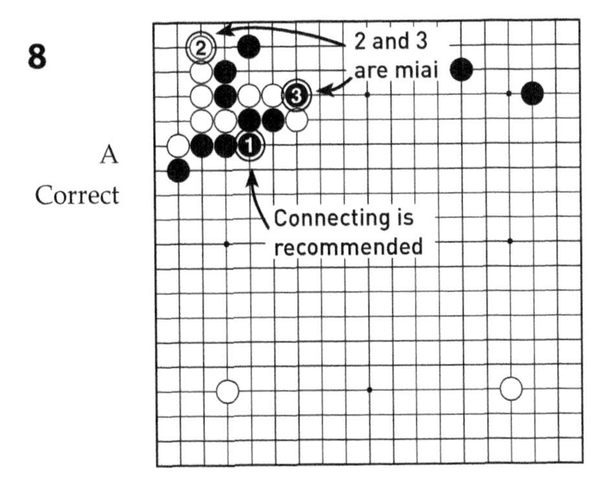

The move of Black 1 is easy to understand. Things that are easy to understand are often rejected because they don't lead to success. That's not the case here. As we can see from the continuation of the game, this is playable for Black. His strategy is straightforward.

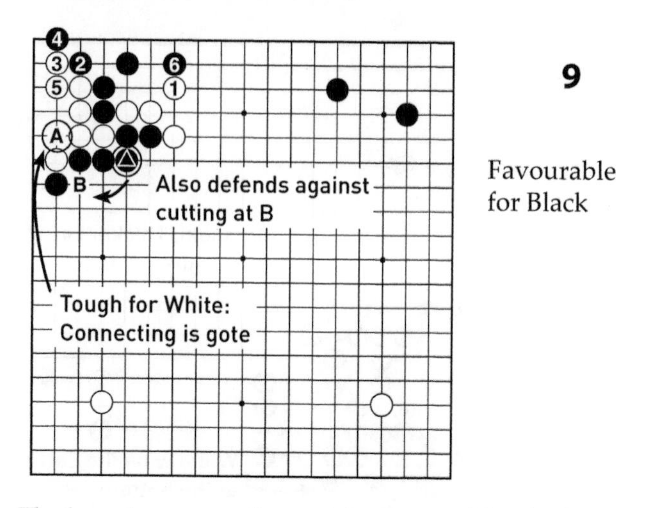

9

Favourable for Black

The hanging connection at 1 is answered by the hane at 2. The result is not acceptable for White. Black now has the advantage, because connecting at A is gote while he is already safely connected, thanks to the marked stone.

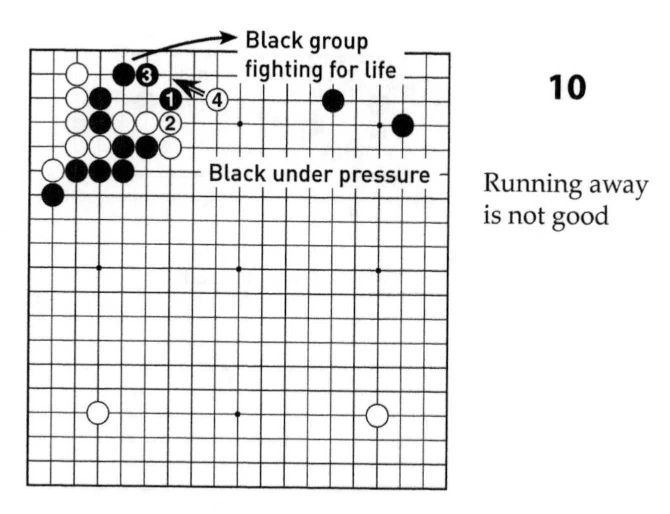

10

Running away is not good

If White plays in the corner, running with 1 is a bad choice. In order to prevent White from capturing two stones, Black must defend at 3. After this he gets attacked by White 4 and ends up with a bad shape.

11

White accomplishes nothing

White needs time to capture 3 stones; the territory is smaller than it looks

Splendid wall for Black

Therefore it is good for Black to cut with the marked stone and then to sacrifice the stones. Although White can make more territory with 1 and 3 than in the game, Black is considerably strengthened after 8. That's why it's better for White to play as he did in the game.

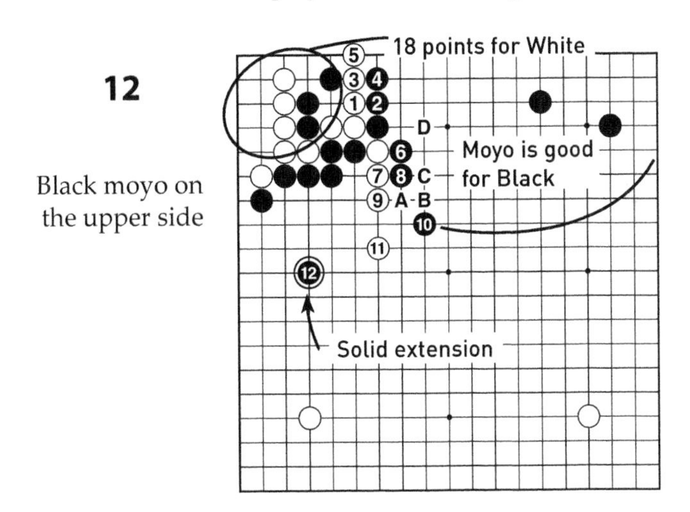

Black moyo on the upper side

In the game, White played 1 to 5 and captured Black. After 9 Black pushed at A, but 10 may also be considered. If White presses here at A, Black blocks at B and the cut at C is answered by D. In the actual game, Black took great care not to expose any weaknesses.

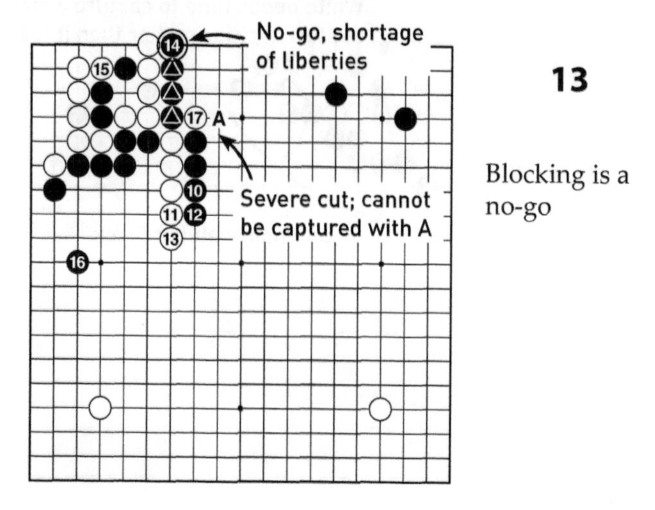

13

Blocking is a no-go

As a continuation of the previous diagram, Black 14 after White 13 is a serious mistake. Due to shortage of liberties, it is now possible to cut at 17. Black cannot capture the cutting stone with A.

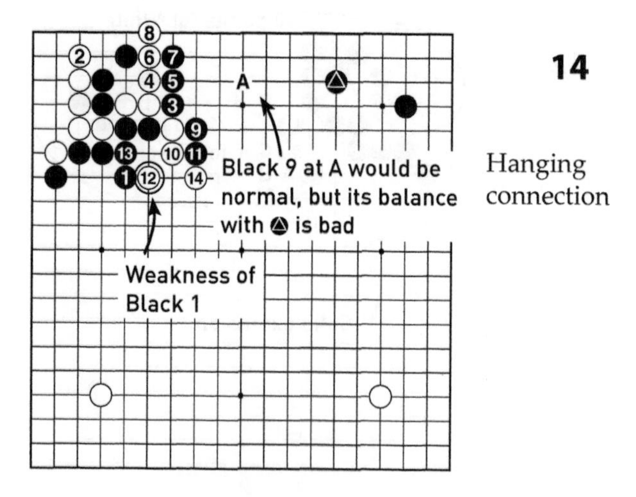

14

Hanging connection

There is also the hanging connection at 1. The continuation up to 8 is the same as in the game. After the atari at 9, however, White responds with 12 and 14. Compared to the game, this is unfavourable for Black. Instead of 9, it is not uncommon to play at A, but in this configuration of stones it's not good.

15

The game 1

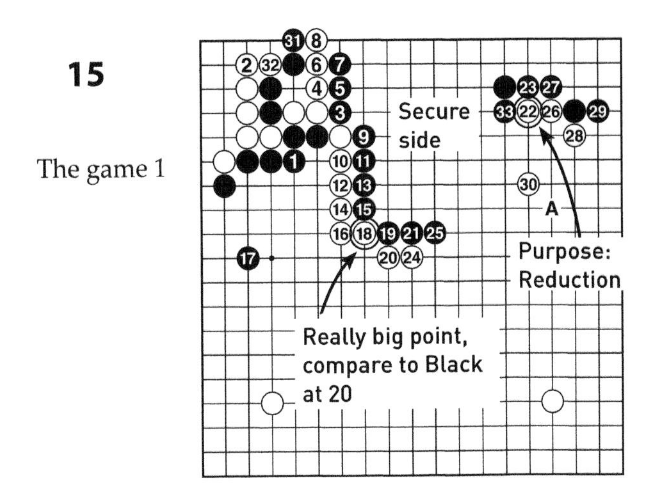

Turning at 18 is big. Black played the hane at 19, then extended, taking secure profit at the top. White began reducing the Black moyo with 22. White 30 is usually played at A, but here it was White's intention to reduce the moyo even further.

16

The game 2

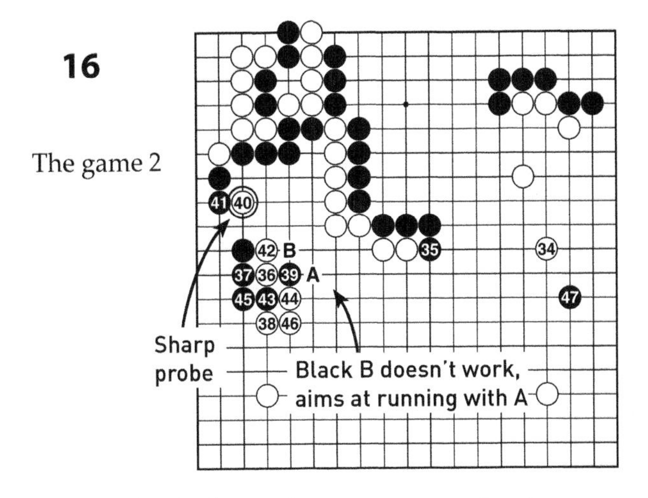

Turning at 35 is also huge. As a response to the clamp at 39, White wanted to see Black's reaction to 40 – this is clever. If Black plays at 41, White can continue with 42. There is still some aji for Black at A.

The game

Moves after 94 omitted.
White wins by 1.5 points.

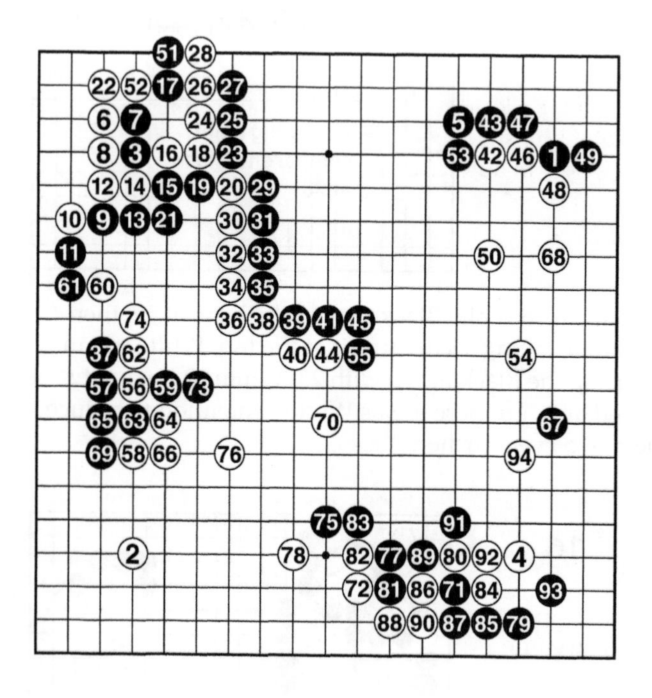

In the next game, Choi Jeong 9p from Korea and Shi Yue 9p from China meet in the preliminary round of the 24th LG Cup.

Column 1

Introduction to tribodian

Tribodian is a game in which a player competes against one and the same opponent in three different kinds of games (9x9 go, shogi, and othello), striving for the best overall result. Once a year, in autumn, there is a tournament. Both go and shogi are games with a long tradition in Japan. Othello, on the other hand, is a game with a shorter history, but the rules that were established in Japan are easy to understand and get comfortable with.

Although all three of them are board games, there are no similarities such as there are, for example, between shogi and chess. They are all completely different games and so overall success requires a good understanding of each. For instance, if a player is only really strong in go, but can survive in the other two games only at beginner level, then that player can only win a round if they achieve an outstanding result in go. This means that a balance of skills is important, too.

Interestingly, the game isn't played at all on wooden boards. Instead it's played on the internet, via smartphone. So the playing itself is a rather quiet affair, without the typical sounds of stones being placed. After each round the game is analysed together.

I joined my first tribodian tournament after I'd heard that such tournaments exist. At the time, I liked playing shogi and so I was looking for a tournament that I could join without having to worry too much.

I don't have a lot of experience with go on a 9x9 board. In shogi, I was at the level of about 1 kyu at the time. As for othello, I knew only one joseki, and so I was unsure how things would turn out. In the end, after six rounds of games, I won five victories in go, three in shogi, and even two in othello. These successes have been fond memories for me.

The tournament is grouped into three divisions, so that players of different strengths can find equal opponents. Prizes are awarded to the best players of each division, and every participant receives a shogi book. There is no participation fee.

* This information relates to the 4th Tribodian Tournament (2018). Tribodian is recommended for people who can also play shogi and othello, in addition to go. I would love to join many more tournaments, and if you hear about any, please feel free to contact me.

Game 4

Choi Jeong is a strong Korean female top player who can also hold her ground in the tournaments that are dominated by male players.

Shi Yue is a Chinese pro who won the LG Cup in the year 2013.

(1 – 11)

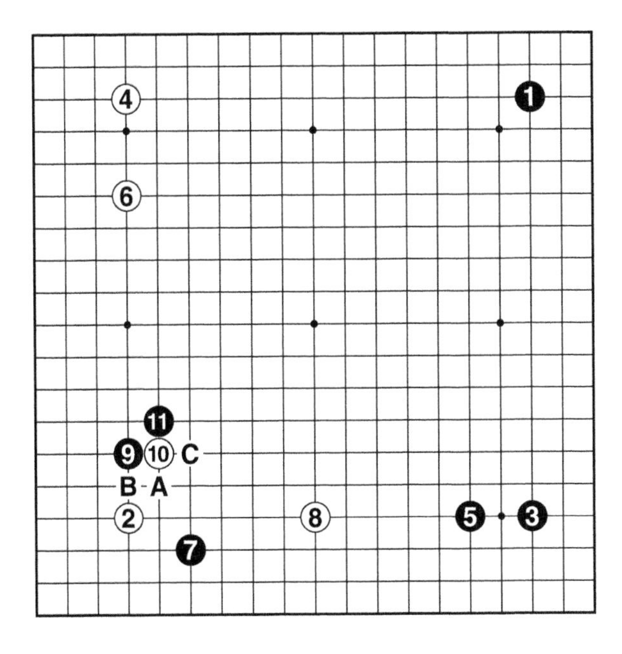

White to play

After the hane at 11, there is the question of how White should continue. Black 9 and White 10 were rarely played until recently. Under the influence of AI they have gained in importance. The next move is not particularly innovative, but it is recommended by AI in this situation.

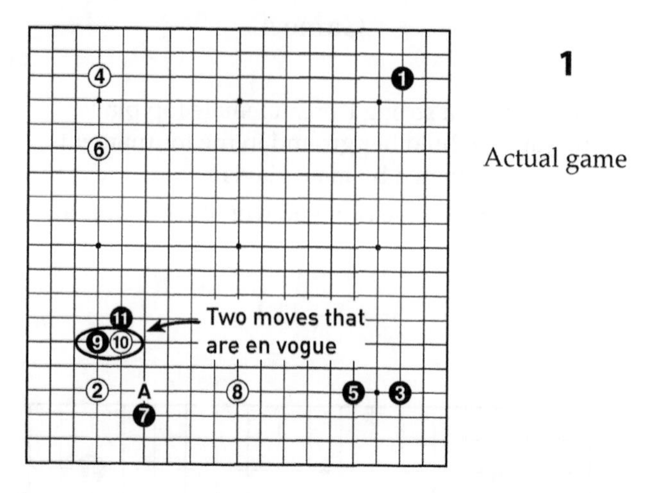

Actual game

As a response to the pincer at 8, the low kakari (left of 9) used to be the popular choice. With the emergence of AI it is now common to attach to the stone at 9 with White 10, instead of attaching to 7 at A as before. Still, these two moves have already been seen in the past.

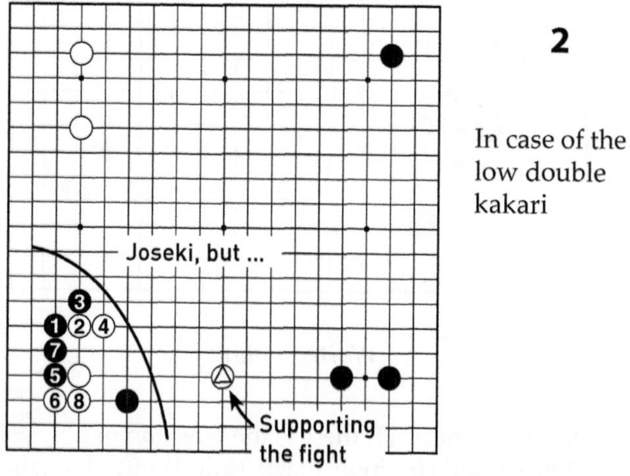

In case of the low double kakari

If the second kakari is played low, then this continuation may be considered. It's one of several possible variations. The marked stone aligns well with White's thickness, which is why Black won't be pleased with this variation.

3

Joseki for thickness of White

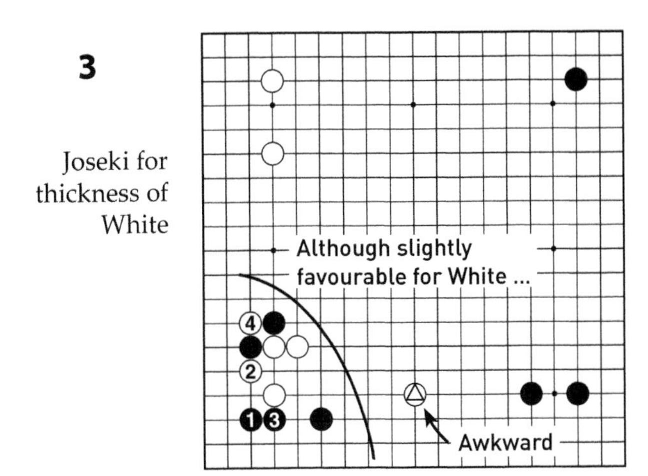

If Black wants to avoid a fight, he can invade at 3-3 with 1. White's position is strong after 4 to some extent, but the marked stone is in a bit of an awkward spot.

4

Playable for Black

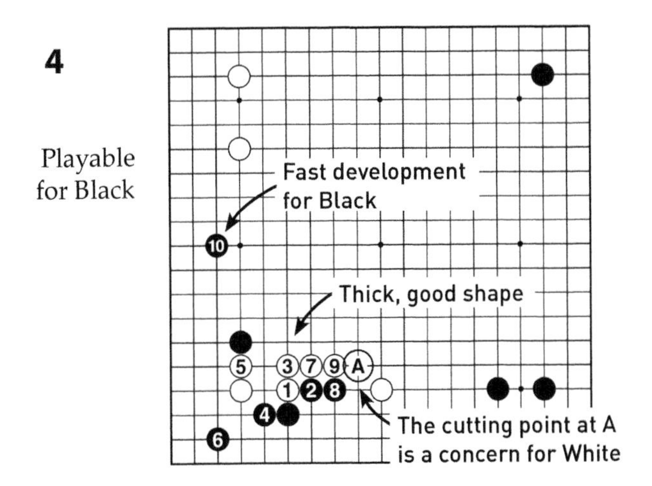

After a high kakari, White 1 was normal in the past. The common perception was that White's position after 9 is not bad. That's why Black rarely played the high kakari. AI however rates the result as not bad for Black.

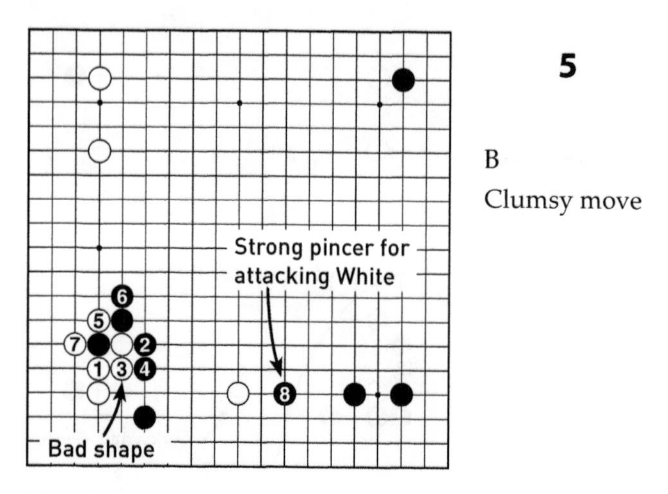

5

B

Clumsy move

White 1 is a clumsy move; also, the shape is really bad after connecting at 3. Black 4 and the follow-up extension build influence. In addition, Black can play the pincer at 8.

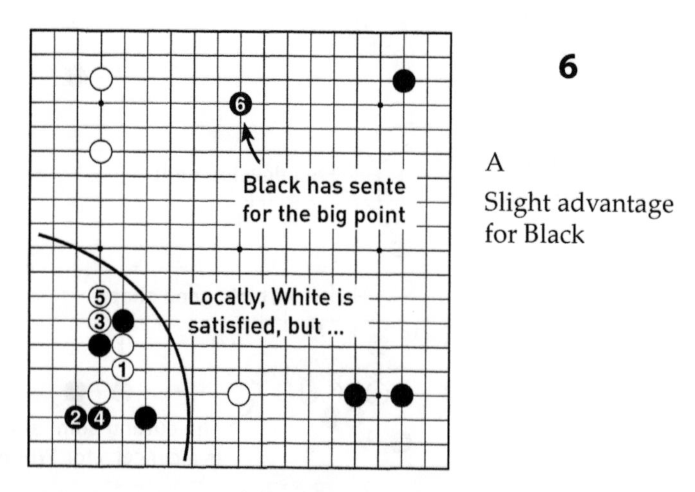

6

A

Slight advantage for Black

White 1 is a standard move that always used to be played in this situation. It was assumed that White is strong after 5 and has no reason to complain. AI however rates the result as slightly favourable for Black.

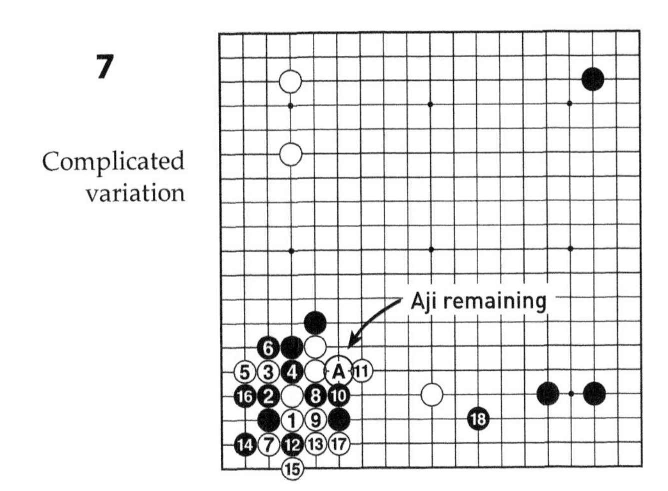

7

Complicated variation

White can also block with 1. Here we see a complicated variation after the hane at 3. The result after the continuation up to 18 is considered even.

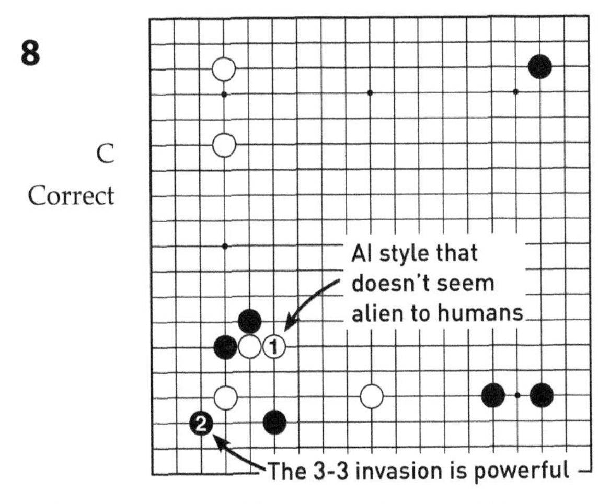

8

C

Correct

Although the extension at 1 is a natural move, it has rarely been seen up until now. Since it hardly came up, it was never studied properly. After this, White 2 is a strong move.

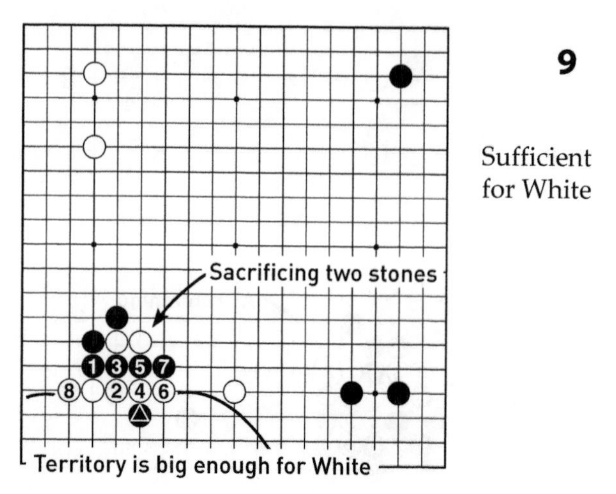

9

Sufficient for White

Bumping at 1 is not a good move, because if White answers at 2, the marked stone is positioned badly. After the continuation to 8 White ends up with a big territory.

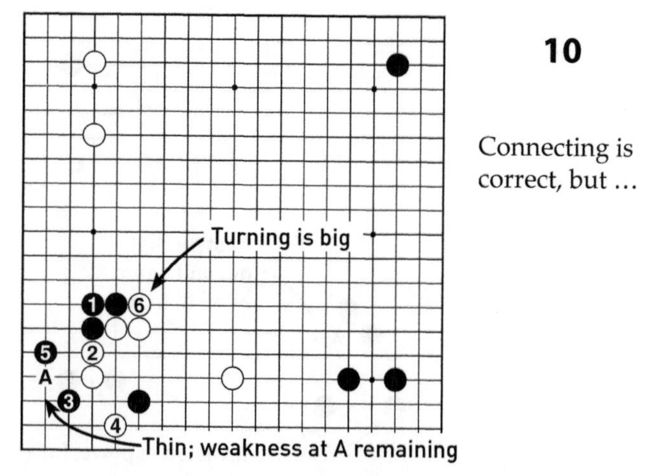

10

Connecting is correct, but ...

Black 1 is a natural move, and White 2 makes good shape as well. If Black now invades at 3 and then jumps to 5, the shape in the corner is thin. White however plays the strong turn at 6; she is not dissatisfied with this.

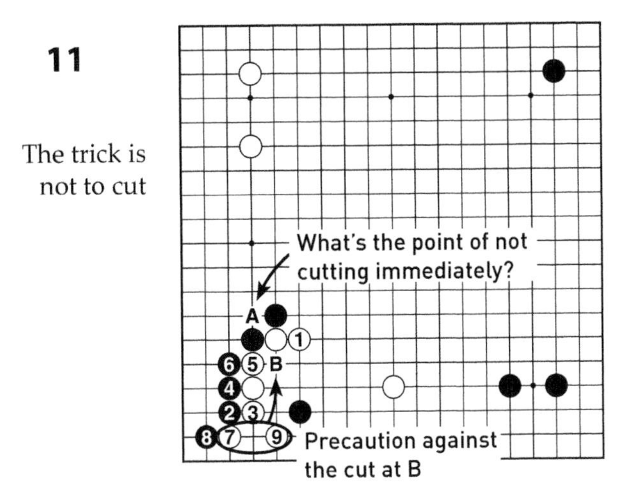

11

The trick is not to cut

This diagram shows the actual game. After White 3, 7 and 9 follow in order to threaten Black's corner. It is of course tempting to play at A, but one shouldn't do so. The reason is explained in the following.

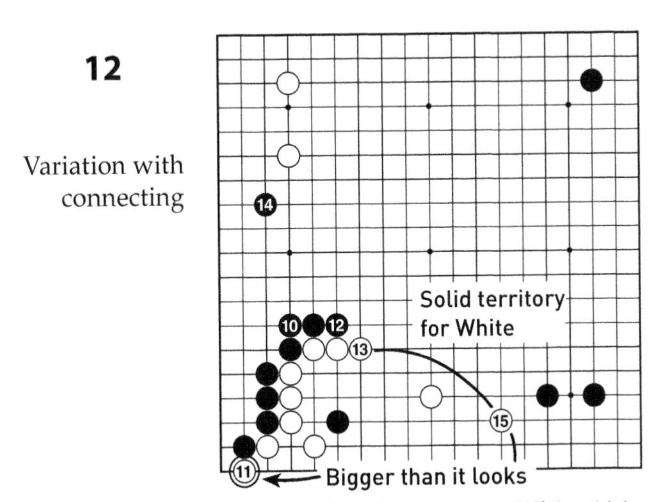

12

Variation with connecting

Next, Black 10 may be considered. However, White 11 is big. After this, the extension to 15 is an option, and White is not unhappy with her magnificent shape.

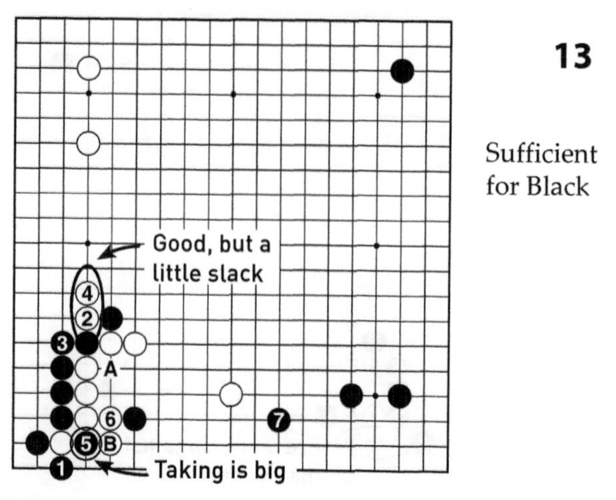

13

Sufficient for Black

If White plays 2 and 4 as a response to Black 1 and lets Black capture at 5, it is a rather slack way of playing. If White, after 7 in diagram 11, had defended against the cut at A with 9, then Black 5, White B and Black 6 would be a very uncomfortable continuation.

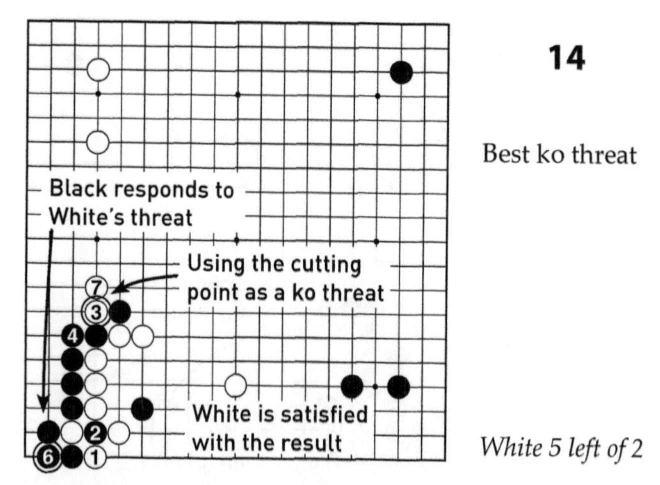

14

Best ko threat

White 5 left of 2

The reason why White didn't cut at 3 earlier is that she can now resist at 1. White 3 now serves as a serious ko threat. If Black defends at 6, White extends at 7. White is satisfied with this result.

(12 – 41)

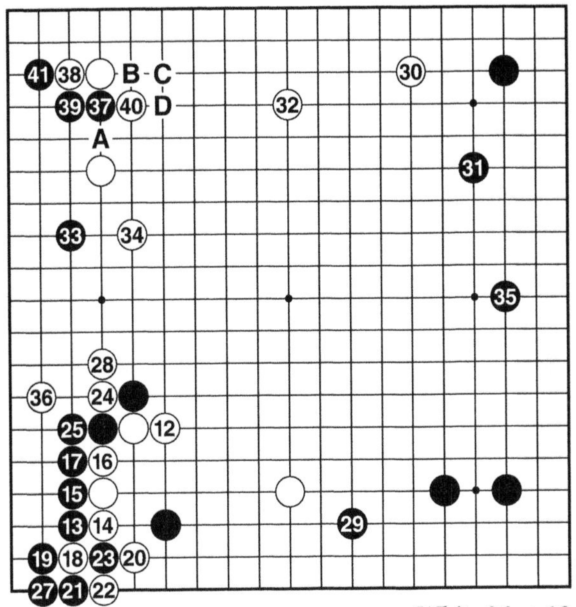

White 26 at 18

White to play

Fighting now shifted to the upper left, with focus being on how Black proceeds in White's sphere of influence. After Black 41, White had to think about how to defend against the cut. Where would you play?

The way of defending shown here here reveals the key to the AI style. Lately it has already been applied in similar situations.

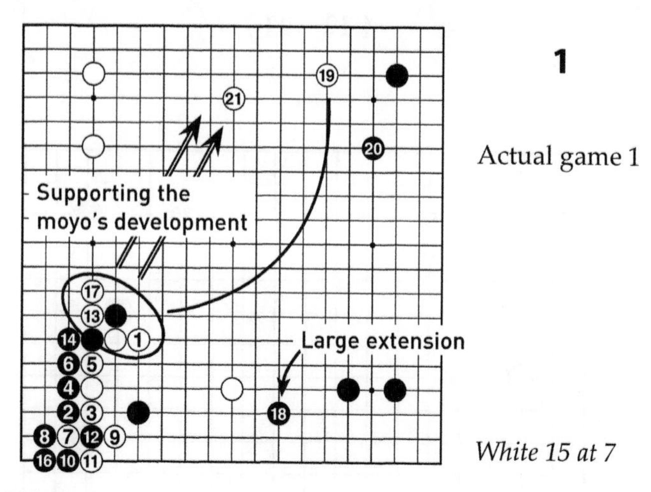

1

Actual game 1

White 15 at 7

White doesn't complain about the outcome in the lower left. Black, however, gets to play the large extension to 18, and the position is even. In return, White 19 and 21 take big points on the upper side.

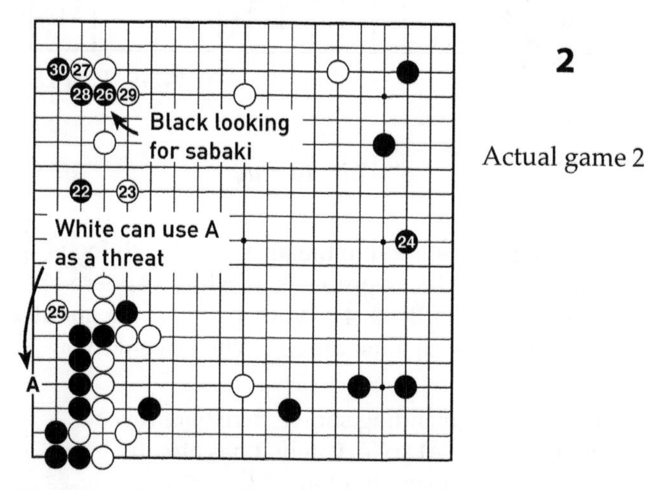

2

Actual game 2

Black invades with 22 in order to scoop out the developing moyo. Black 26 is a typical AI move and is very often applied in pro games. Today it is the standard move for approaching the large high shimari.

3

Variation for hane below

Badly positioned

Waiting to start running

The hane at 1 is answered by Black with the counter-hane at 2. The sequence up to 7 is often seen, even without the marked stone being present. These moves offer an advantage, although a subtle one, as the kosumi is rather badly positioned. With 12 begins a fight for Black, but it's playable.

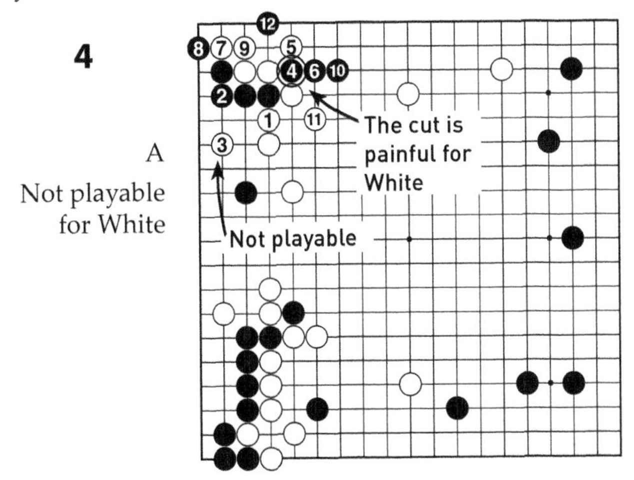

4

A

Not playable for White

White 1 is not a playable variation, because Black 10 works perfectly and after 12 the local fight ends in a victory for Black.

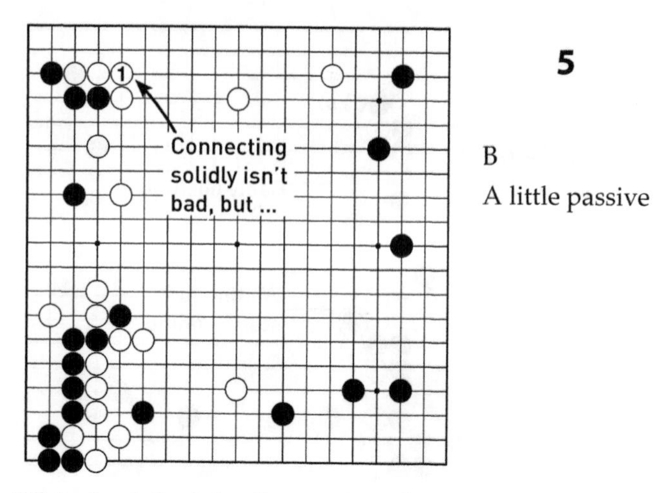

White 1, while defending against the cut, seems a little honest. White would like to play more actively.

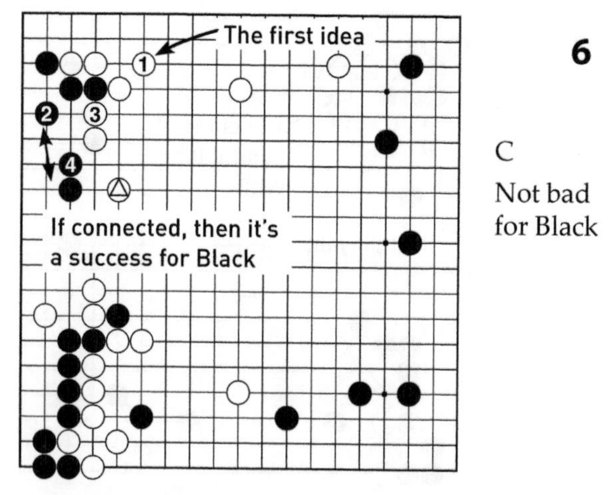

Connecting with a tiger's mouth is a standard defensive move. If there is no additional stone in the area, such as White's marked stone, then that move is correct. Black 2 is the expected response. If White now plays 3, then after 4 Black has nothing to complain about.

7

D

Actual fight

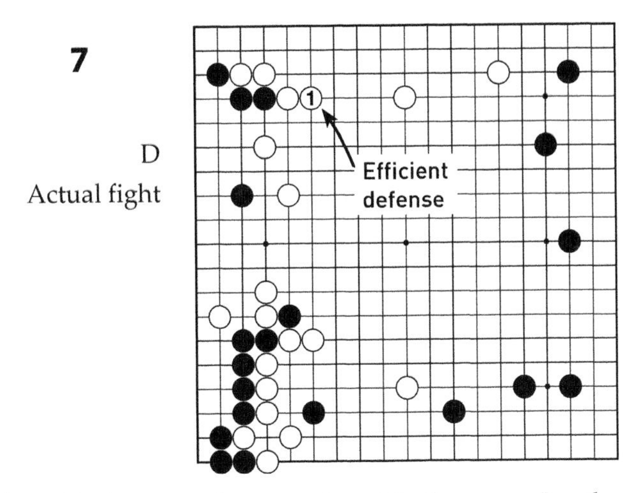

White 1 is the move that was played in the game. In other problems, this diagram would be marked "Correct", but here it's just "Actual fight". The reason is that this move is heavily influenced by AI. It is a very efficient method for defending against the cut.

8

Actual game

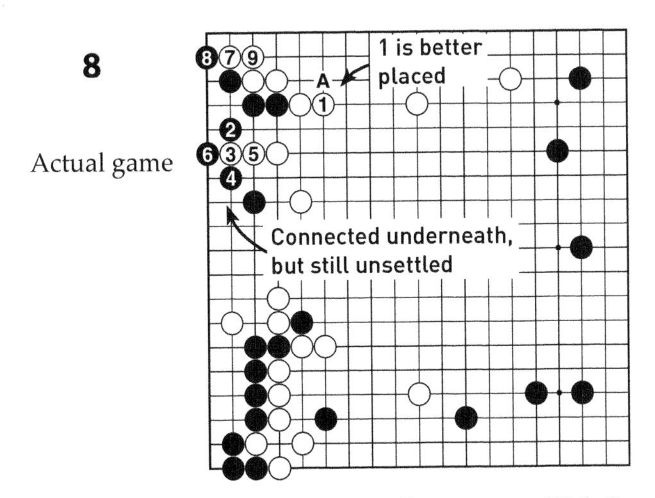

White 3 is a move that doesn't actually separate. With 7 and 9 White removes the possibility for Black to make eyes in the corner. This sequence is a result of defending at 1. It's more efficient for attacking than connecting at A. Here we witness AI style defending in a real life game.

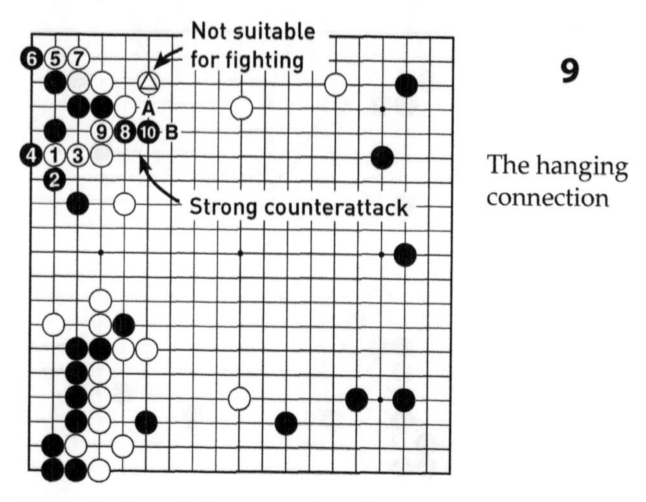

9

The hanging connection

After the hanging connection, this sequence could also be considered, but the marked stone is not in a good position. A counterattack with Black 8 and 10 is hard to fend off. If there was a stone at A, White could turn at B.

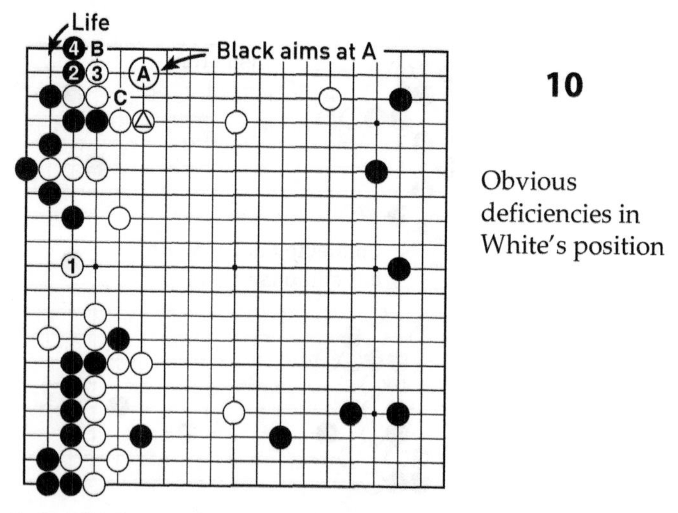

10

Obvious deficiencies in White's position

Instead of 7 in diagram 8, attacking with 1 is a variation for coercing Black into the corner with 2 and 4. This sequence is not good in view of the marked stone, because now there is the threat of the peep at A. Should White even play at B, then Black will cut at C.

11

Influence for Black

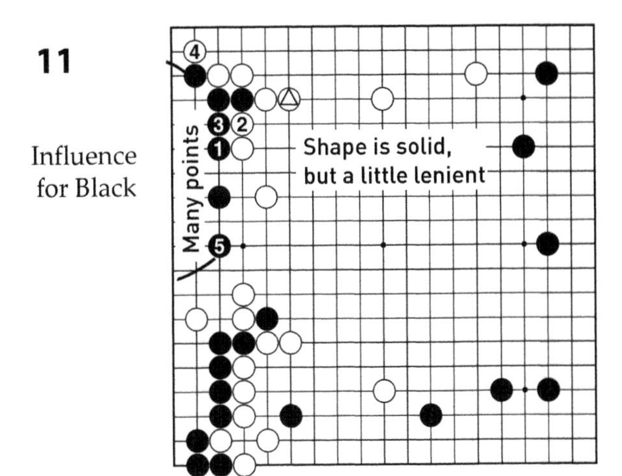

According to AI analysis, the attachment at 1 is a good response to the marked stone. Black is even slightly better.

12

Giving up two stones is skilful

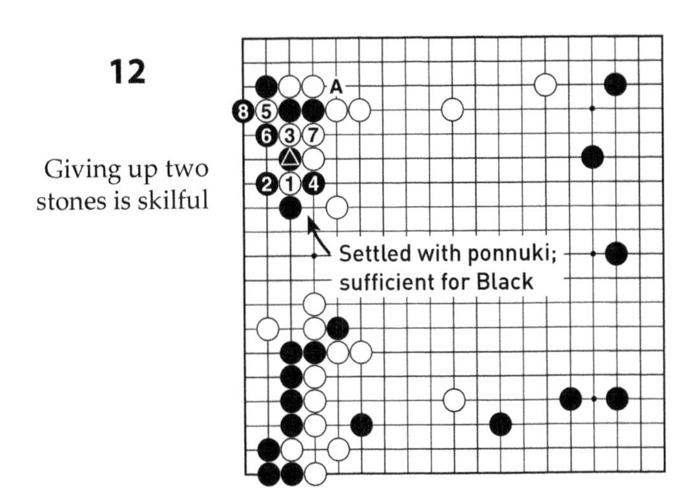

The wedge with 1 is uncomfortable for Black. But if he gives up two stones, the result won't be bad for him either. White's three moves that defend against the cut at A are not good, because they allow Black to connect to the marked stone.

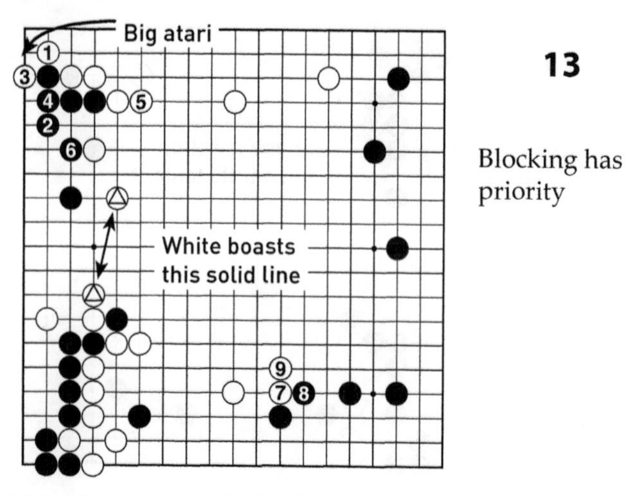

13

Blocking has priority

The AI recommends blocking at 1. The atari at 3 is big and White seems to achieve a better result here than in diagram 11.

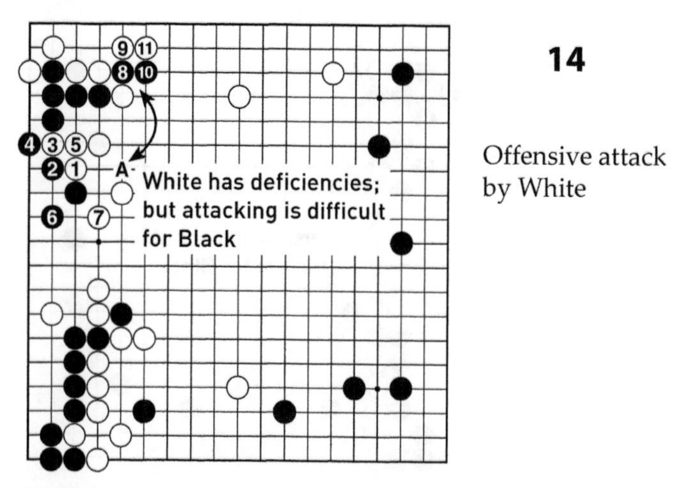

14

Offensive attack by White

If White wants to play more aggressively then this sequence can be considered. It leaves cutting points such as 8 and A and is thus clearly more risky. However there doesn't seem to be a good move for Black right away. For the moment, he's having a hard time making life in good shape.

15

The game 1

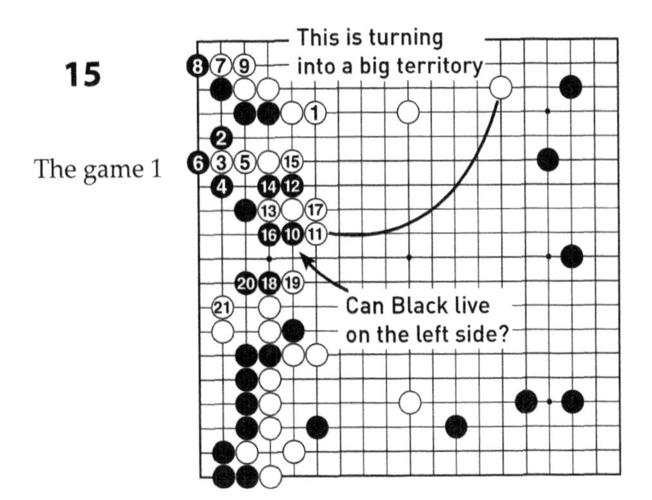

Diagrams 13 and 14 have shown that not hurrying to defend against the cut is a strong way of playing. But if you'd still like to defend it directly, then 1 is a good move. Black is struggling to make life for his group. Now White should attack Black with precision.

16

The game 2

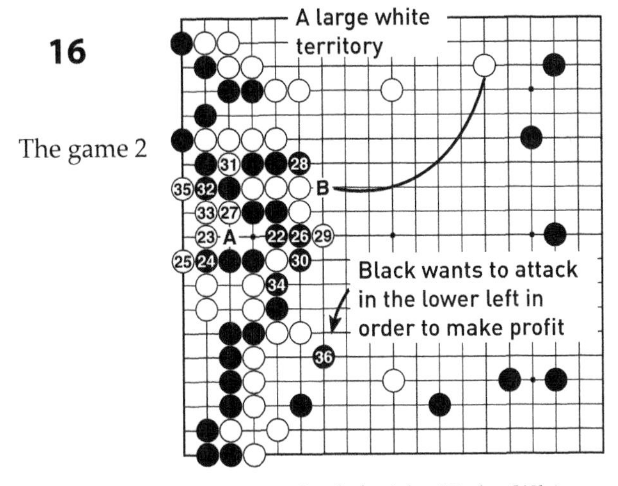

Eventually Black gave up on the left side. He let White play at 29 (31 forces 32, A and B are miai) so he could connect at 34. With this he aimed at attacking on the lower side. The left side, however, is big – White's position is now a little better.

The game

Moves after 87 omitted.
White wins by resignation.

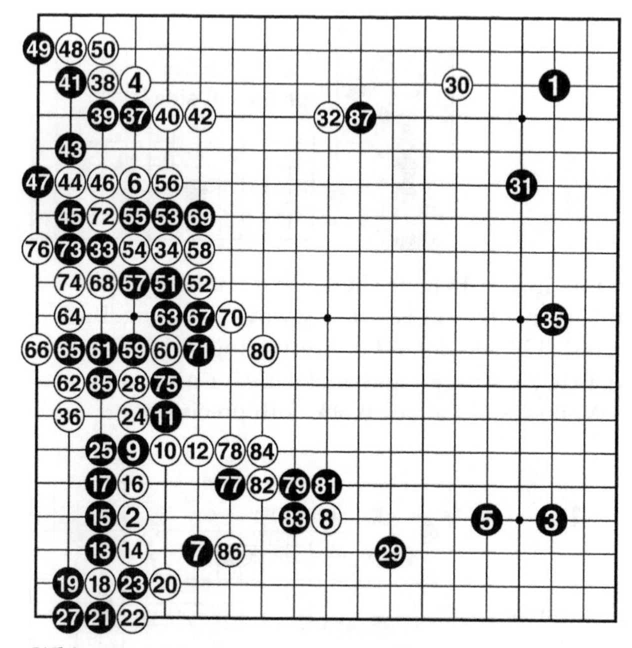

White 26 at 18

The next game is an encounter between two young pros, from Korea and China respectively: Shin Jinseo 9p and Ding Hao 5p.

Game 5

Shin Jinseo won the final of the Asia TV Cup against Ding Hao in June 2019. Shortly before, in April, they already came up against each other in the Globis Cup. In this game, a new AI joseki was applied in the top right corner.

(1 – 18)

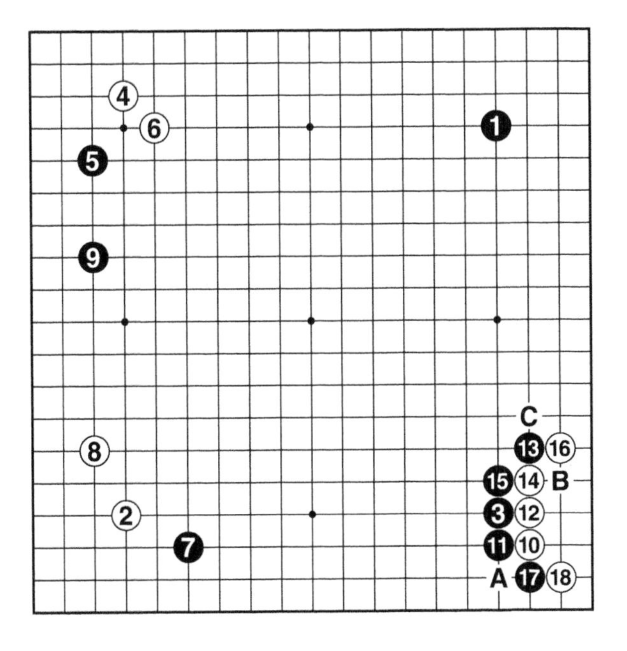

Black to play

In this game, White plays the 3-3 invasion with 10. They present another variation here, in which Black chooses the hane at 17 and White blocks at 18. The resulting sequences are quite popular and en vogue.

Where should White continue: At A, B, or C?

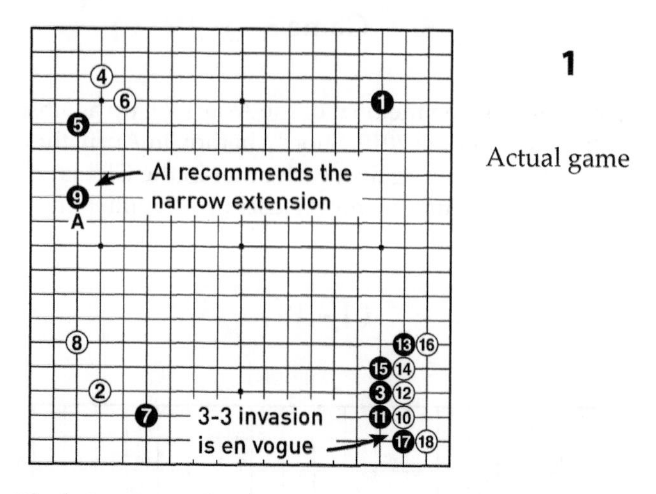

1

Actual game

Black 9 at A used to be the common extension in this position, but now, under the influence of AI, the close extension to 9 is played more often. After this, White invades the corner in the lower right at 3-3.

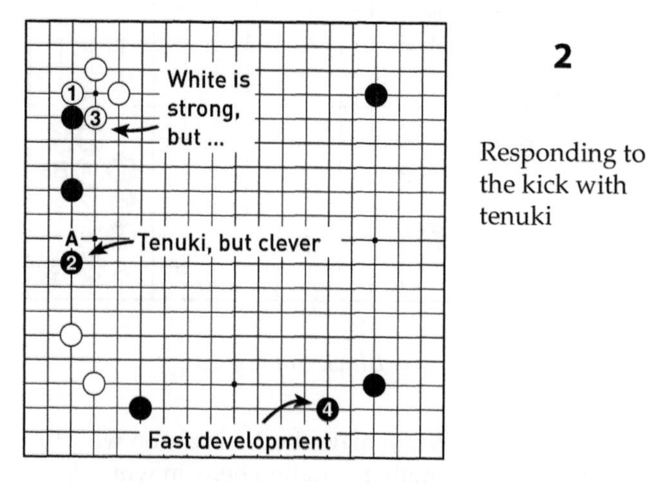

2

Responding to the kick with tenuki

The tenuki at 2 is a skilful response to the kick at 1 and paves the way for a fast development of Black. If Black plays at 2 instead of 3, White will attack at A. Depending on the situation there are various options; here, Black 2 is a good choice.

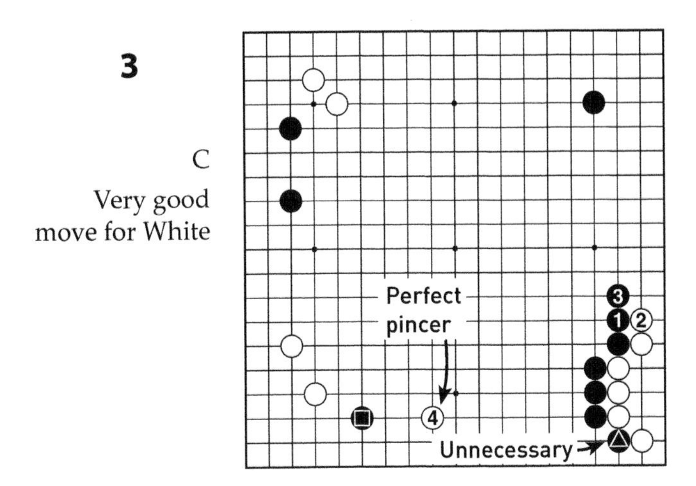

If Black extends at 1, he fails to make use of the marked stone in the right corner. White 4 is a move that serves two purposes: pincering the marked stone on the left, and impeding Black's moyo.

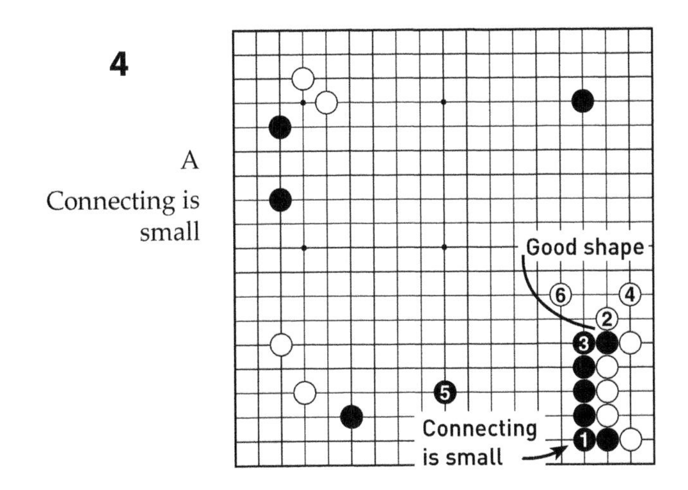

The hane was not played in order to then connect at 1. At this point, connecting is still too small and too slow for Black.

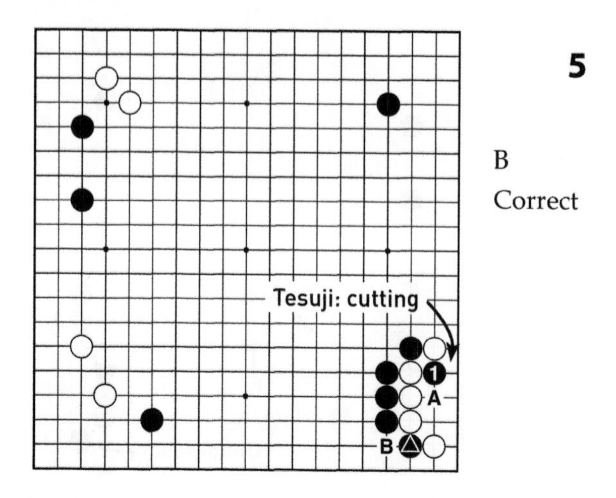

5

B
Correct

Cutting at 1 capitalises on the marked hane. White can now answer at A or B. Let's first look at option A, not taken in the game.

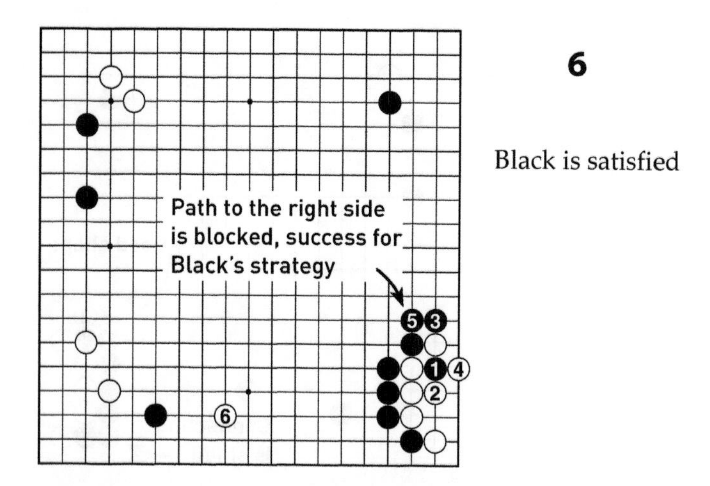

6

Black is satisfied

If White goes for A, he will be forced to take the Black stone with 4. This is not good for him, but it's a possible way of playing. Black is happy to be able to block access to the right side with 3 and 5.

7

Black can fight

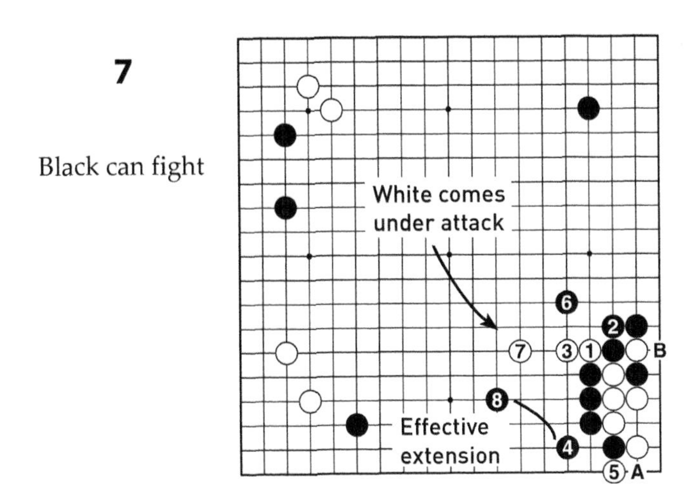

Instead of capturing a stone, another variation for White is playing the atari at 1. Black counters the attack with 4 and 6. If White plays away from the corner, Black can start a ko with A or B. This fight is playable for Black.

8

Slack play
by Black

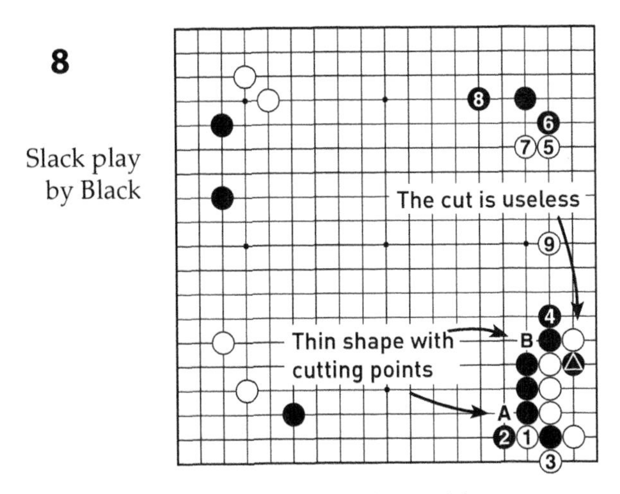

Instead of White 2 in diagram 6, cutting at 1 is strong. Black 2, on the other hand, forces White to capture at 3, only resulting in a shape with weaknesses. Black has to worry about the cutting points at A and B.

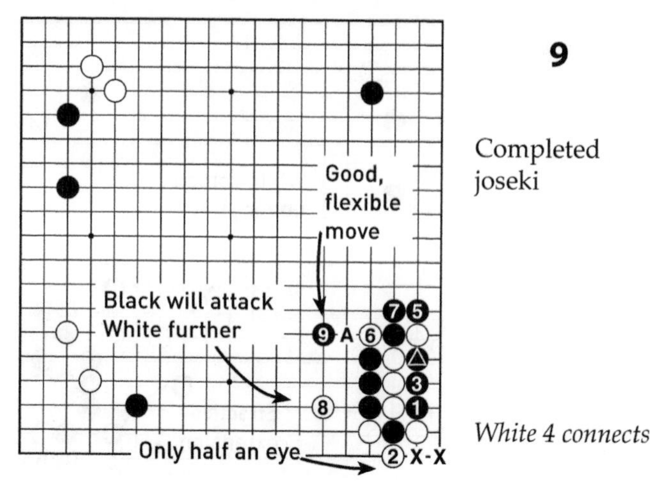

9

Completed joseki

White 4 connects

Black cuts with 1, forcing White to take the Black stone. This is the continuation after the marked stone (Black 1 in diag. 6). If the ladder works, Black can capture with 9 at A. If it doesn't, then Black 9 is the better move.

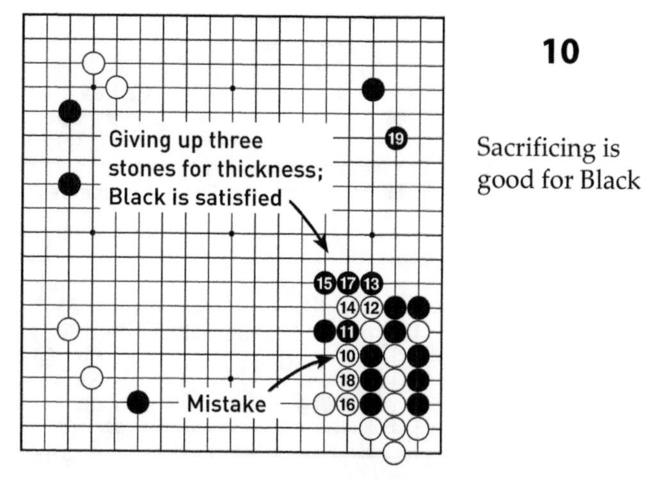

10

Sacrificing is good for Black

White wants to take advantage of the ladder not working and plays the attack with 10. Black, however, sacrifices three stones with 11 to 15 and builds a thick wall. With 19 he finally consolidates his moyo on the right side.

11

As a response to tenuki, attack

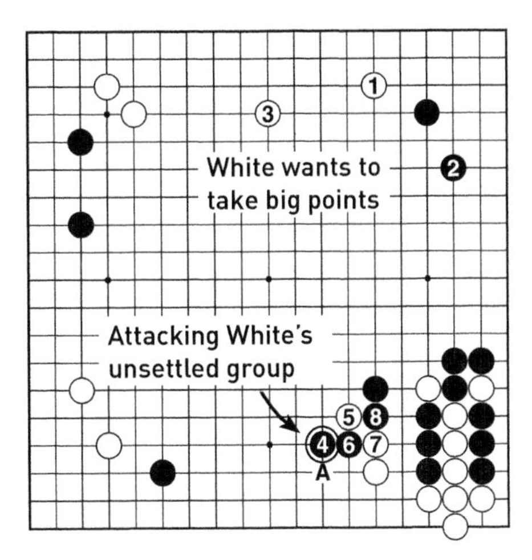

In the game, after diagram 9, White plays at 4 right away. If he'd play tenuki instead, then Black should attack at 4. As White still doesn't have two eyes, Black can fight by cutting at 8.

12

Weak extension

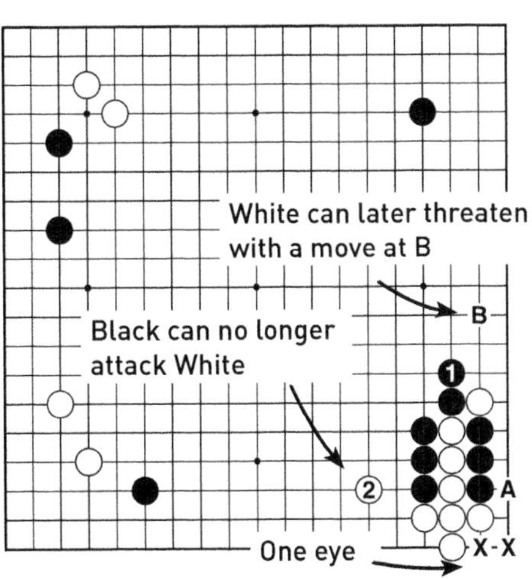

Instead of 5 in diagram 9, extending is a natural move, but it is very rarely played. White now lives in the corner, as A is sente. As a consequence, Black can no longer attack White's group the way he could in the previous diagram. Now it's not going to be easy for Black.

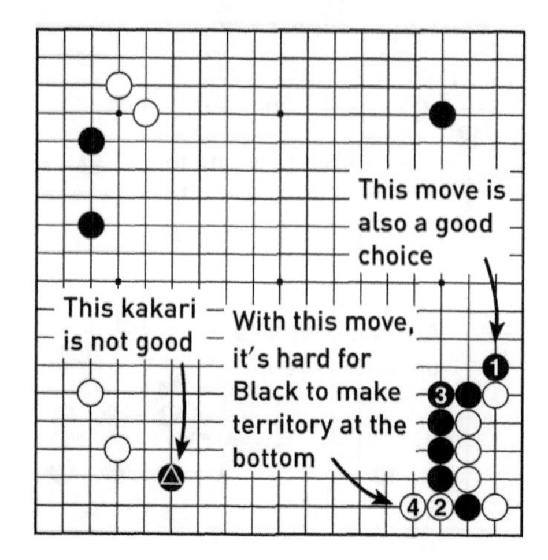

13

Addendum: Variation with hane on the outside

The hane at 1 is also often played. After the continuation to 4, Black and White are locally even. Looking at the whole-board situation however, it is inadequate, as White 4 devalues the lower side, thwarting Black's ambitions in the area.

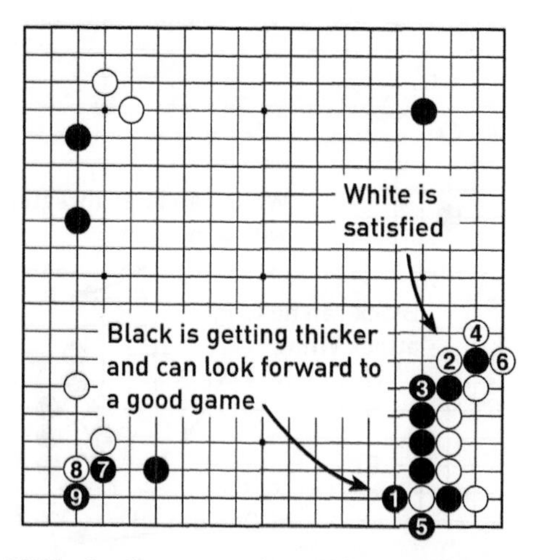

14

Just what White hoped for, but…

If Black plays at 1, then White can develop on the right side with 2 and 4, thanks to the sacrifice stone. Black takes a stone with 5, gains in thickness, and a moyo emerges on the lower side. The game is even.

(19 – 38)

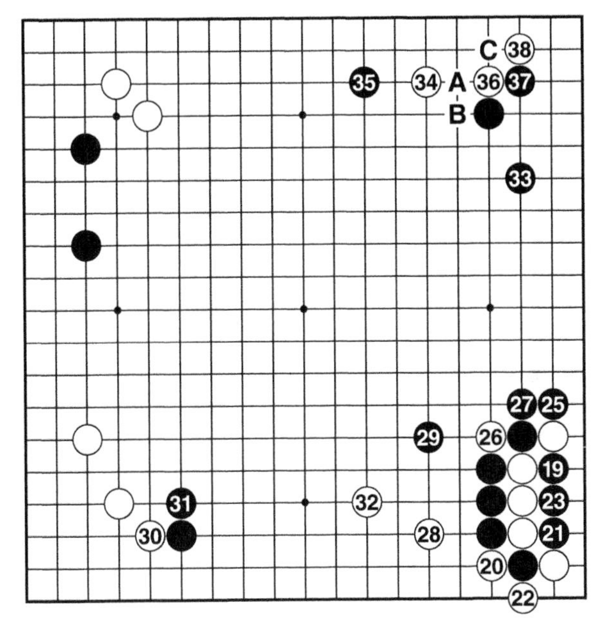

White 24 connects

Black to play

White just played the hane at 38. After that, Black applied a new AI technique. You shouldn't play this variation before having understood its meaning. It's a very powerful way of playing.

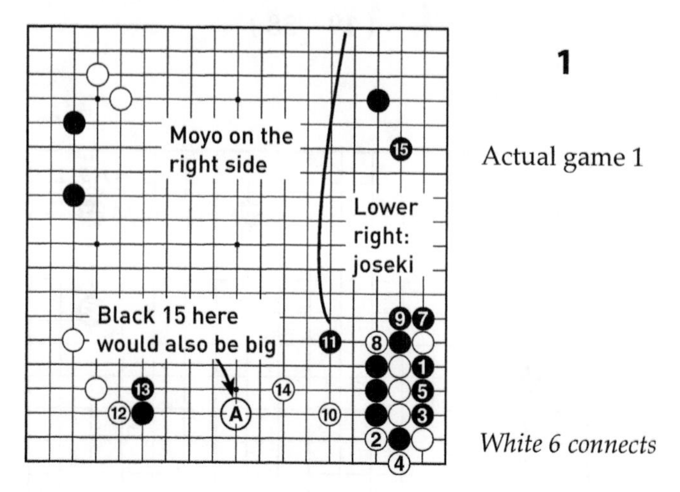

1

Actual game 1

White 6 connects

Kicking at 12 and playing the extension to 14 are a good plan for White. For Black, the extension to A would also be big, but here he reinforced the moyo at the top with 15.

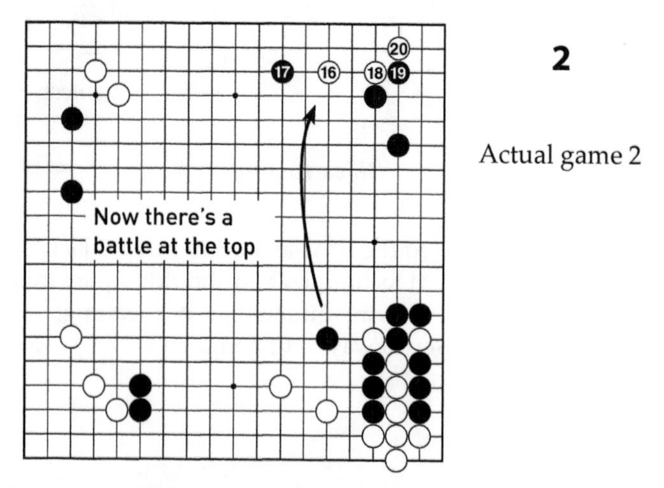

2

Actual game 2

Instead of White 16, playing a pincer on the lower side could also be considered. But a move on the upper side is big, too. So White immediately played at 16, with the intention of making a base in light shape, responding to the pincer at 17 with 18.

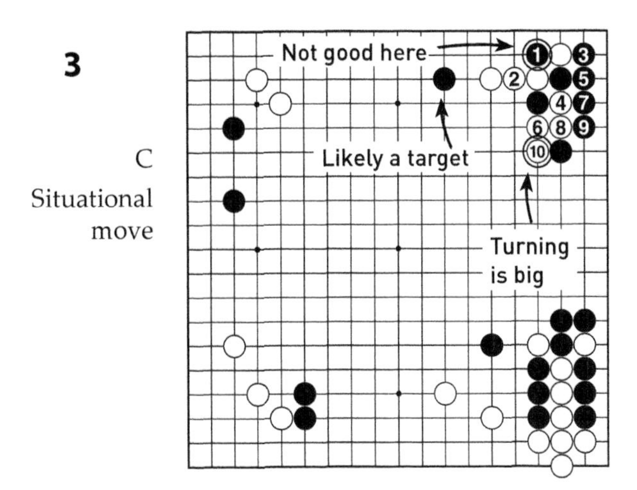

3

C

Situational move

In certain situations, Black 1 may be a feasible move, but these are very special. If Black continues here with 7, then White will have reduced the moyo effectively after 10. The result is not good for Black.

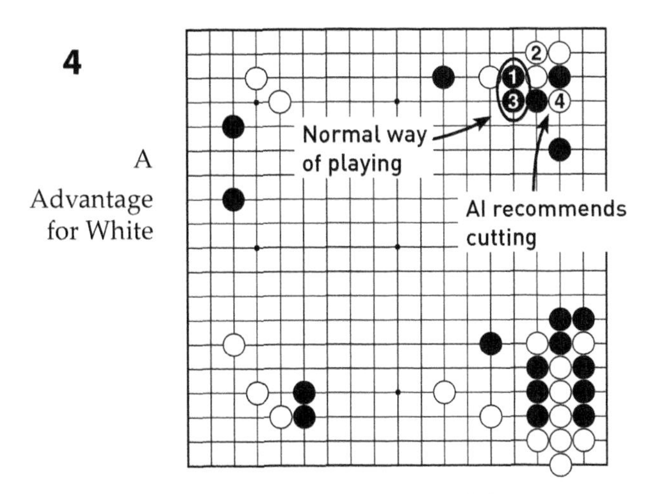

4

A

Advantage for White

Until now, Black would usually have played the atari at 1 and connected at 3. That's not uncommon in this situation. According to the AI's assessment, however, White is a little better after the cut at 4.

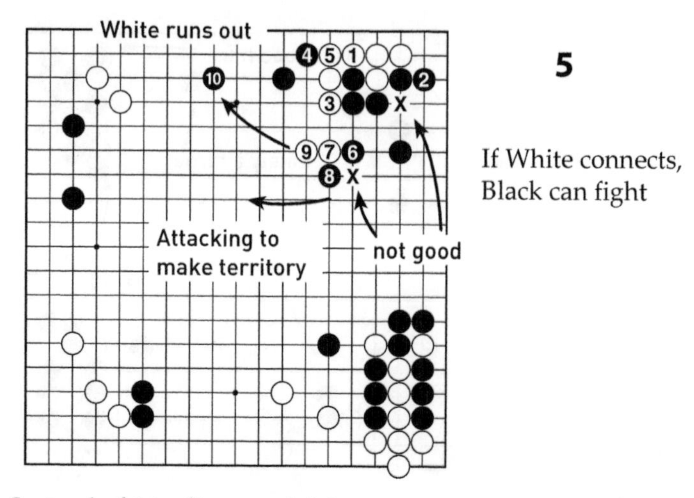

5

If White connects, Black can fight

Instead of 4 in diagram 4, it is common to connect with White 1. For Black it is sufficient to take territory on the right side and play the extension to 10 at the top. Black still has to worry about the two marked cutting points though.

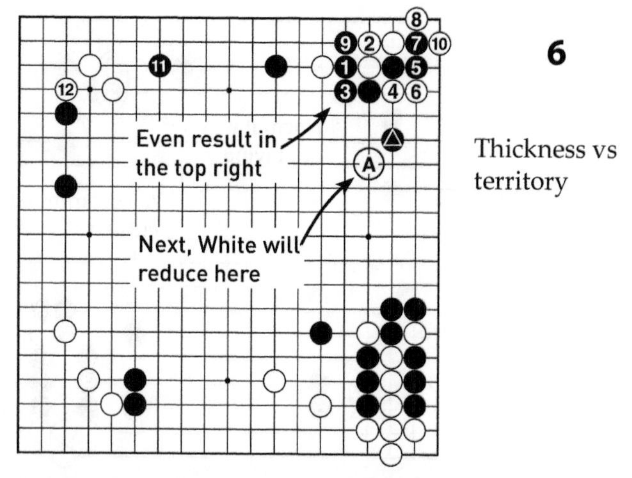

6

Thickness vs territory

So White cuts at 4. It seems that Black gets thickness in exchange for territory, but the territory in the corner is very big. The marked stone is only loosely connected and so Black probably cannot expect much territory there.

7

Gote for Black

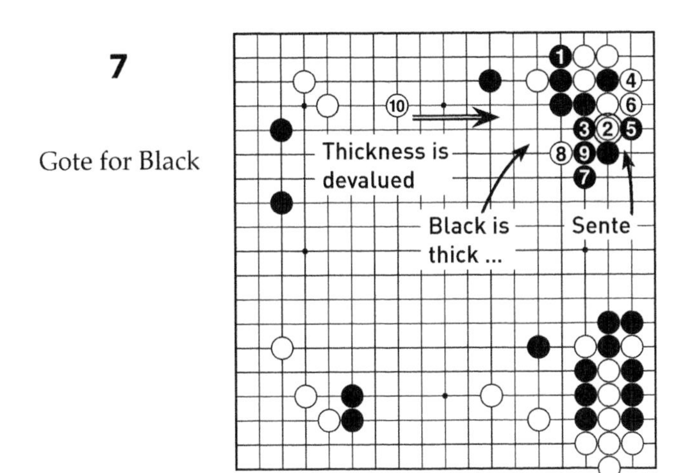

After Black 1, pushing with 2 is sente for White. Black defends the cutting point with the hanging connection at 7. The extension to 10 is now a big move, and the result is good for White.

8

B

Correct

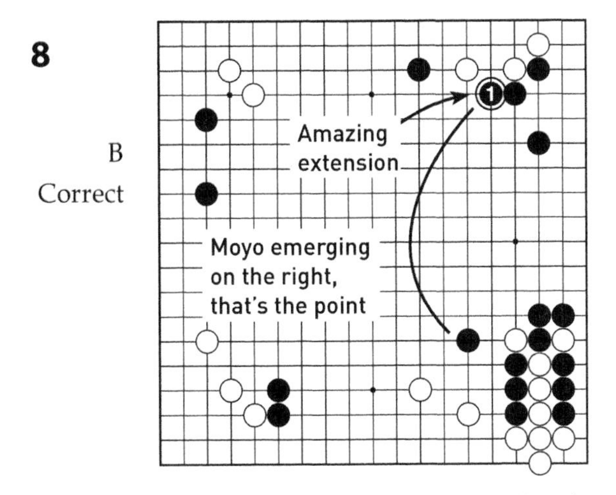

Extending at 1 is one of the sensational moves in AI style. When I first saw that move I couldn't believe my eyes. But its purpose is clear. You can easily apply this move yourself. It is also seen in pro games.

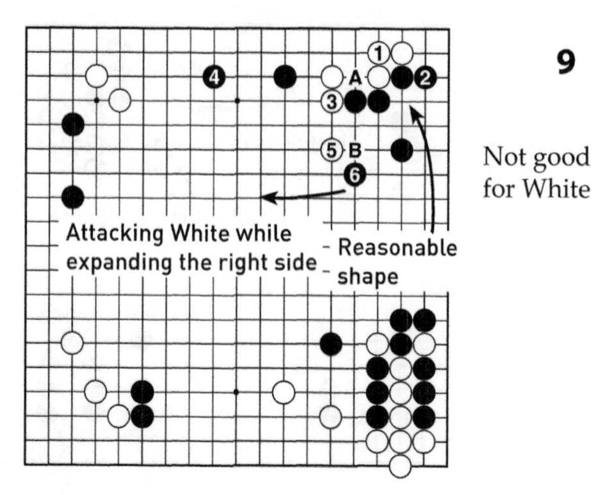

9

Not good for White

If White connects at 1, Black extends at 2. This sequence is better for Black, as with A he has one more liberty. This means that White B is now less threatening for Black.

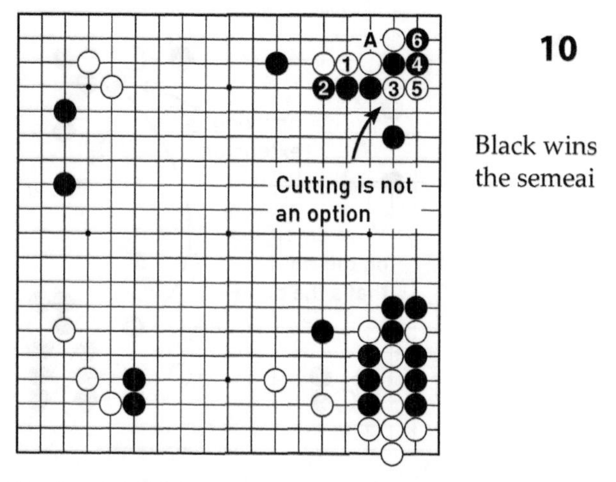

10

Black wins the semeai

That's why White connects at 1. Cutting at 3 doesn't work, because Black turns at 6 and threatens to play at A. Black wins the semeai. Here we see the effect of Black's extending at 1 in diagram 8.

11

Moyo on the right side

Acceptable result for both parties

The moyo is impressive

The atari at 1 is an alternative for White. After Black 4 White defends at 5. This concludes the fight for the time being. After White moving at A, Black further expands his moyo with B. This is a possible continuation after the marked stone.

12

First hane in the corner

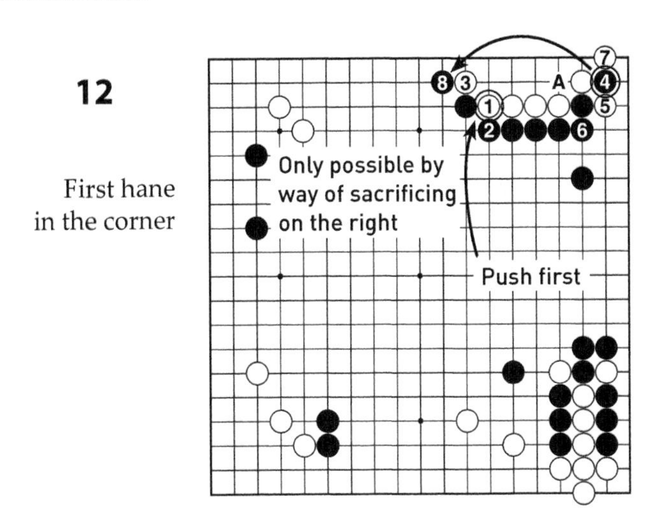

White pushes at 1 in order to make big life. Black plays the hane at 4 and threatens to cut at A. Therefore, White plays 5 and 7.

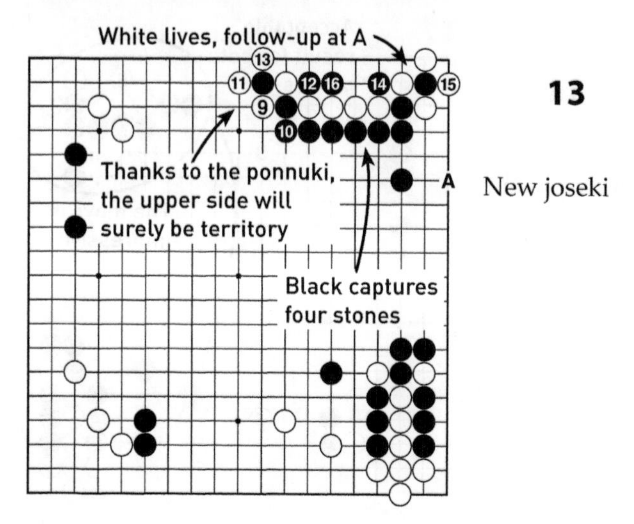

13

New joseki

White takes one stone, Black captures four stones. The result is an interesting trade-off that has also been seen in other pro games. Even though the position drastically changes, the result is even. So it's probably going to be a new joseki.

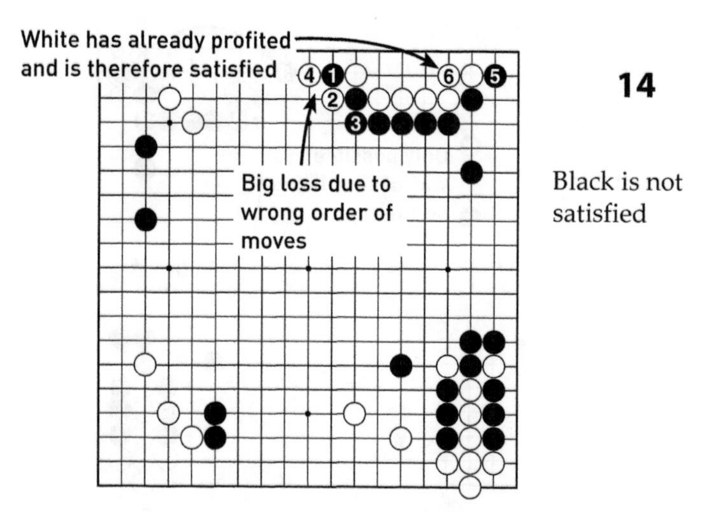

14

Black is not satisfied

If Black first plays 1 on the outside, then the result after 5 is unsatisfactory, as White now defends at 6. However if Black begins with 5 and White defends at 6, then it's enough for him to extend at 2. Black would then have good shape.

15

The game 1

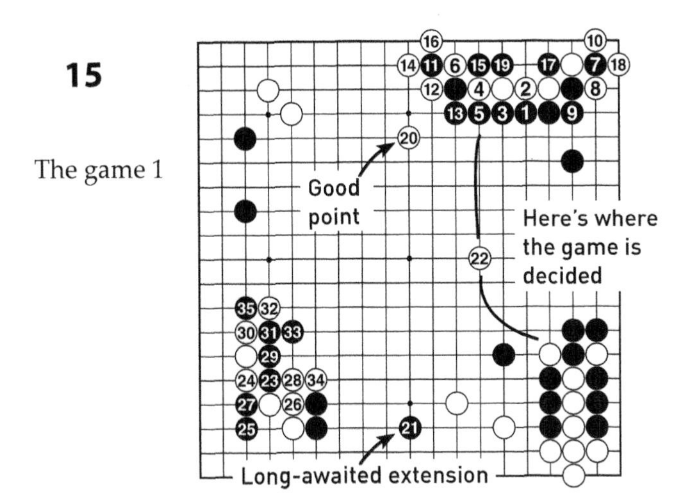

White 20 and Black 21 are extremely big moves. With 22, White aimed for a gentle reduction of the right side. His reaction to Black's counter-move at 23 was a strong one. A complicated fight developed.

16

The game 2

White 58 at 52
White 59 at 39

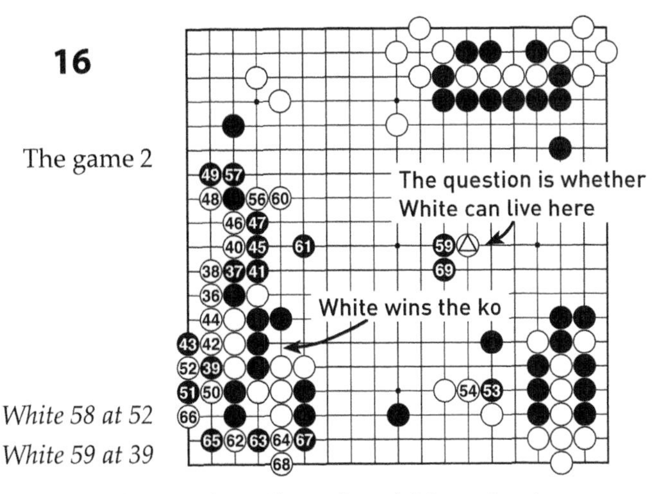

The cut at 50 led to a ko. White played 56 as a ko threat. However, White cannot respond to Black 59. Black used 69 as a ko threat in order to capture the marked stone. After that, a new fight began.

The game

Moves after 115 omitted.
Black wins by resignation.

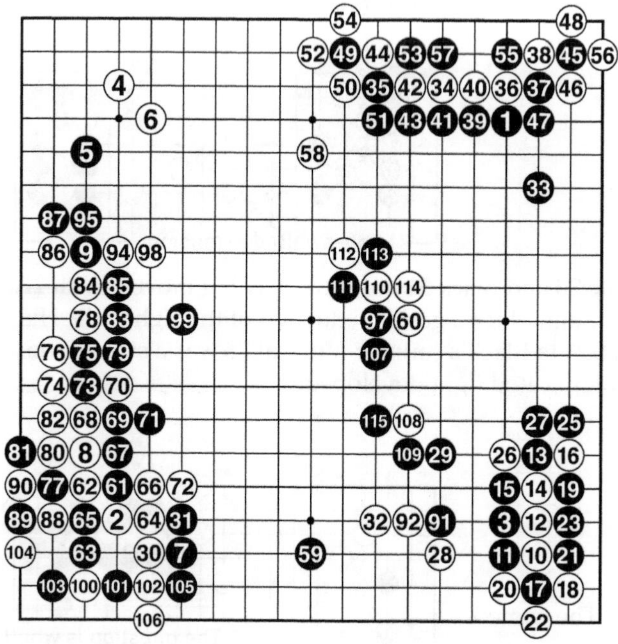

White 24 at 17, Black 93 at 77, White 96 at 90

In the next game, Mukai Chiaki 5p encounters Choi Jeong 9p, the world's strongest female player, at the IMSA Elite Mind Games.

Game 6

Lately one hasn't seen Choi Jeong, as the world's strongest female player, lose a game against other female players, but here Mukai wins against Choi. Although this book focuses on the opening in AI style, the middle and end game are also fascinating and worthy of examination.

(1 – 5)

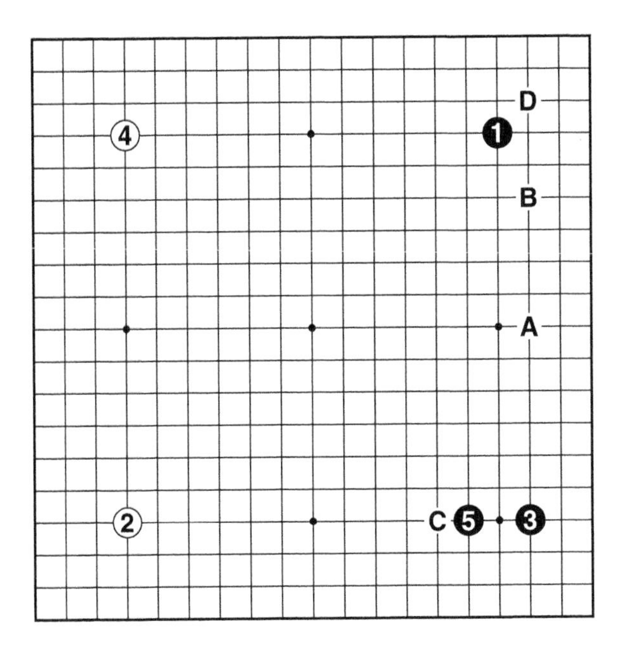

White to play

This position could often be found in collections of opening problems where in each case only one specific move was seen as correct. However, in recent times the situation has changed, with a variety of moves coming into consideration. Here, of course, we take a look at the AI move.

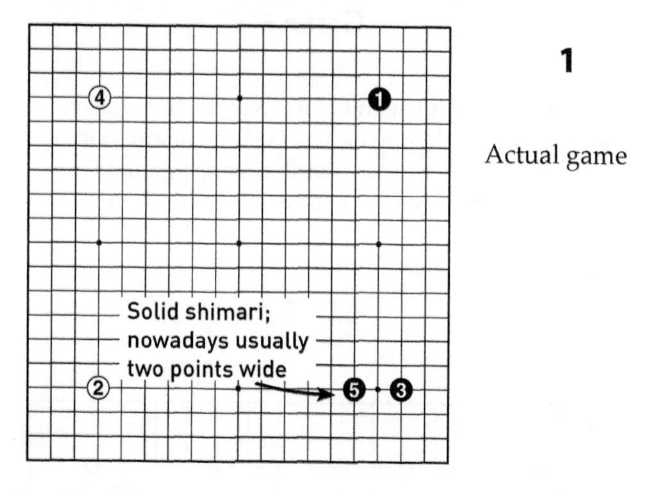

1

Actual game

For Black 5, AI recommends the large two-point shimari. The shimari at 5 is also good and is still often played. It has its benefits and also its drawbacks.

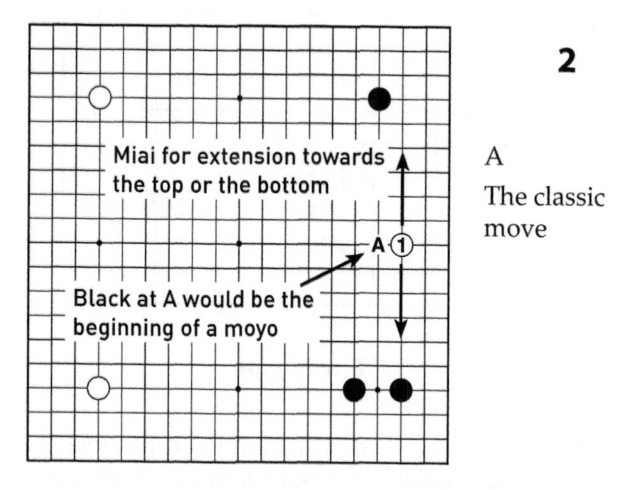

2

A
The classic move

In the past, the response was almost exclusively the move at 1. If Black gets to play at A, the position on the right side is virtually ideal. White 1 prevents that. It is the natural move and nowadays regarded as not bad.

3

The reason why breaking up the side isn't played anymore

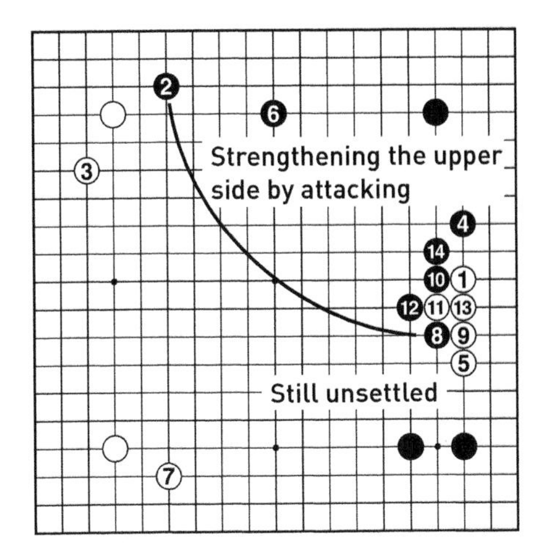

The sequence shown here, however, has established itself. The number of pros who dislike that move has been increasing. As a result, other moves are being considered.

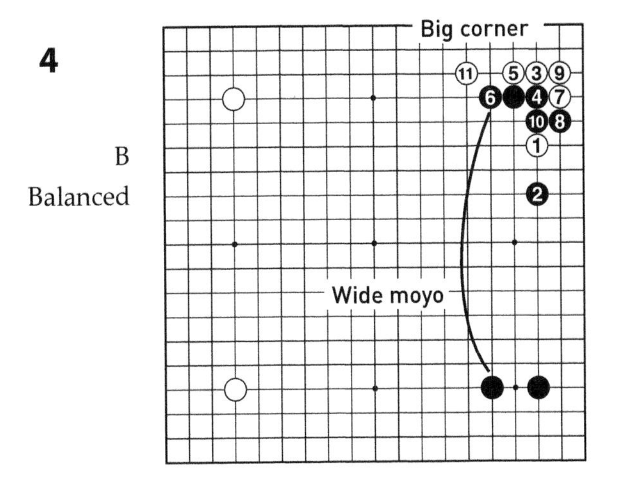

The kakari at 1 is chosen as a consequence. Black's pincer at 2 is seen as the perfect response. White gets a big corner and the result is generally regarded as balanced.

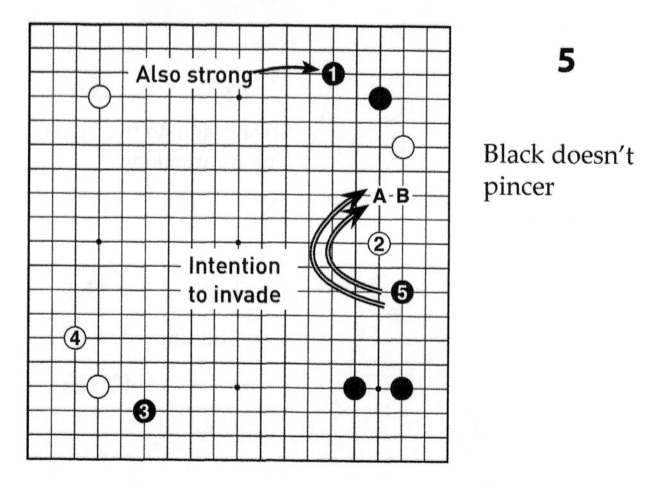

5

Black doesn't pincer

A common response to White's kakari is Black 1. After White 2, Black prevents a further extension of White with 5, additionally exerting pressure by threatening to invade at A or B.

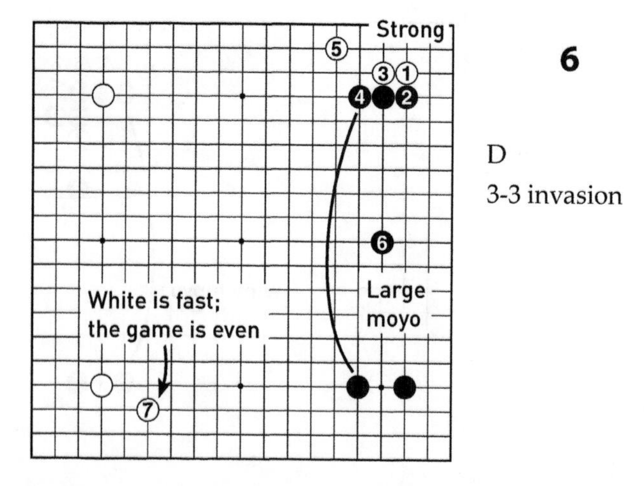

6

D

3-3 invasion

The AI style of play, of course, is the invasion at 3-3. It is therefore no surprise that it is frequently played. Up to this point, the diagrams are not that different from one another, and so you can pick your favourite.

7

C

Correct

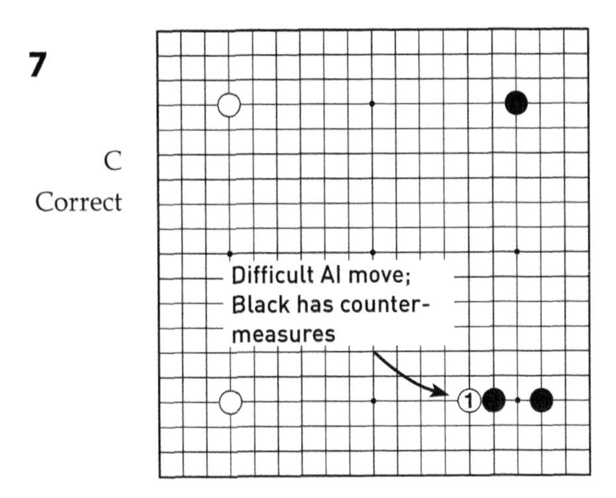

The unusual move at 1, a new move in AI style, is a probe to gauge Black's reaction. Black has a variety of strong responses. That's why this move seems difficult to master for White.

8

Extending towards the edge

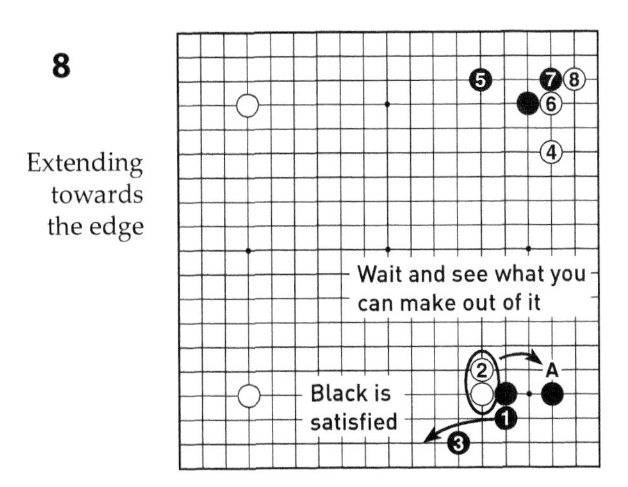

Extending at 1 leads to a variation with the low shimari. You could say that the kakari has worked out so far.
If White extends at 2 next, Black jumps to 3. This continuation is normal.

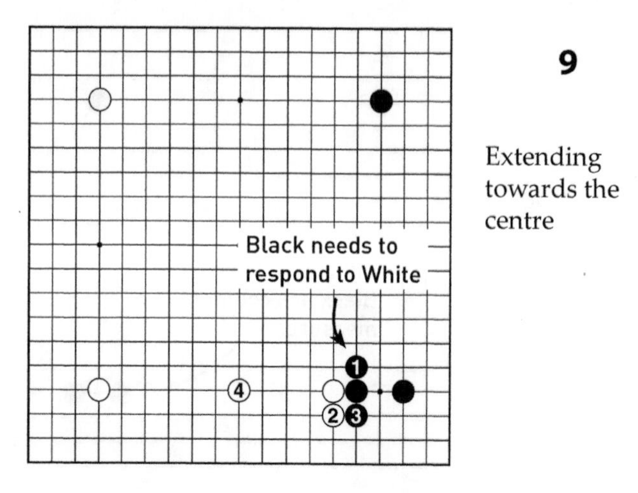

9

Extending towards the centre

Extending upwards isn't played. White extends towards the bottom and when Black blocks at 3, White jumps to 4. For Black, this way of playing is too slow.

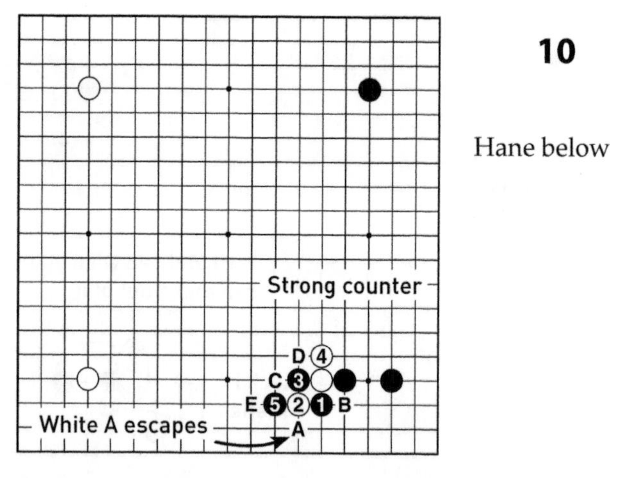

10

Hane below

After the hane below, Black 3 and 5 are a strong continuation. White can throw away the two stones above with the sequence A to E. This is a strong way of playing.

11

Sacrificing one stone is also good for White

Black 4 connects

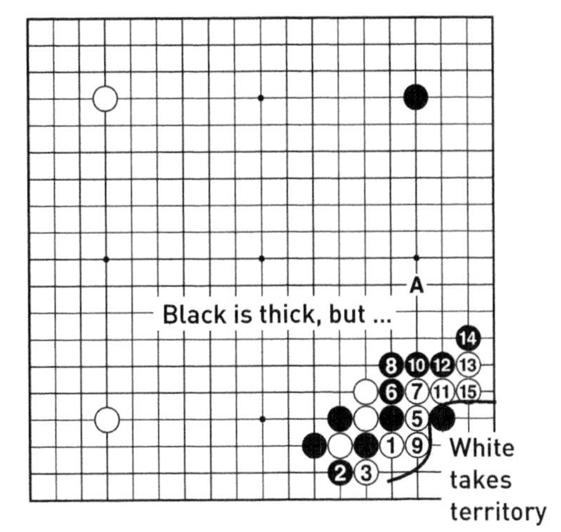

Instead of the sequence in diagram 10, cutting at 1 is an interesting variation. With regards to thickness, Black clearly gained. But the corner is big, especially since Black was here first. If Black plays at 9 instead of 6, then White first follows up with 6 and then jumps to A.

12

Hane above

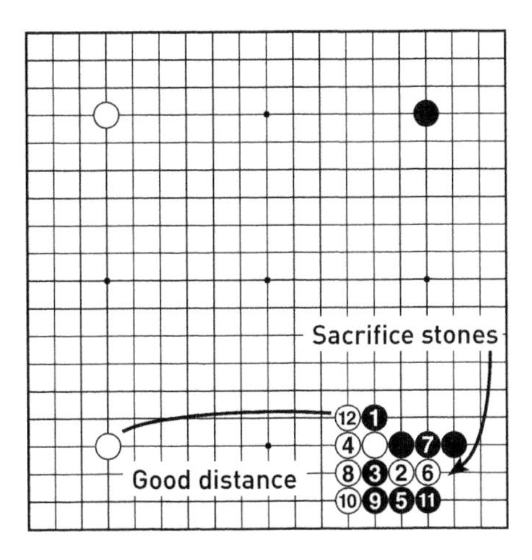

White's response to the hane above is to counter-hane below at 2. White need not worry about the cut at 3, as White can sacrifice two stones. After 12 the result isn't bad for White.

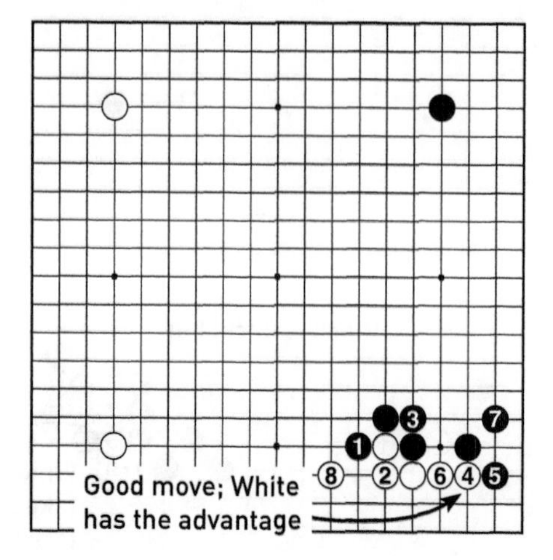

13

White's attachment is a success

Instead of 3 in diagram 12, Black 1 and 3 are natural moves. If White now immediately plays at 6 and Black blocks at 4, then Black's position won't be bad. But White can penetrate one step further into the corner with the attachment at 4.

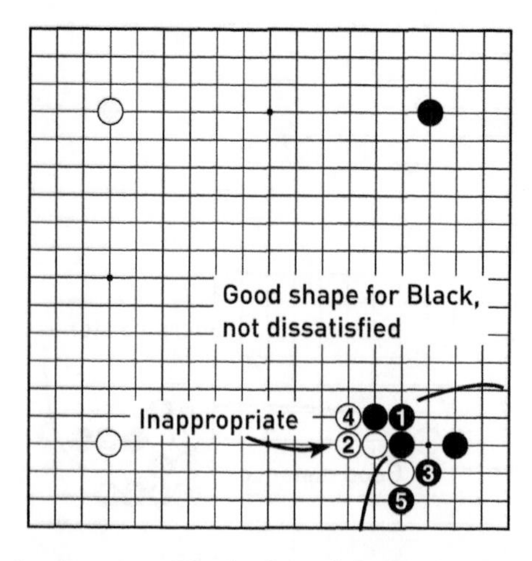

14

Good shape for Black

In the game Black played 1. If White extends at 2, Black having skipped the atari, Black makes good shape with 3 and 5. Black is not dissatisfied.

15

The game 1

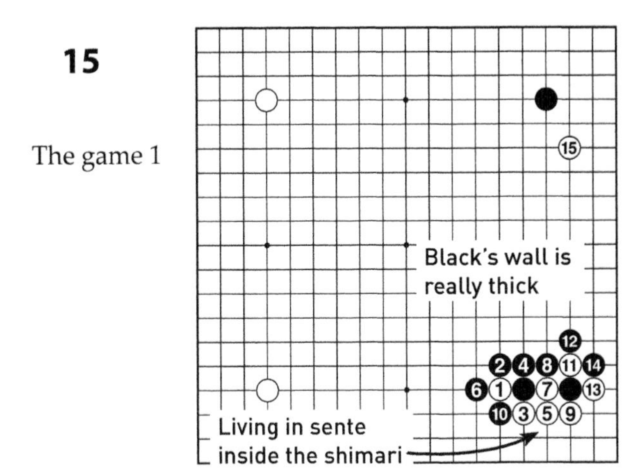

White countered the atari at 6 with 7 and penetrated into the corner. This new joseki concluded with Black 14. Black is looking thick, but the result is regarded as even.

16

The game 2

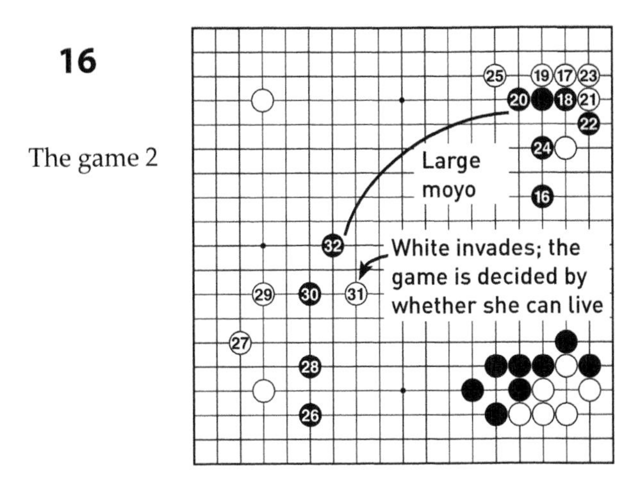

An enormous moyo emerged, reaching from the top right corner to the lower side. White invaded the moyo with 31 and the game hinged on how strongly Black could actually attack this stone.

The game

Moves after 93 omitted.
Black wins by resignation.

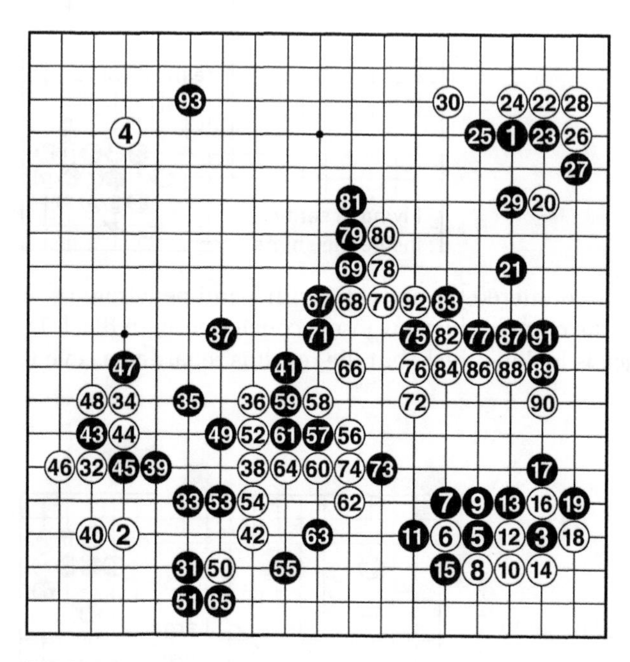

Black 85 at 3

The next game shows the encounter between Byun Sangil 9p from Korea and Tao Xinran 7p from China, in the second round of the 24th LG Cup. Byun ranks among the strongest Korean players. Tao is showing similarly strong results in China.

Game 7

In the opening, a position arises in the upper left corner that is not easy to play without previous study. The two players boldly embarked on a battle defined by difficult development.

(1 – 10)

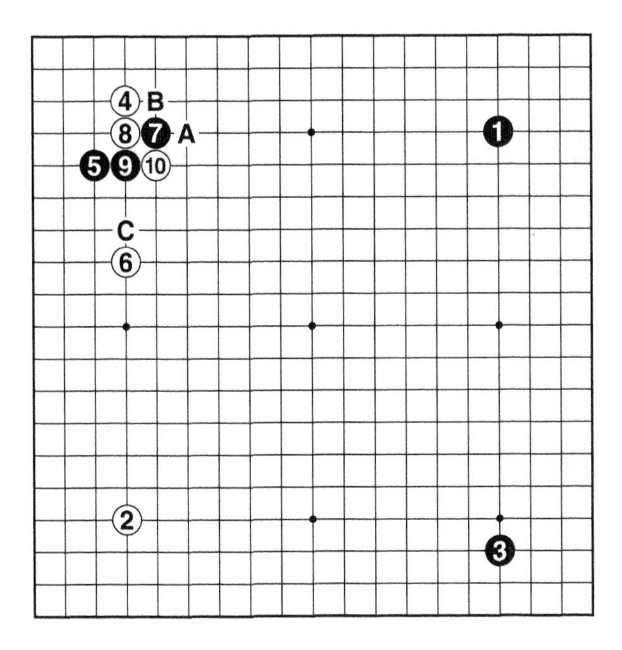

Black to play

The number of pro games in which White plays the pincer at 6 has considerably declined. The main reason for this is that the AI has pointed out a severe response for Black. It is difficult to come up with a suitable countermeasure.

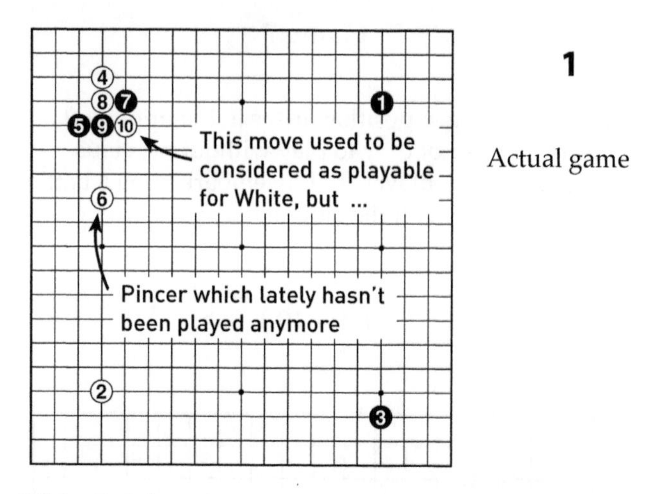

1

Actual game

White 6 and cutting at 10 are a strategy in which White deliberately invites the playing of a new AI move, letting himself come under attack, and striking back only then. Today this way of playing is regarded as advantageous for Black, but because there are difficult variations, this assessment may still change in the future.

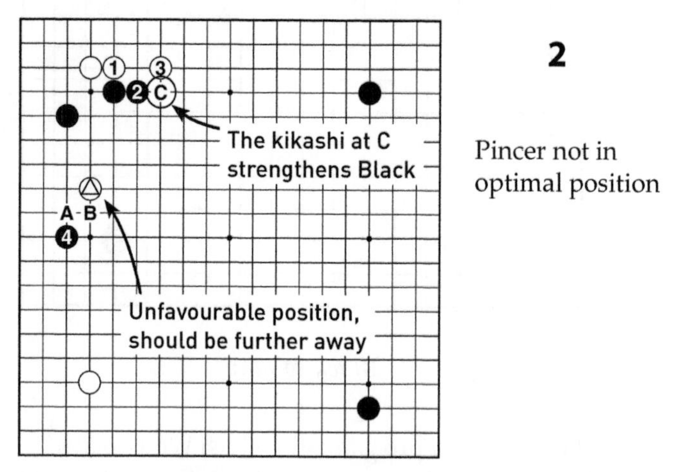

2

Pincer not in optimal position

White 1 is hardly playable, as the marked stone is in an unfavourable position. If you wanted to play like this, the stone would be better placed at A or B. If White starts with the high two-point pincer, he should proceed like in the game, cutting Black.

3

C
Peaceful division

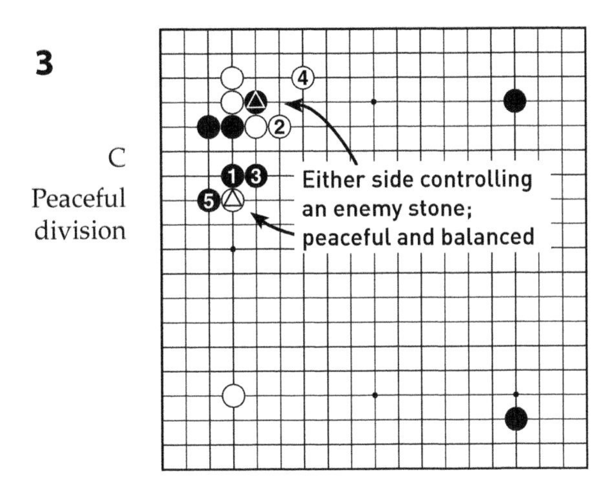

The contact play at 1 is a good move. The continuation up to 5 used to be played often. If you want to play a smooth game then this is a suitable way of playing.

4

Complicated variation

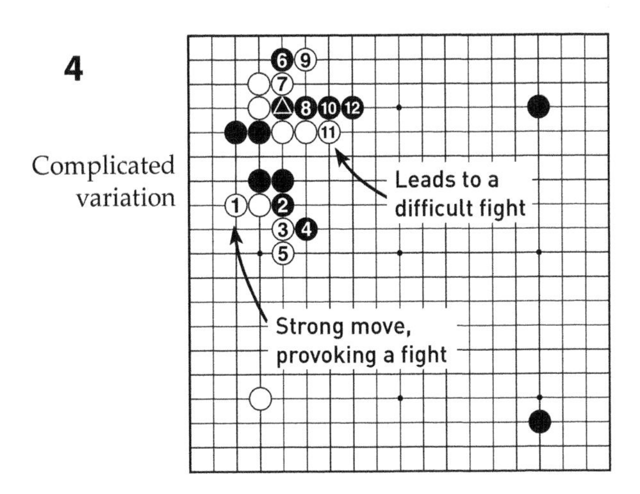

While the previous diagram shows a peaceful way of playing, White can also take a harder path with 1. This sequence was popular for some time. After the marked stone has been cut, fighting cannot be avoided if one of the players is bent on it.

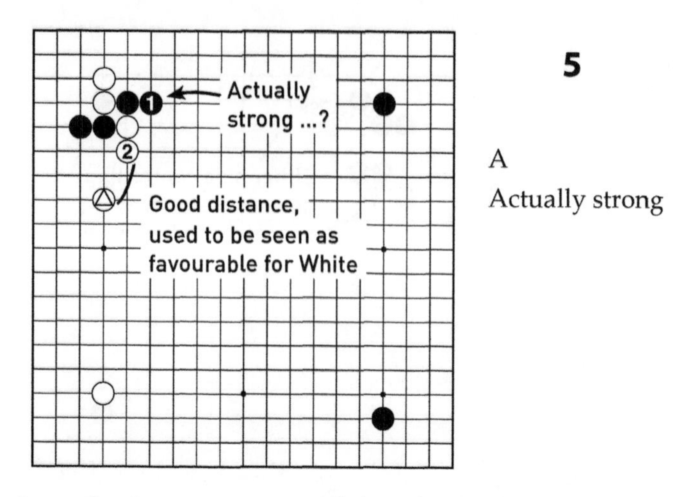

It used to be uncontroversial that after both sides extend at 1 and 2 respectively, White has the advantage in this fight. AI however rates extending at 1 as good for Black and sees no advantage for White.

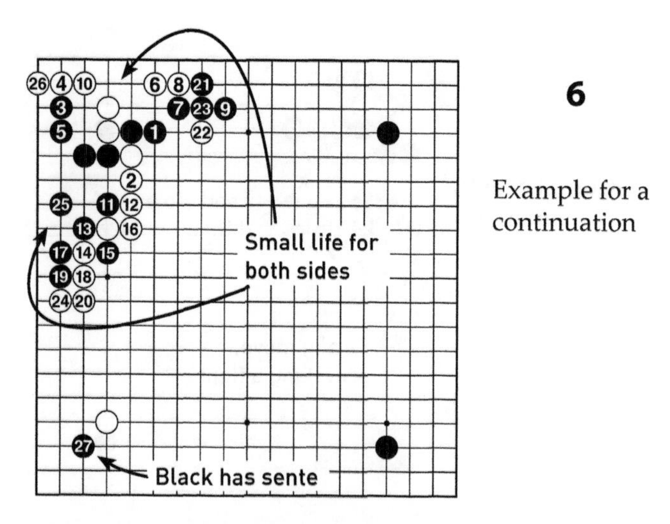

Taking this continuation as an example, we can see that the result is not bad for Black. Black 1 might gain in importance in the future. In the game, however, Black played 1 in diagram 7, presenting White with some different challenges.

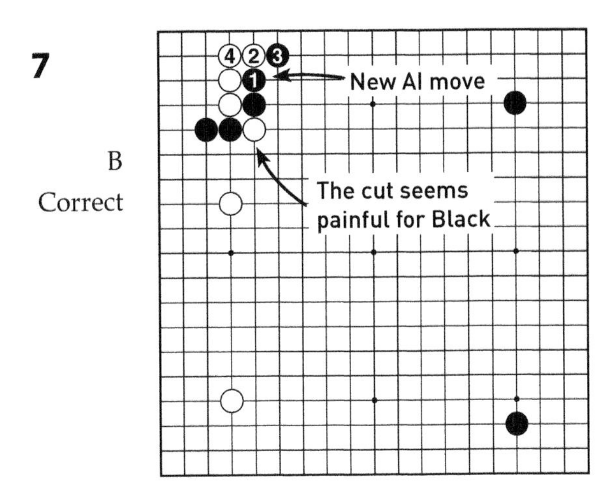

Blocking at 1 is a strong move brought up by AI and resulting in the pincer being played less often. At first glance it looks like a trick move by Black which cannot work.

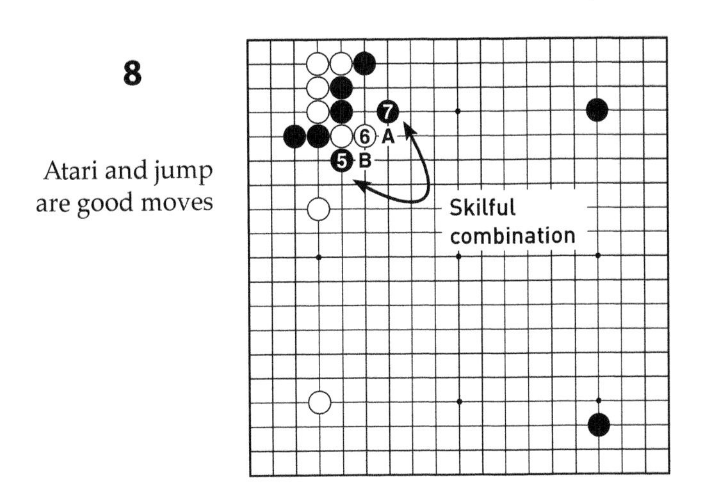

After that, Black follows up with the skilful moves of 5 and 7, and White is in trouble. For White, a move at A or B is the natural response. But Black can extend and make good shape.

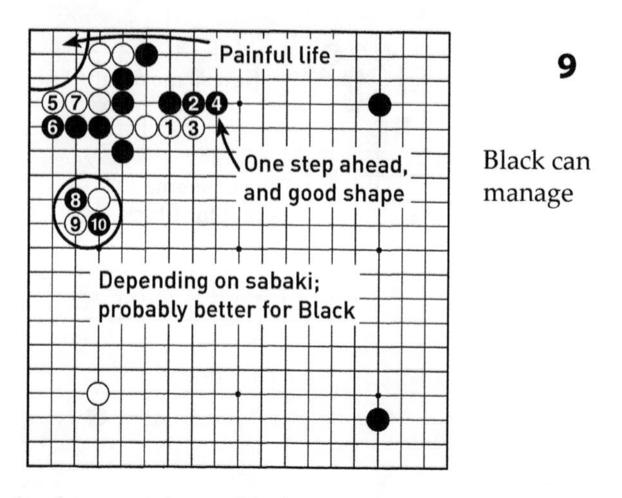

9

Black can manage

Pushing at 1 forces Black to play at 2, improving his shape. However, it doesn't mean that this is clearly good for Black. Living in gote with 7 is bitter. After cutting with 8 and 10, Black seems to manage quite well here.

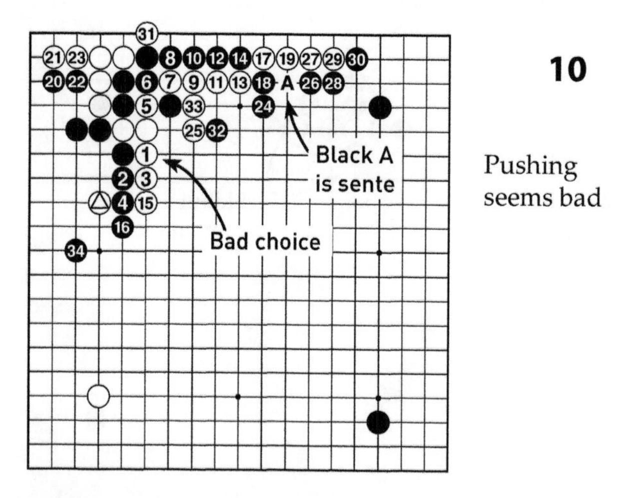

10

Pushing seems bad

Pushing with White 1 looks like a bad way of playing, as the marked stone is given up. There are a variety of options, but if you play like in this diagram, then it doesn't look bad for Black.

11

Seems like a difficult fight for Black

Probably going to be captured

If White lives after cutting at A, then Black gets thick; this is bitter for White

Good move

White 1 is a move that dampens Black's momentum but is not strong enough for Black having to answer. So Black jumps into the corner. This position seems like a tough battle for White, but it's not that simple.

12

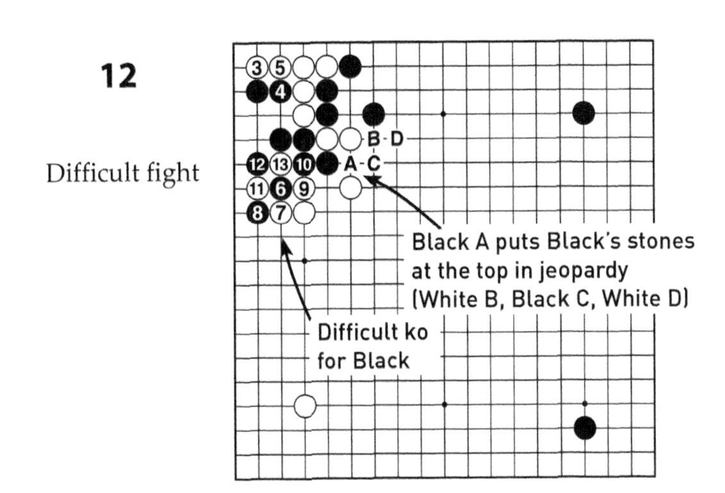

Difficult fight

Next, White 3 as well as Black 4 and 6 can be expected. White 7 and 9 are surprisingly powerful and lead to a difficult fight. Because White's cut at 10 is sente, Black wants to connect at 10. But now a ko begins and Black is not completely alive yet.

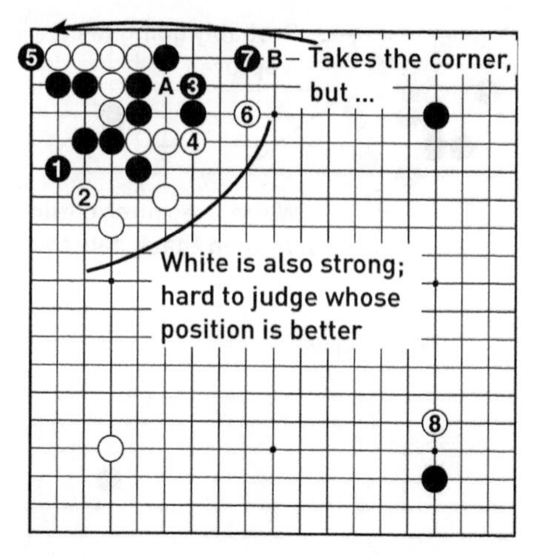

13

Sacrifice stones

Instead of 6 in the previous diagram, Black can play the solid move at 1, but things remain difficult after White 2. Black is worried about A and therefore plays 3 and 5. This means that White gives up six stones in the corner and keeps an eye on the aji at B for later.

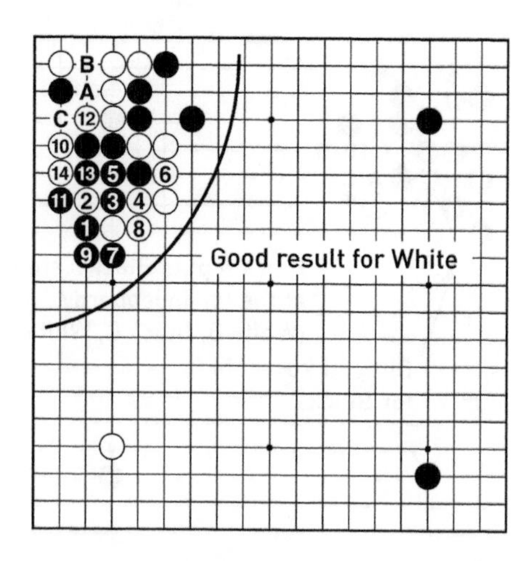

14

The meaning of the attachment

Black 15 at 2

In the game Black neglected exchanging A for B and played the attachment at 1. The reason might be that Black expected this sequence, which then wouldn't leave a cutting point at C. That would be very bad of course.

15

The game 1

Black getting enclosed; looking good for White

A and B are miai

At first glance, the position looks better for Black, as A and B are miai. But it actually isn't satisfactory for him. This shape offers several strong continuations for Black, but it can't be said that his position is therefore better, because this shape has not yet been studied sufficiently.

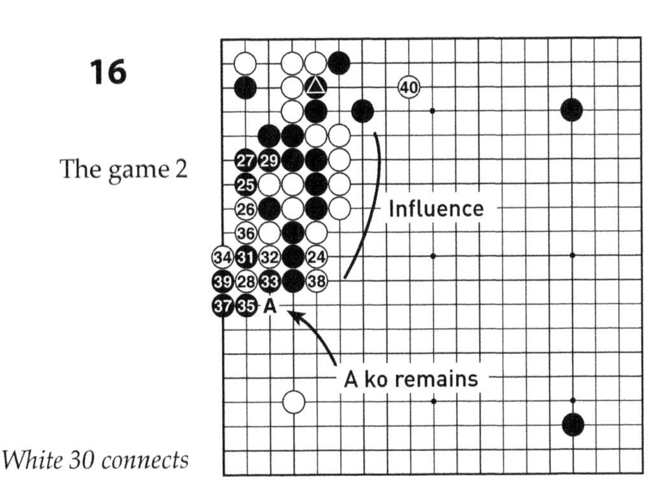

16

The game 2

White 30 connects

White was captured on the left side but got to play the pincer at 40. That isn't bad for White. On closer inspection there's even a ko remaining. The new AI move (marked stone) is strong, and therefore it's normal for White to try and prevent it.

The game

Moves after 92 omitted.
Black wins by resignation.

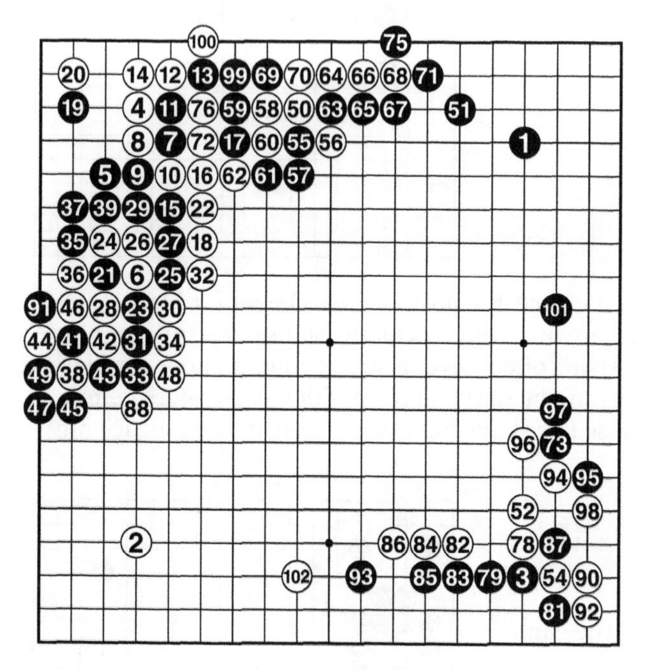

White 40 at 21, Black 53, 77, 89 at 41,
White 74, 80 at 38

The next game was played by Oomote Takuto 2p and Numadate Sakiya 6p in the Shinjin O Tournament.

Column 2

Go and shogi

Rather than two rivals, the relationship between the world of go and the world of shogi is better described as one between two good brothers. A friendly relationship between the two has been established over a long period.

I only play shogi as a hobby, and recently I learned that the oldest record containing a specific tactical position, the "rook (chariot) on the 4th line" (右四間飛車, *migi shikenhisha*) comes up in a shogi book by Ōhashi Sōkei and Honinbō Sansa (founder of the Honinbō house, also a strong shogi player).

I was surprised, as I didn't think I would find the name Honinbō Sansa in a shogi book. As for special terminology, there is a lot that both games have in common. The most well-known example is keima, a go term derived from the knight's move in shogi (桂馬, *keima* = cassia horse).

There are a lot more terms for which the exact origins are unclear. Terms such as sabaki and hiraki are also used in shogi. It's hard to think of this as a coincidence. It seems plausible enough that some ancient player found them interesting and worthy of adopting, and that they became established later as years went on.

For me, shogi is a hobby – although it is not only a hobby, but also a great complement to my activities as a go player. The reason I wrote this book was that I took part in a tribodian tournament (a go-shogi-othello tournament) which was sponsored by the Mynavi Publishing Corporation, and they approached me. When I was writing the book, I recalled my viewpoint as a reader of shogi books, which are easy to understand because of their style of diagrams and the way they are written. These were valuable insights that I gleaned from my experience as a reader of shogi books for amateurs.

Another plus is good sleep. I used to suffer from sleep disorders at night in the past, but when I began reading shogi books in bed, my troubles vanished. Novels weren't conducive to sleeping, as I would always be concerned about how things might continue. Although in places, shogi books can be rather heavy mental fare, I fall asleep before I know it. Perhaps some readers have had a similar experience with this phenomenon. I'd be happy if somebody reads my book and finds good sleep at night as a result, haha!

Game 8

The Shinjin O Tournament is a big stage for young pros. As as result, they usually shy away from trying out new techniques. Here, though, both players apply them confidently. The opening shown here was popular for a while, especially in online games.

(1 – 7)

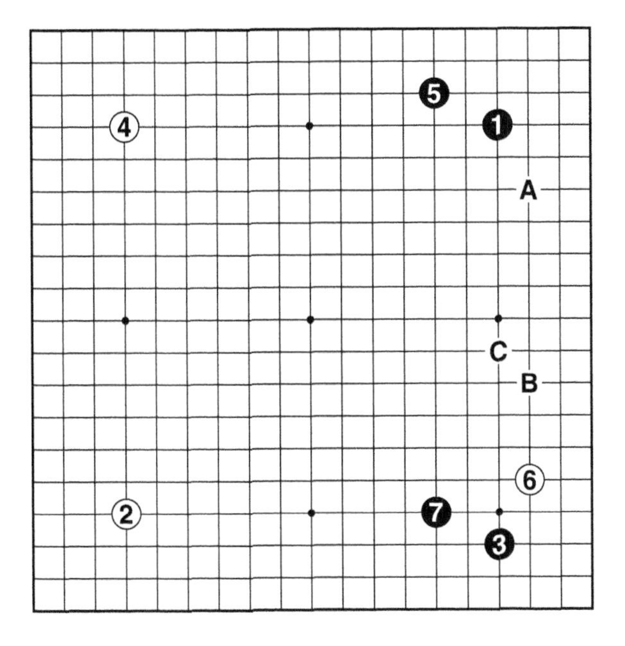

White to play

Black responded to White 6 with the keima at 7. Then White chose a special AI move that differs from the traditional way of playing. Not only this next move, but also the following plays are remarkable.

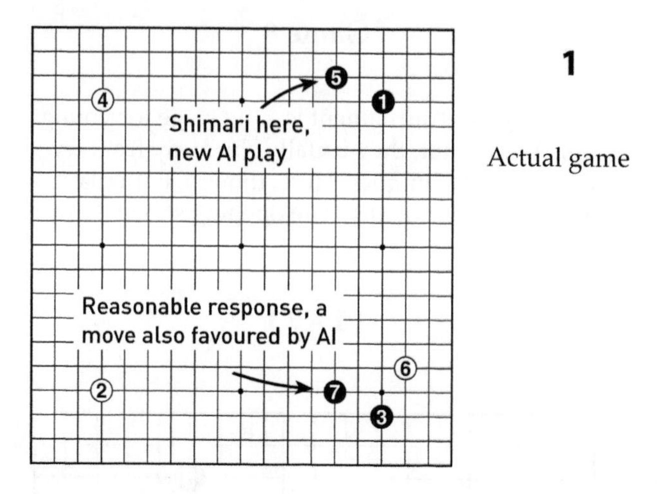

1

Actual game

The shimari at 5 is another move that came up through AI. Until now it was normal to play the shimari at 6. This opening was chiefly popular in online games.

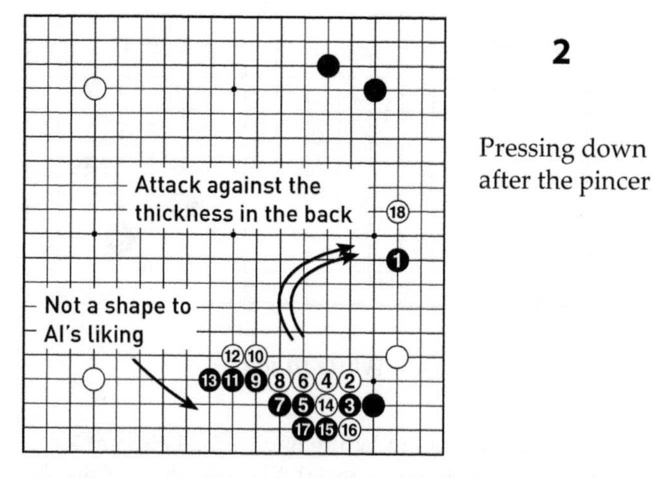

2

Pressing down after the pincer

Black wants to attack with the pincer at 1, but then White presses down with 2. AI rates the shape after White 2 up to Black 5 as good for White. That's why this variation is rarely played anymore.

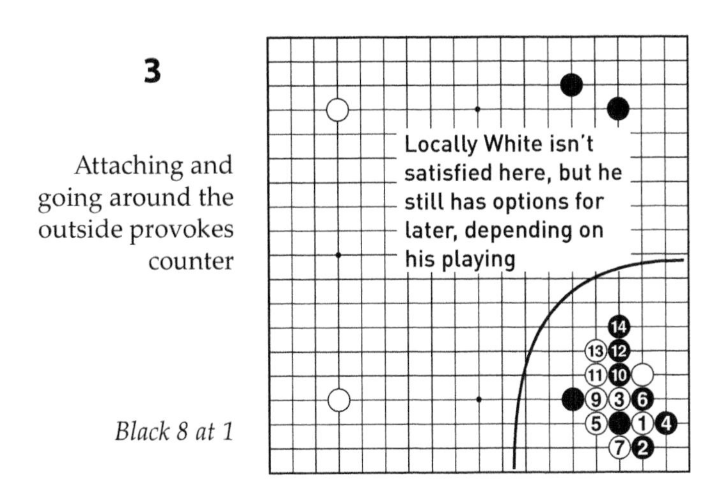

3

Attaching and going around the outside provokes counter

Black 8 at 1

White 1 and 3 are countered by Black 4. In the end Black cuts at 10. That's a disadvantage for White.

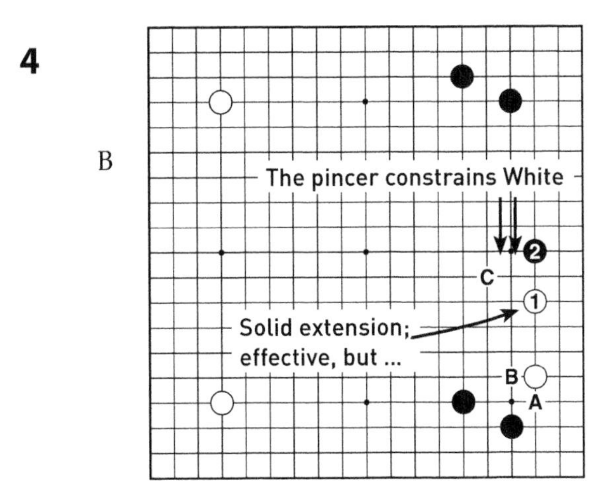

4

B

The two-point extension is a normal, solid move. But after Black comes close with 2, the extension isn't broad enough. White could get attacked with A to C.

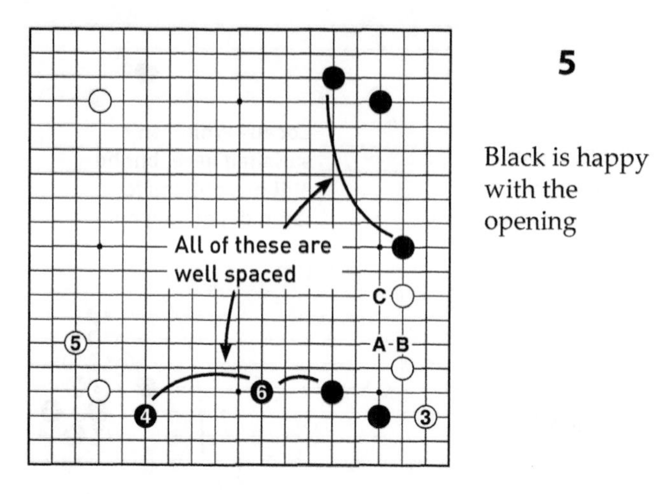

5

Black is happy with the opening

Jumping into the corner with 3 is big, but Black 4 and 6 take the lower side. Next, the sequence of Black A, White B, Black C is looming, which would create a moyo reaching from the lower edge to the right side.

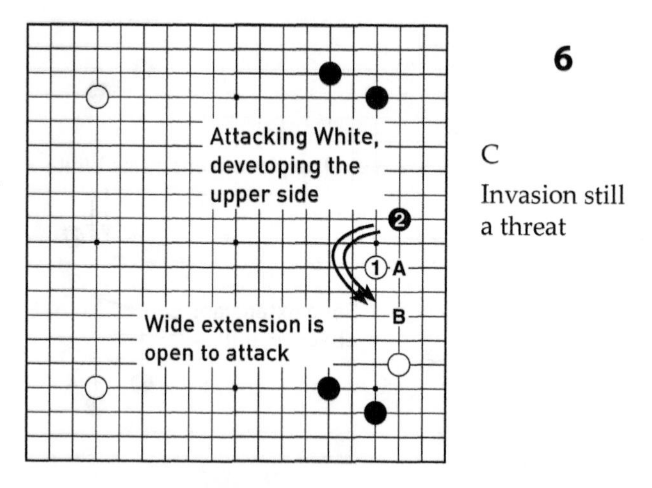

6

C

Invasion still a threat

White 1 is a wide and open extension. Black prohibits further extension of White with 2 and aims at an invasion. In order to prevent that, White needs to play once more, which is bitter. White A has a small advantage compared to 1, but the weak point at B remains all the same.

7

Possible way of playing

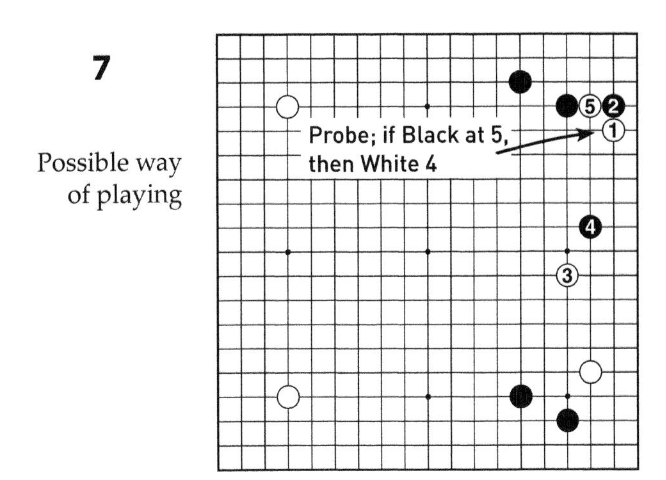

It's also interesting for White to play at 1 first, if he has the wide extension to 3 in mind. After Black 4 White squeezes in between the Black stones with 5. Even though this is an uncommon sequence, it has been played in games before.

8

A Correct

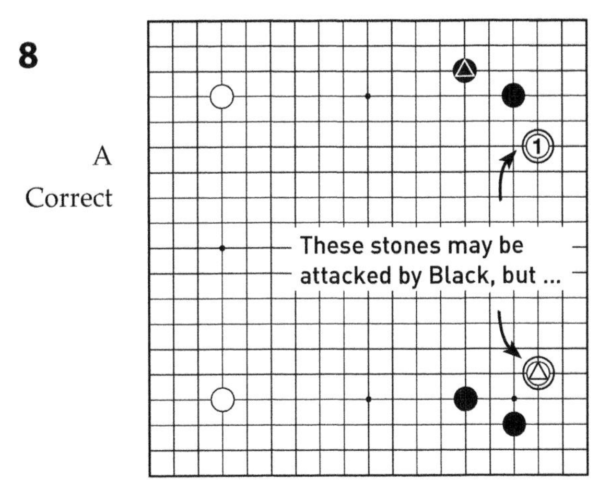

In spite of the marked stone already being present, White plays at 1. This is the AI method, which at first seems a little odd. Both of White's stones might come under attack; however, White can be flexible.

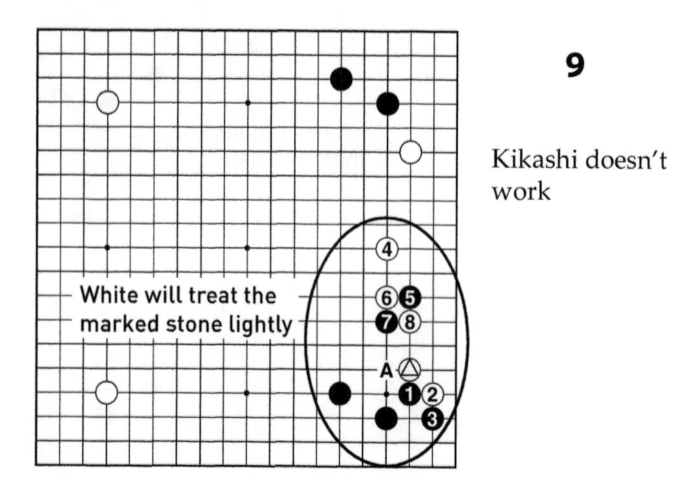

9

Kikashi doesn't work

The kick is intended to force White into bad shape. White won't respond though. Maybe White can sacrifice the marked stone and be satisfied if the continuation proceeds like in this diagram.

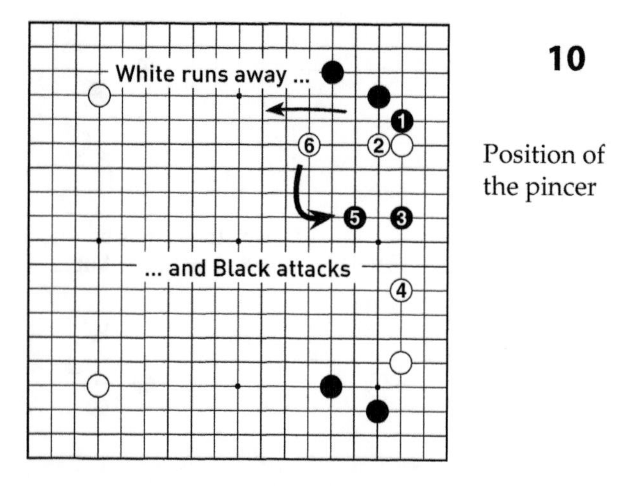

10

Position of the pincer

After the kick, White can't play tenuki, as Black's hane at 2 would be bitter for him. It's hard for Black to find the proper pincer. Black 3 is a normal move locally, but now White can play the extension to 4. The attack against White with 3 and 5 is feeble. Black is in need of a creative idea.

11

Black's wish

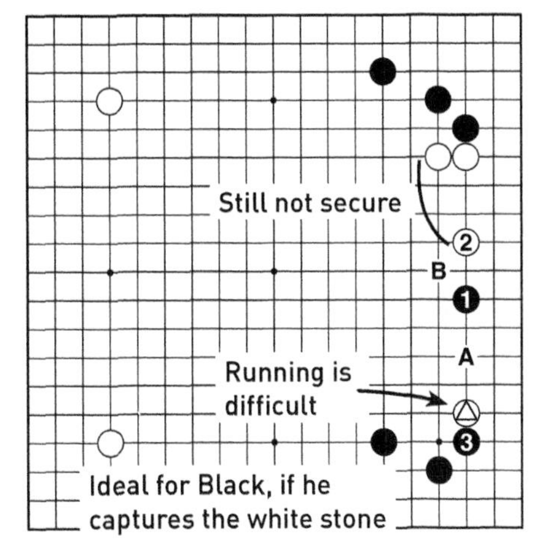

Black 1 is the creative pincer. Playing the extension to 2 is common, after which the kosumi below is a strong attack. Because White's group at the top is still not settled, White cannot start running at the bottom. With the continuation of White A and Black B, White becomes heavy and Black has the advantage.

12

Surprising two-point jump

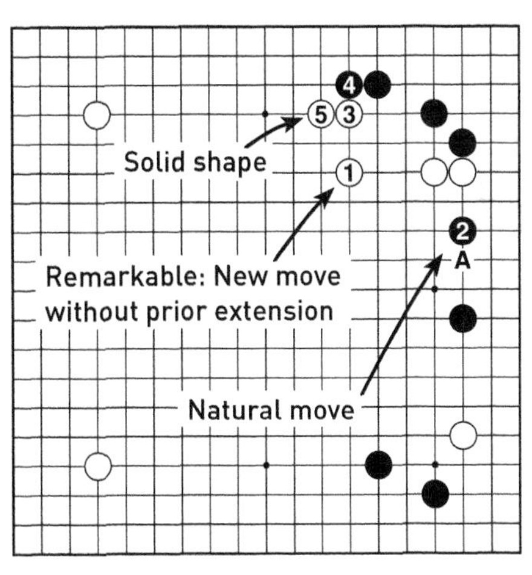

Although the extension at A is possible, White unexpectedly jumps to 1. If Black now grabs the extension on the side, White fortifies himself with 3 and 5. Now White is more solid at the top and can also play more flexibly at the bottom.

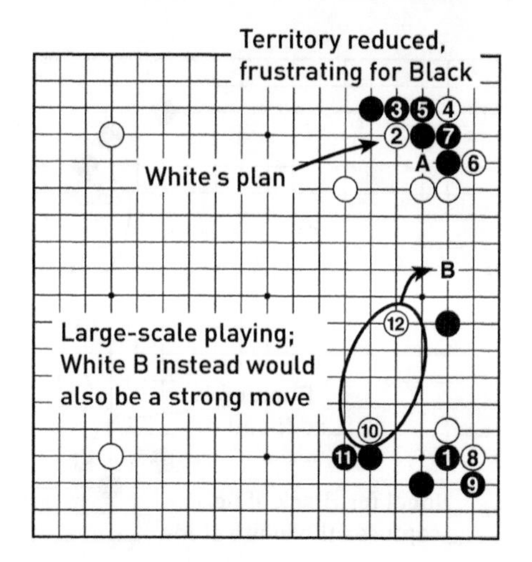

13

White's kikashi works

If Black attacks with 1, White plays the sente moves of 2 and 4. Black A instead of 5 is risky, as White cuts at 5. Connecting is therefore correct, but White still gets to play 6, as Black has to pull back at 7. This result is sufficient for White.

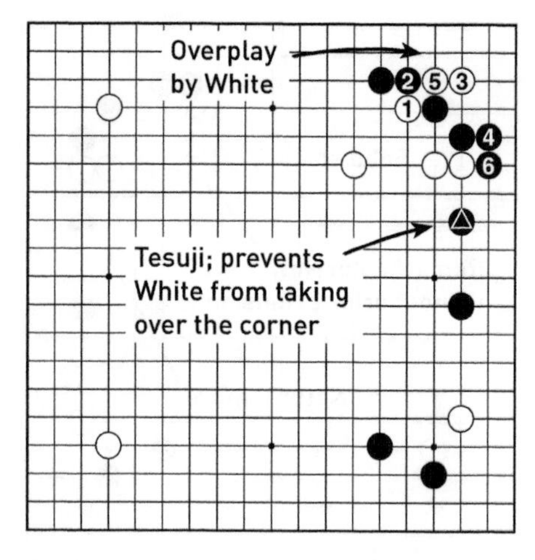

14

The meaning of Black's extension

The marked extension makes sure that White 1 won't work. White 3 is frustrated by Black 4 and 6. Now White has neither good shape nor a follow-up. The marked Black stone prevents White from making a base and fortifies the corner at the same time.

15

The game 1

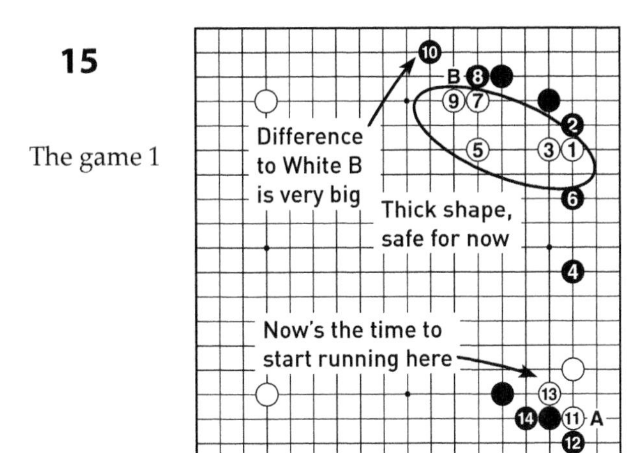

Black 10 is a big move; White plays a kikashi in the corner with 11. What happens if Black plays at A instead of 14 and then White at 14 is shown in diagram 3. As the stones at 4 and 6 are not in a favourable position for this, it's playable for White in this case.

16

The game 2

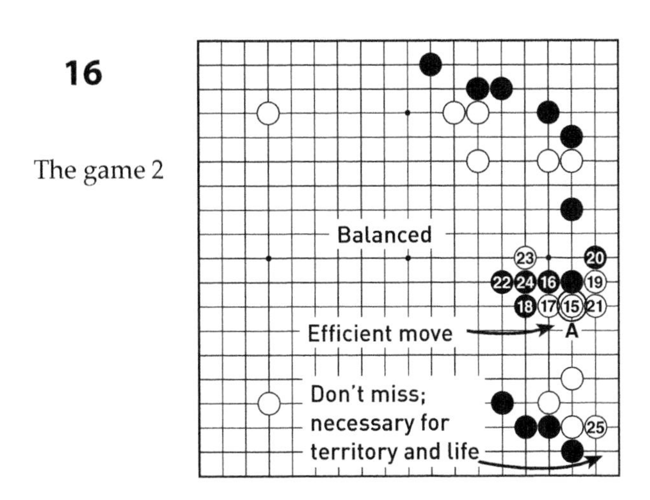

White 15 looks unusual, but with this White prevented Black's extension to A. There are many continuations similar to this one up to White 25. This shape is already well analysed.

The game

Moves after 50 omitted.
White wins by resignation.

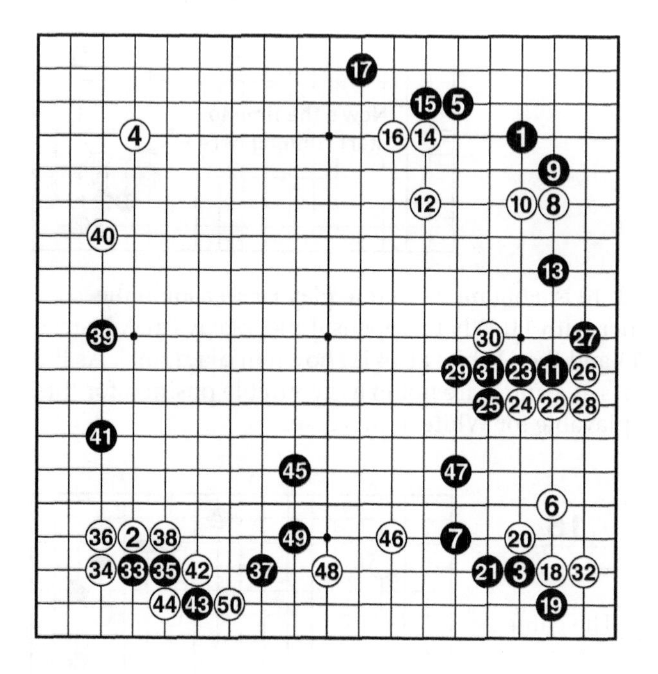

In the next game the two top pros, from Korea and China respectively, confront each other: Park Junghwan 9p and Ke Jie 9p. The encounter took place during the IMSA Elite Mind Games.

Game 9

Park Junghwan was already a go prodigy in elementary school. He became a pro at the age of 13.

(1 – 20)

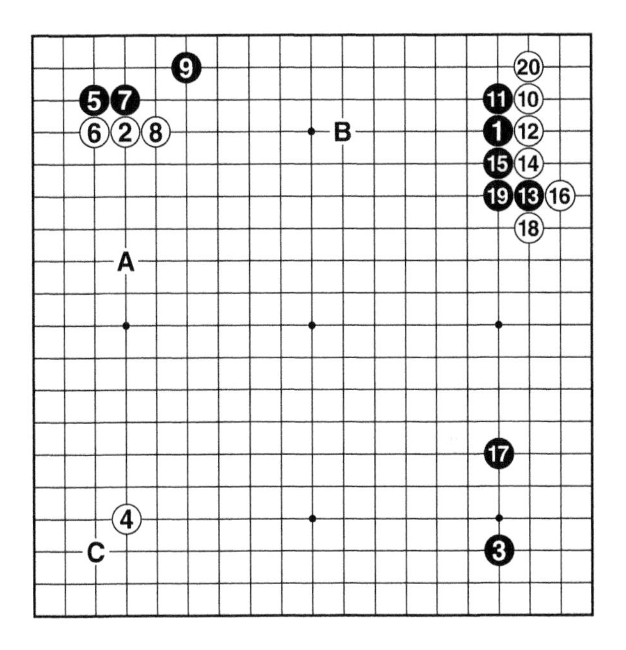

Black to play

The topic of this chapter is "After the 3-3 invasion". A 3-3 invasion has already been played in the upper left and also in the upper right. Can these two be regarded as completed? You'd like to hurry and play a big point if nothing urgent takes priority.

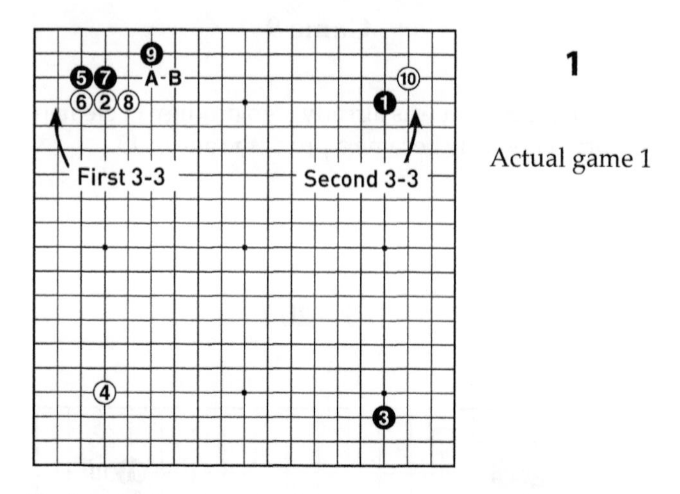

1

Actual game 1

Black quickly plays the first 3-3 invasion with 5. Instead of White at A and Black at 9, White opts for extending at 8, taking sente for the second 3-3 invasion.

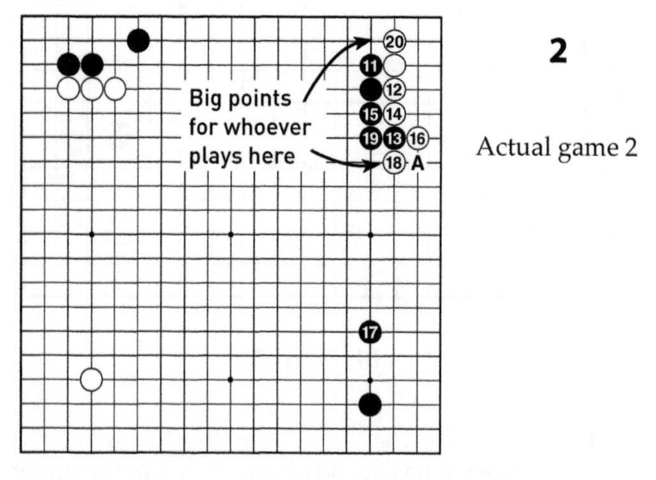

2

Actual game 2

Black plays the keima with 13. If White continues at 16 instead of 14, Black will strongly attack, and Black A, White 14, and Black 19 will follow. Here, Black occupies a big point with 17 and White takes ample territory with 18 and 20.

3

Possible continuation for Black

The marked stone is in perfect position, spaced properly

If White plays tenuki instead of 18 in the previous diagram, then Black will take advantage of this by playing at 2 and 4 without hesitation. Should White comply with the sequence to 7, then Black will get good shape on the right side and be satisfied.

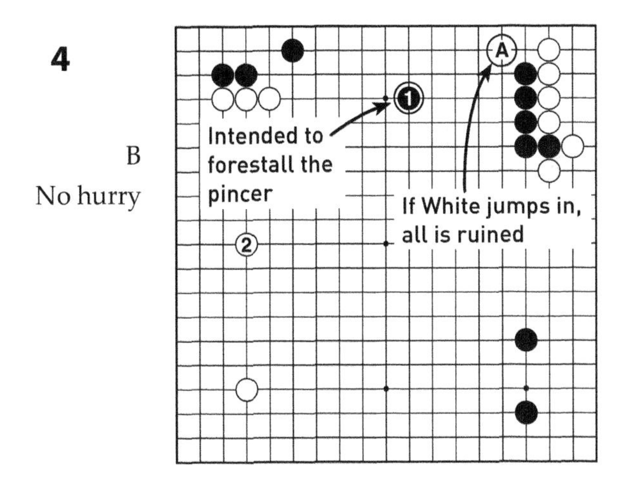

4

B

No hurry

The extension to 1 is not an urgent move. White can still jump in at A. The territory won't be big, even if Black succeeds in surrounding it.

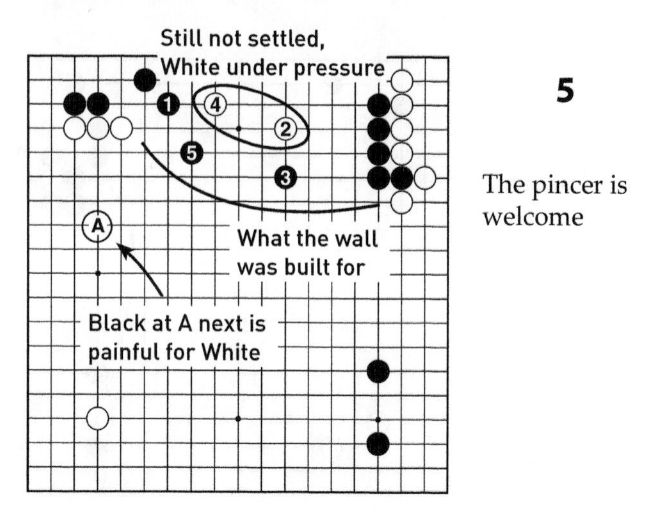

5

The pincer is welcome

In case Black wants to play on the upper side, then 1 is reasonable move. If White now attacks with 2, Black responds with 3 from above. Instead of 2, White should play an extension on the left side at A.

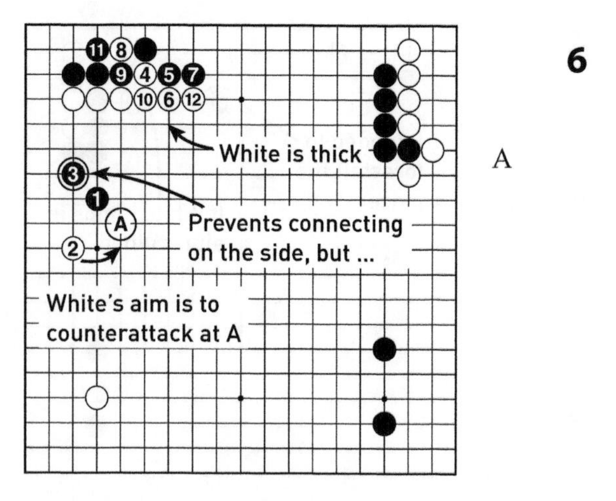

6

A

Here, Black attacks with 1, which is not the move chosen in the game. But it's a move that can be considered in this situation. White's counter is the attack at 2. Black plays 3 in order to prevent White from connecting. But this is an overplay. White fortifies himself with 4 to 12 and is no longer easy to attack.

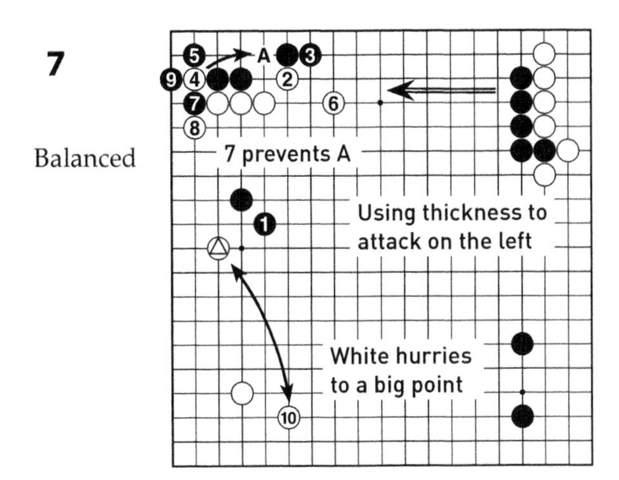

The kosumi at 1 is a good response to the marked stone. The same is true for Black 3 after 2. White 10 is good for quick development, but White's group at the top is not yet secure. Black might be able attack this group, which is why the situation is still balanced.

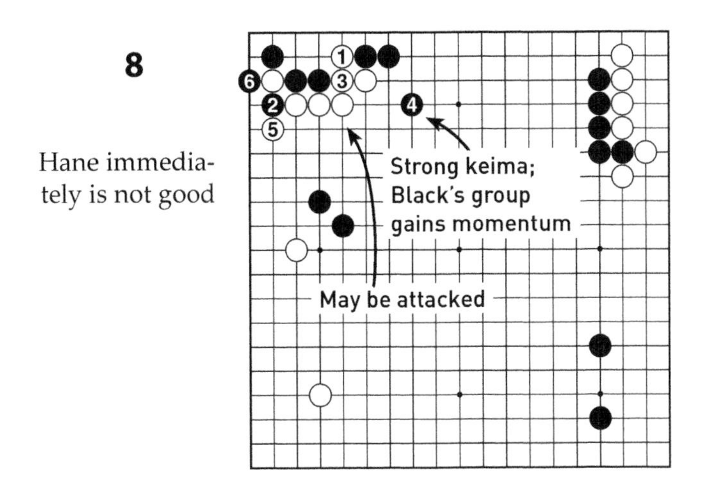

If White wants to play the hane, he shouldn't do so immediately. Black 4 is the perfect response. Even though White separates with 3, White's group ends up with a somewhat clumsy shape.

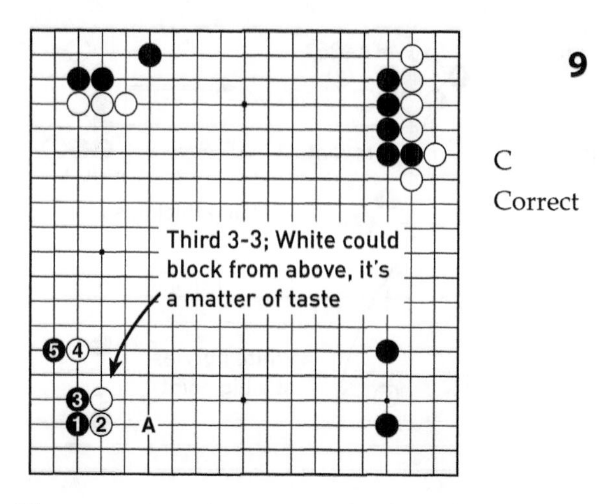

9

C
Correct

The sequences of moves on the top left and top right are completed for the time being. Black now played the third 3-3 point with 1. For continuations in the lower left, A and 4 are also good moves apart from 3-3.

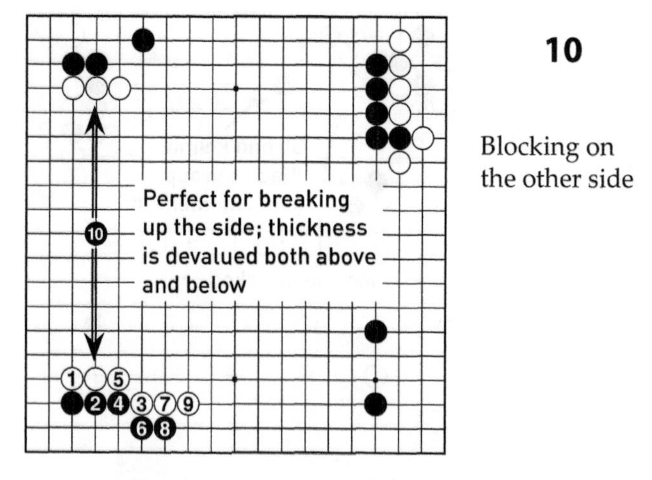

10

Blocking on the other side

White can also block with 1 on this side. If White extends at 7 after Black 6, Black will take the perfect spot with 10. This isn't necessarily good for Black, but it is certainly unsatisfactory for White.

11

Moyo vs moyo

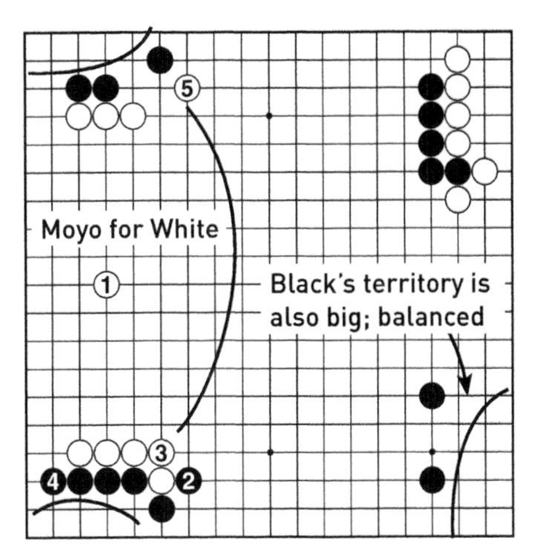

If White plays at 1 in order to link both walls, a nice moyo emerges. This development is more natural for White than the previous diagram. The game is even.

12

Questionable choice of joseki

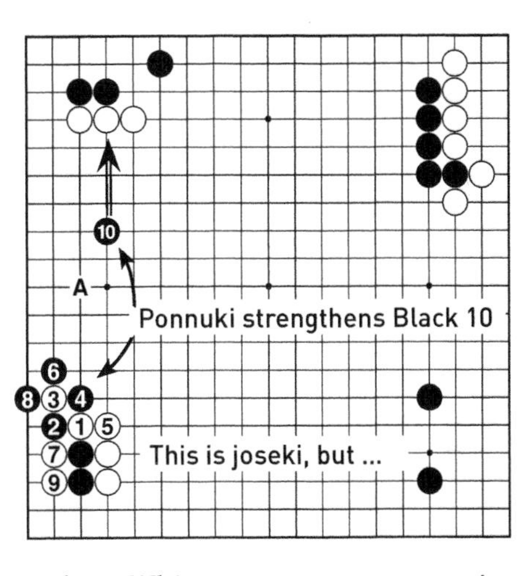

The joseki variation where White captures two stones is locally even, but Black can pincer with 10. Because there is now a ponnuki in the lower left, White can no longer launch a counterattack at A.

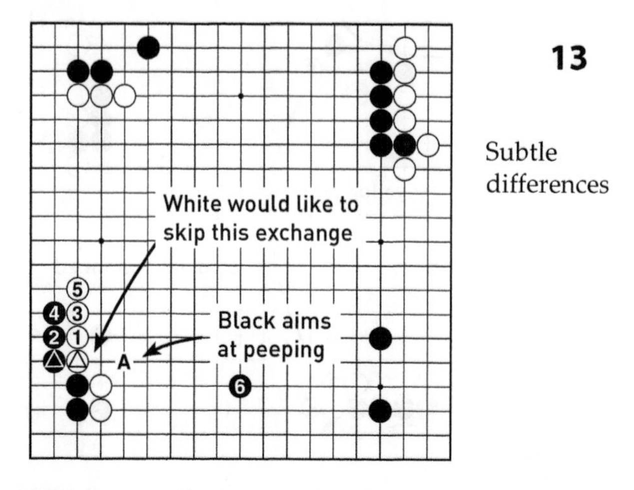

13

Subtle differences

If White extends at 1, it's the same as in the actual game. At this point White has already played the marked stone. Although it's hard to understand why, AI recommends against White playing this move.

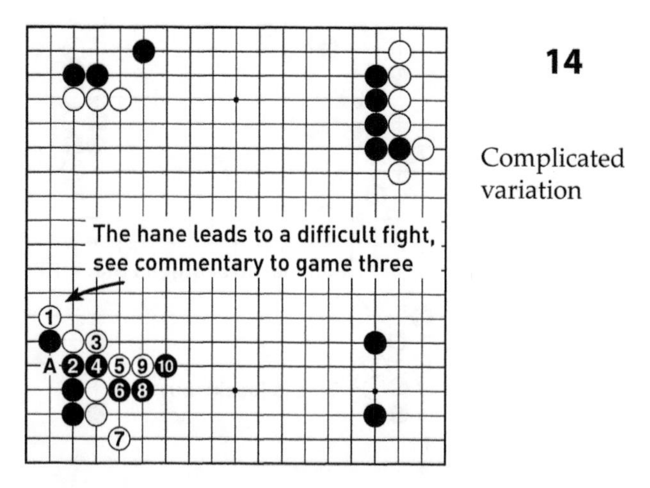

14

Complicated variation

As a continuation from diagram 9, blocking with 1 is an ambitious move. Instead of 2, Black can also play at A. If Black resists with 2, a complicated fight ensues.

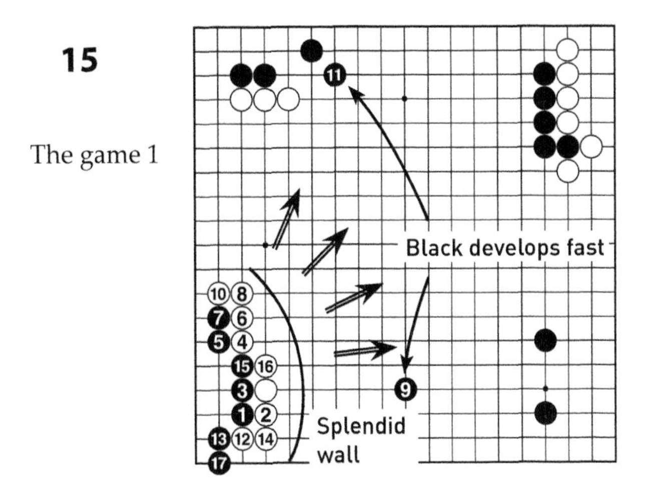

The game 1

In the lower left, a straightforward joseki was played. White surrounded the corner with 10, 12, and 14. Black answered at 15. White gained thickness, but Black developed quickly.

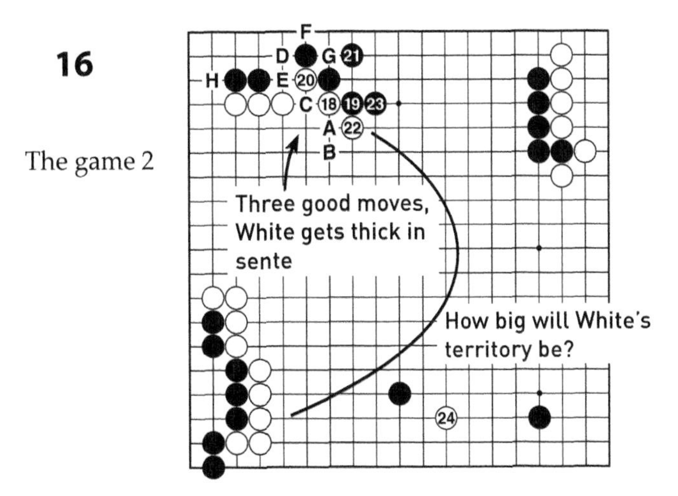

The game 2

White 18 through 22 is a follow-up to the joseki. It doesn't hurt to memorize it. If Black then cuts at A, White sacrifices a stone with B. Should Black play at A instead of 23, then White connects at C. If Black then follows up with 23, White has the good sequence of D through H. That's why Black A is not really playable.

The game

Moves after 50 omitted.
White wins by resignation.

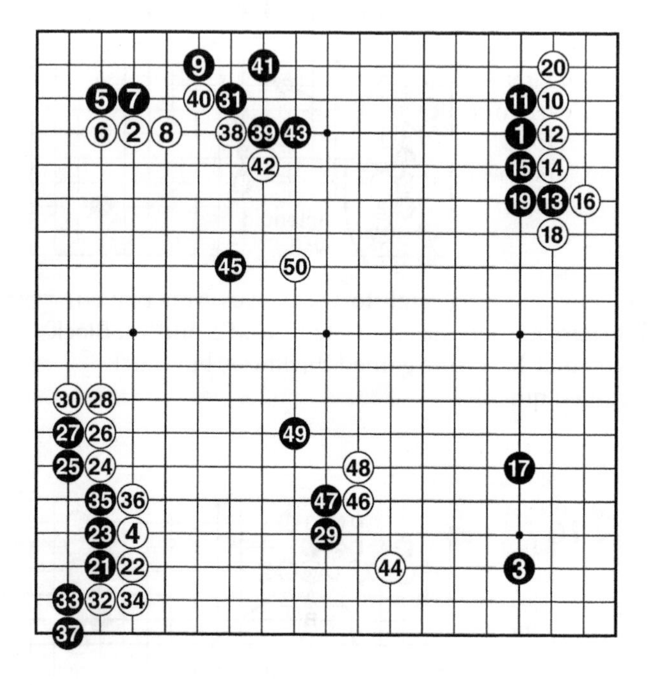

The next game was played by two heavyweights in the Japanese world of go: Takao Shinji 9p and Kono Rin 9p.

Column 3

Appreciating game records at the board

This book gives a detailed explanation of the playing style of AI in game openings. It presents actual game developments from the opening to the early middle game. They provide inspiration even for players who are having a hard time understanding professional go games. The book is structured in such a way that those players too can gain an understanding of these new techniques.

For this book I picked game records of the world's best players, such as Iyama Yuta (Japan), Ke Jie (China), and Park Junghwan (Korea), but also games of other fascinating go players.

Although you can of course just read the book, I would recommend you lay out the games and the variations on a go board. During my training as a professional player – I studied at the Ryokusei Gakuen (緑星学園) go academy – the two most important training modules were playing games and laying out games. Besides that, I read go books about tsumego and the opening. I really enjoyed playing games and reading go books. But I wasn't good at laying out games. I often couldn't find the next move number on a kifu, and so it took a long time until a game was laid out on the board. It was rather tedious.

Initially I had a lot of difficulty adjusting to the task, but little by little I got the knack of laying out games faster. The knack was the following: When I couldn't find the next move, I simply guessed where the next move may have been. "Maybe here." And often, quite unexpectedly, I hit the right spot!

Sometimes the moves I guessed were even better than the moves that were played in the actual games. Because of this, I am convinced that my feeling for playing go was refined by laying out game records.

Unlike in the past, we now have computers that help us study game records with ease, without having to look for the next move. Laying out stones on a board may therefore seem irrational at first, but looking back at my own period of training, it did have a positive effect.

Game 10

With an AI technique, a fight begins in the upper left. Today the sequence is recognised as a joseki, played in a variety of situations in games. Although AI has be around for only a few years, its techniques are already applied by humans.

(1 – 19)

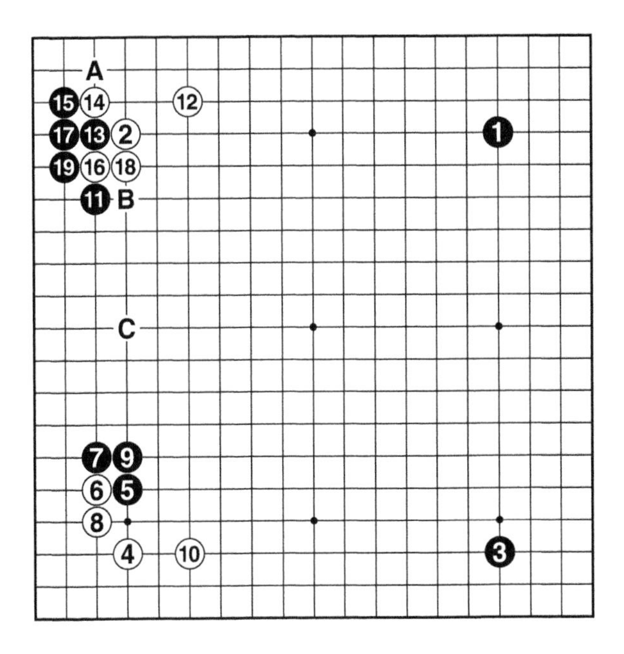

White to play

With 13 and 15, Black plays a variation that is currently en vogue. The sequence up to 19 is played very often. Now White can choose between two continuations.

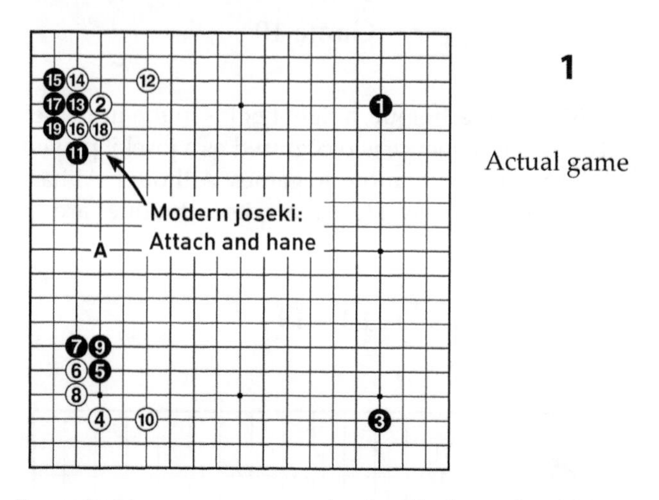

1

Actual game

It used to be common practice for Black to play 13 at A. White 16 and 18 are the standard follow-up after Black 13 and 15. But there are also other options.

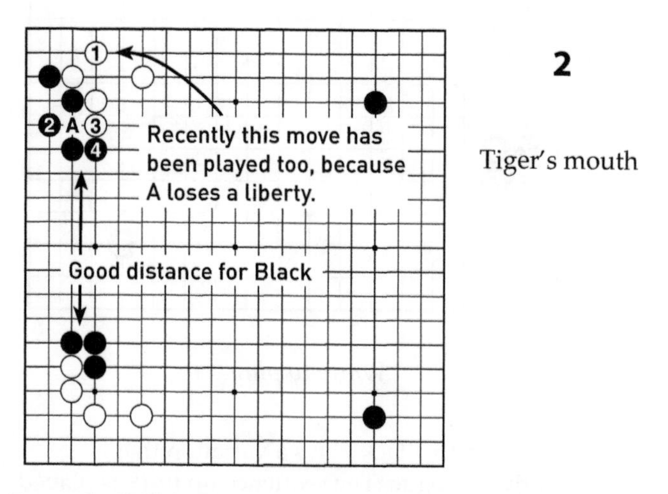

2

Tiger's mouth

Instead of White 16, you occasionally see 1 played here. White's burden is small since he doesn't take his own liberty at A. After 2 and 3, Black will push at 4 in order to develop the left side.

3

White is busy

White is separated

Key point for either side

White can push in further with 1; Black will then fight with the moves up to 10. The crucial question is whether and how Black can involve the three marked stones. Should White get to play at A, they might also come under attack. But White still has a weak group at the top, so he's busy.

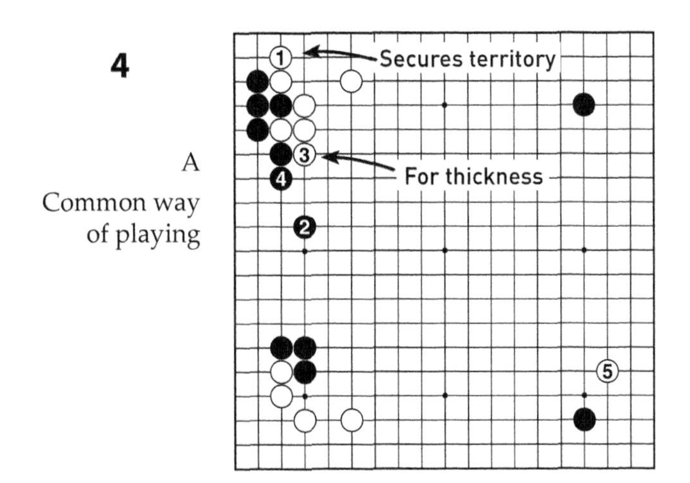

4

A

Common way of playing

Extending towards the edge is often played and is good for securing points. If Black plays the extension to 2, White presses at 3 and then takes the big point at 5. White will be satisfied with this development.

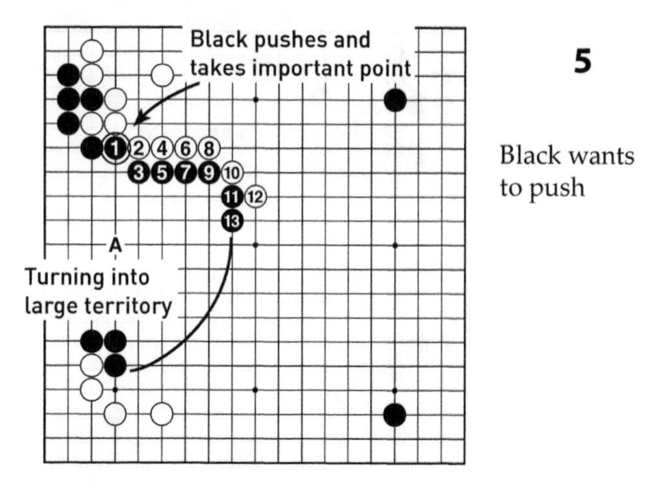

5

Black wants to push

It is better for Black to push at 1, thus exerting pressure on White's group at the top. At the same time, he surrounds the left side. For White, it's dissatisfying to see territory forming on the left side without the need for a move at A. White should avoid the sequence up to 13.

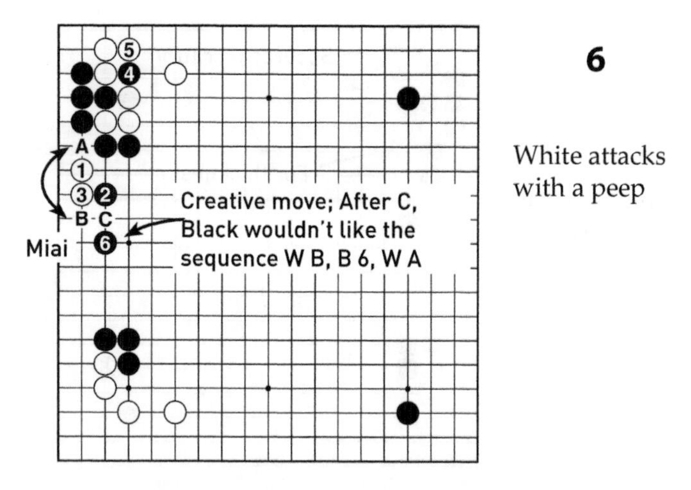

6

White attacks with a peep

As a response to the push, the peep at 1 is a strong move. If Black simply connects at A, White will play the extension to 6. So Black counters with 2 and, after cutting first at 4, he finally jumps to 6.

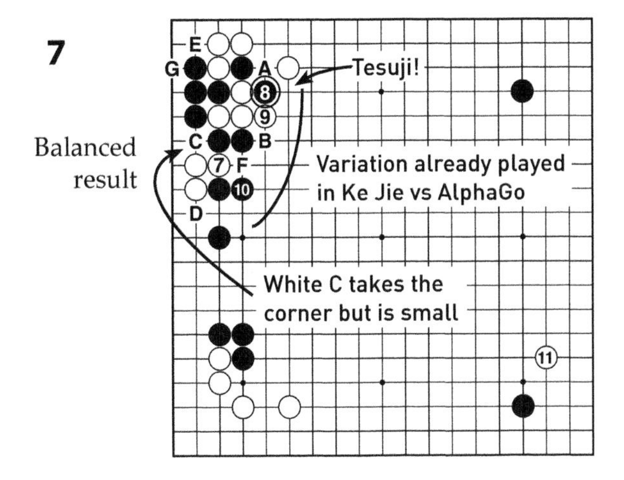

If White next tries to run out with 7, then Black has the tesuji of 8. White A is not an option because Black plays at 9. Therefore White has to run with 9, which turns B into sente for Black. So Black extends to 10. White C to G capture the corner, but that's still too small at this point.

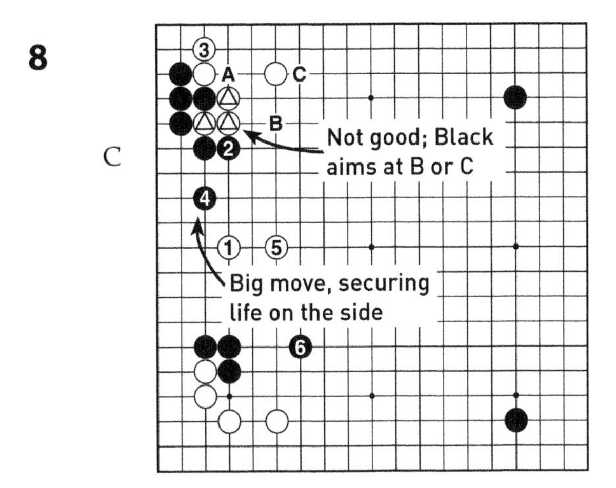

As a response to White 1, Black again pushes at 2. Next a cut at A would be dangerous, and so White extends to 3. The course of the game depends on how this fight will develop. If you'd like to play at 3 after 2 anyway, you had better do it right away.

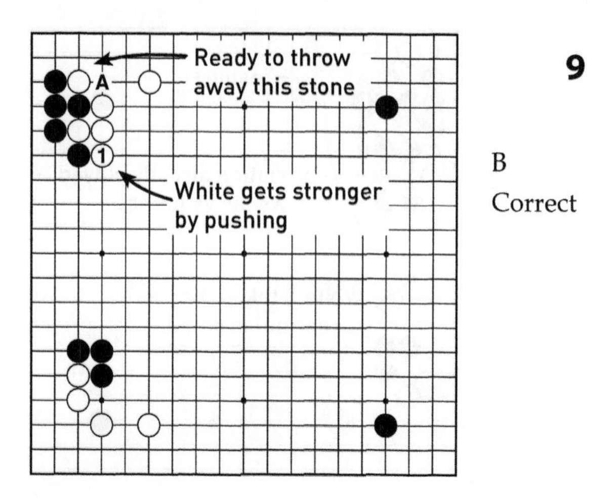

9

B
Correct

Pushing at 1 is a powerful move. If Black can play here himself, then cutting at A becomes a threat. But it's different when White gets stronger.

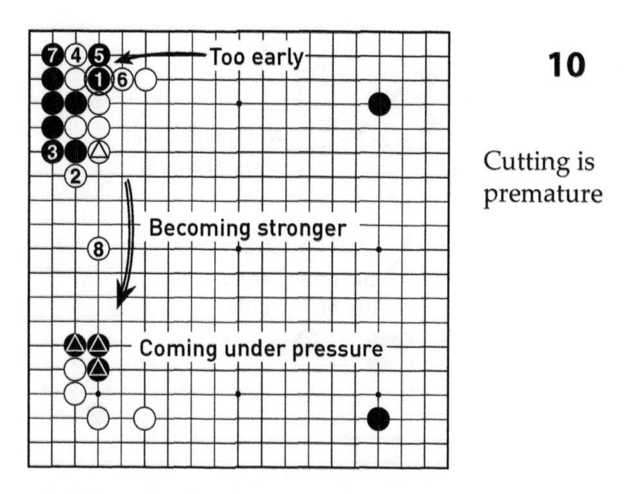

10

Cutting is premature

Black can cut at 1, but after the marked stone has been played already, it's only relevant in terms of territory. With the sequence up to 8, White gets strong on the outside, and Black's marked stones may come under attack.

11

Black is in trouble

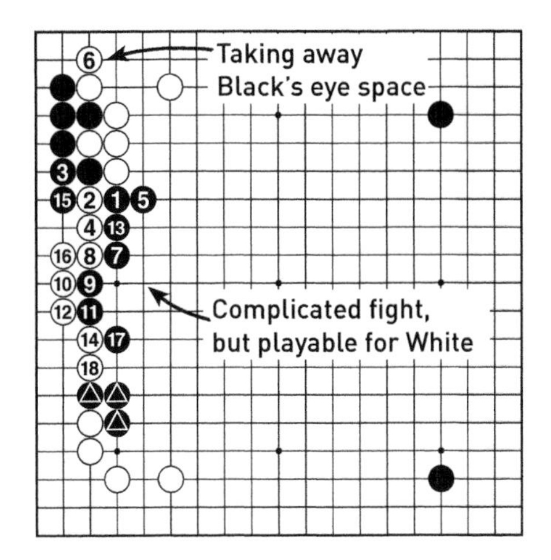

If Black plays the hane at 1, White counters with 2 and 4. With the marked stones already in position, the fight seems to be a difficult one for White, but he can start a semeai with 6. This fight is good for White, because Black has fewer liberties.

12

Alternative for White

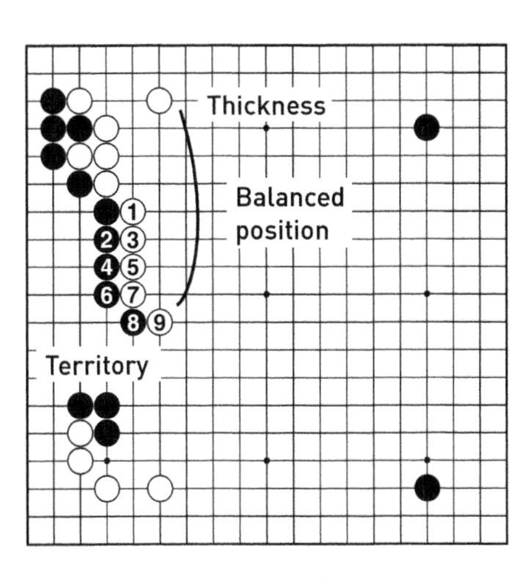

Diagram 11 is playable for White, but if a fight seems tricky because of the surrounding positions then White 1 is a safe way of playing. White concedes the left side in exchange for thickness.

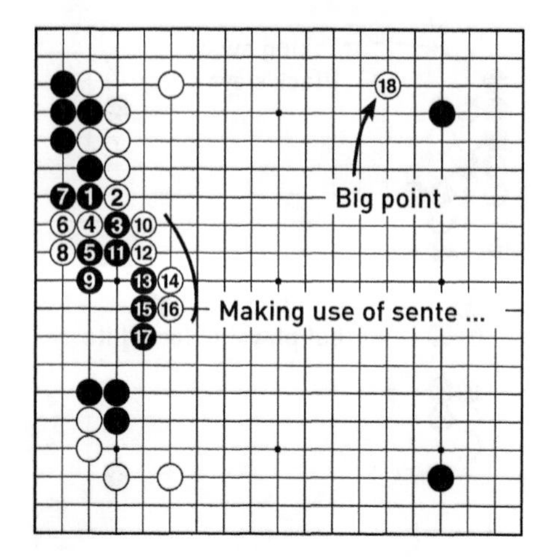

13

Skilful sacrifice

If Black first plays at 1 and then 3, then White will cut at 4. This doesn't look playable at first, but White intends to sacrifice skilfully. If Black now plays atari with 5, White 6 to 16 follow. Compared to the previous diagram, White's position is better, and he is satisfied.

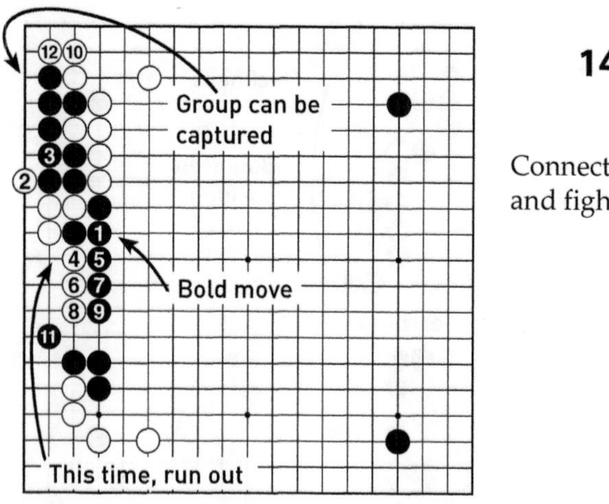

14

Connect and fight

Should Black connect at 1 instead of 9 in the previous diagram, White 4 follows. If White extends at 10 then Black has no eyes, and after Black 11 and White 12, White wins the race for liberties.

15

The game 1

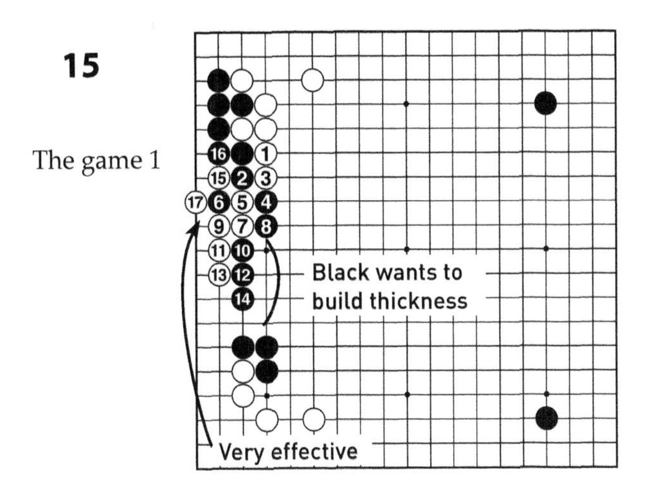

In the game, Black played the atari from below and White turned at 9. Black extended with 10 up to 14 and let White live. After White captured a stone with 17 he was safely alive on the left.

16

The game 2

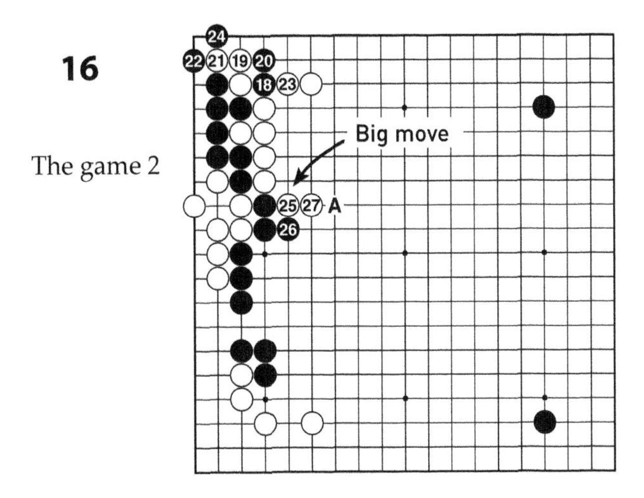

Next, Black 18 is an urgent move, as White must not get to play 19 first. The sequence from White 1 in diagram 15 to Black 24 here is often played in games. White 25 is big and also needs to be played urgently, otherwise Black will play at 27 or A.

The game

Moves after 55 omitted.
White wins by resignation.

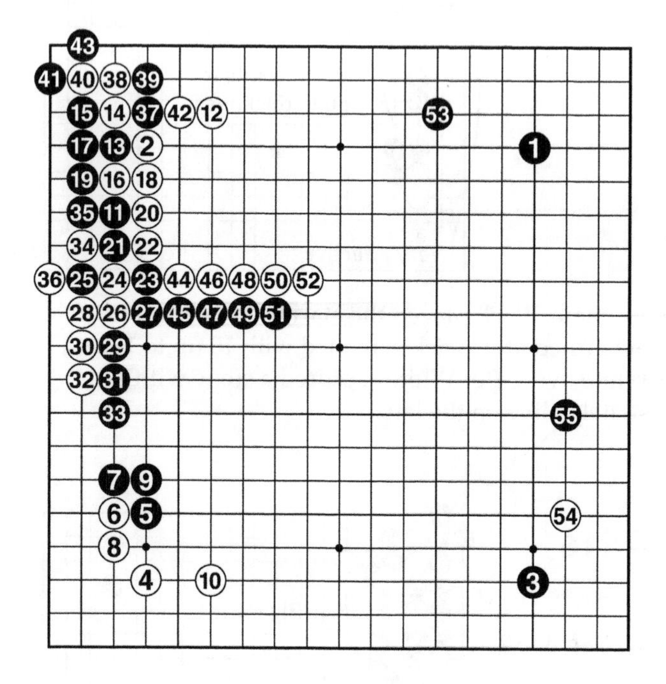

The next game was selected from the final round of the Kisei title tournament, in which Yamashita Keigo 9p encountered Iyama Yuta 9p.

Game 11

I suppose many of you will remember the fierce final of the Kisei 2019, where the winner was decided only after seven games. This is the fifth game of the final, in which an interesting development appeared, starting with an AI move.

(1 – 9)

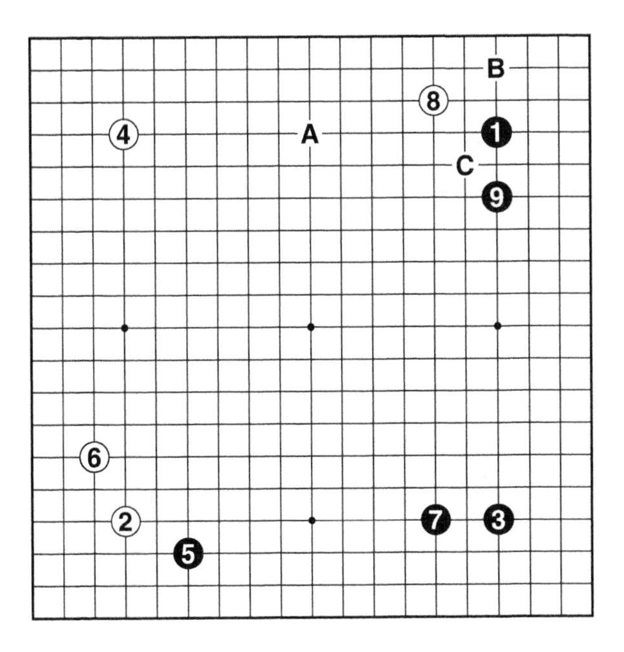

White to play

This position resulted after White 8 and Black 9. Now White played a move in AI style. This move would never have been considered in the past, whereas today it seems almost natural.

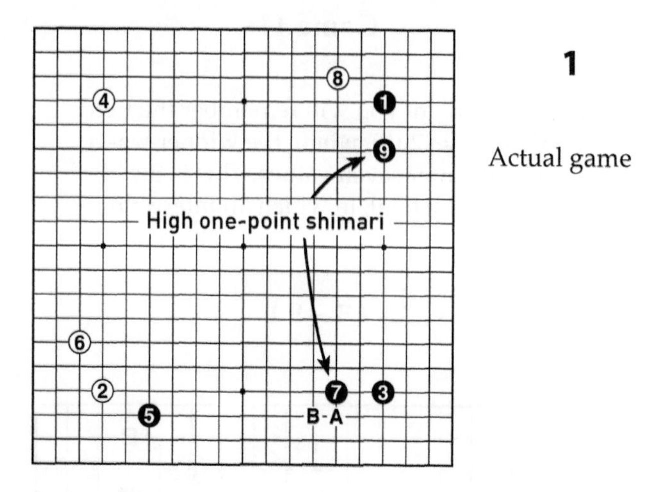

1

Actual game

Black starts off with nirensei, the opening on two star points. The high shimari with 7 is a bit unusual. More common here would be A or B.

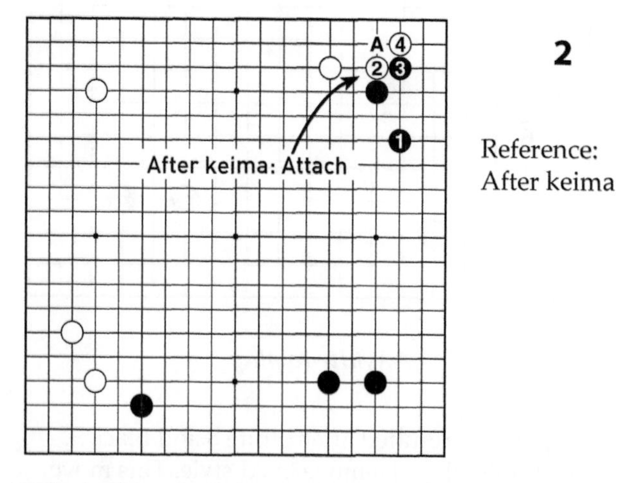

2

Reference:
After keima

If Black plays the keima at 1, then AI usually responds with White 2 and 4. Sliding at A is also possible, but nowadays this move is seen less frequently than it used to be. In response to the high shimari, it's a very likely choice to play the move that was also played in the game.

3

A

Normal move

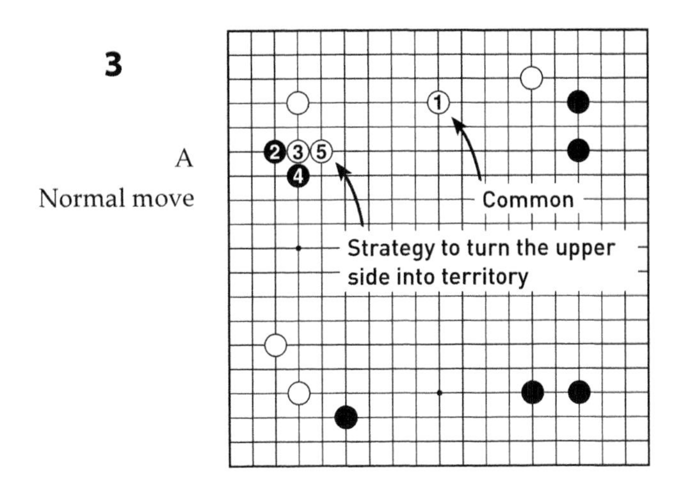

The extension to 1 is a common and, without doubt, a good move. After Black 2, White 3 and 5 conform to AI style for keeping up at this stage.

4

B

Another option

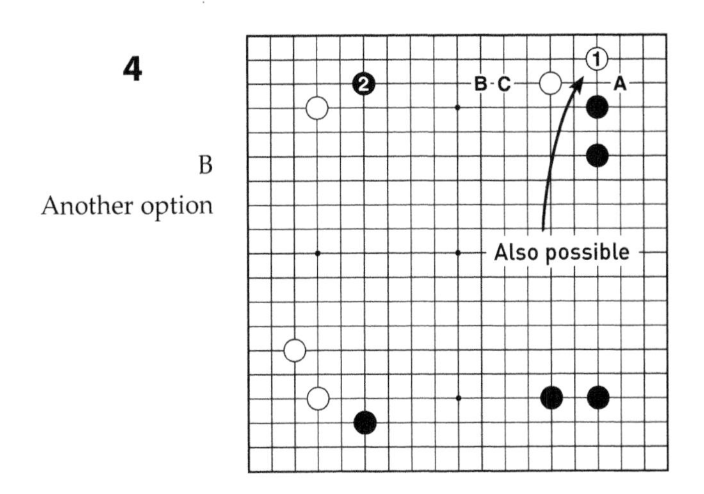

White 1 is joseki. For Black to answer at A would be a bit unsatisfactory, White playing the extension to B. That's why Black usually opts for the kakari at 2, aiming at pincering with C next.

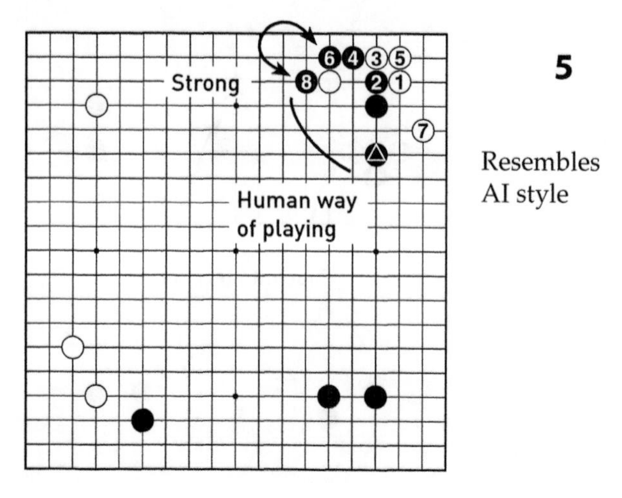

5

Resembles AI style

With the marked stone already present, the 3-3 invasion was also played before AI came up. The AI's recommendation for Black is to crawl at 6 and to follow up by turning at 8.

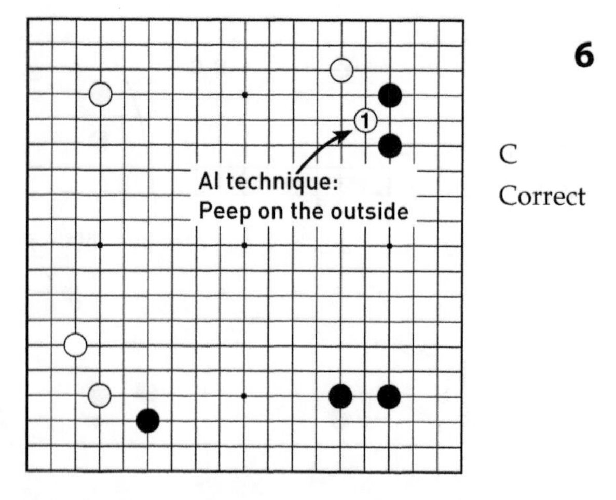

6

C
Correct

The peep at 1 is a surprising AI play. Before the appearance of AI, this way of playing would have been unthinkable, but today this move is seen in many games. For me this move is now the first choice.

7

Variation with connecting

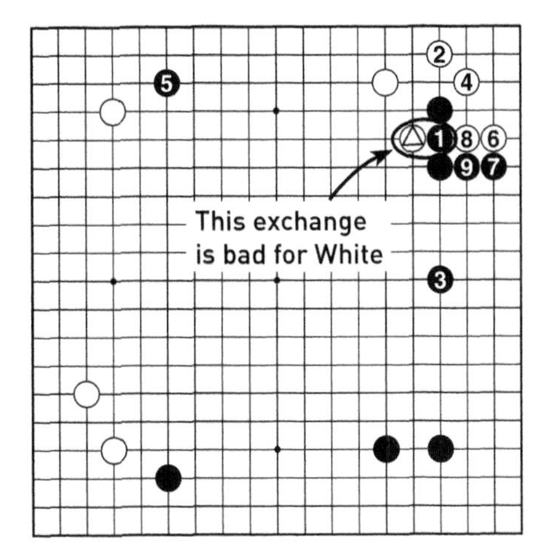

Connecting at 1 is safe. White tends to jump to 2 immediately. To then also jump to 6 is the wrong direction though, because the exchange of the peep for Black 1 turns into a bad combination as a result.

8

Making the most of the peep

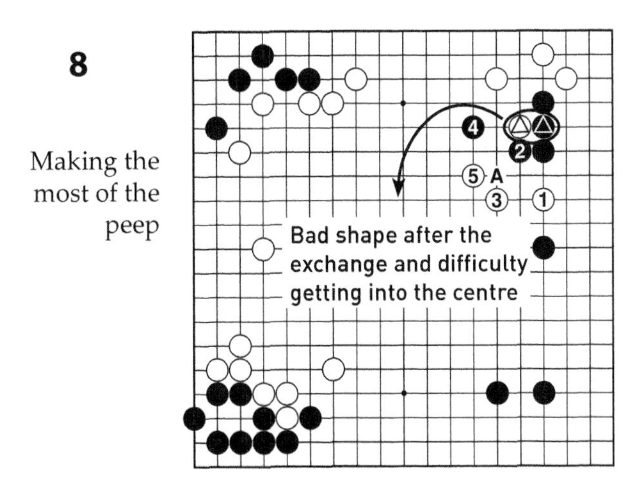

Having arrived at the position in the diagram, it is time to attack with White 1. In a development like this, the marked exchange has made the Black stones clumsy. In order to exploit the peep there is also the option to develop the centre with 4 or A instead of playing at 1.

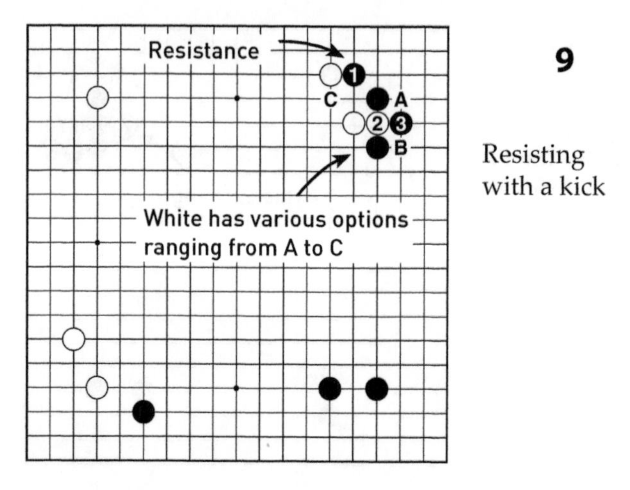

9

Resisting with a kick

Often Black's choice is to kick. White breaks through with 2 and then either cuts at A or B in order to fight, or plays at C if he prefers a peaceful division.

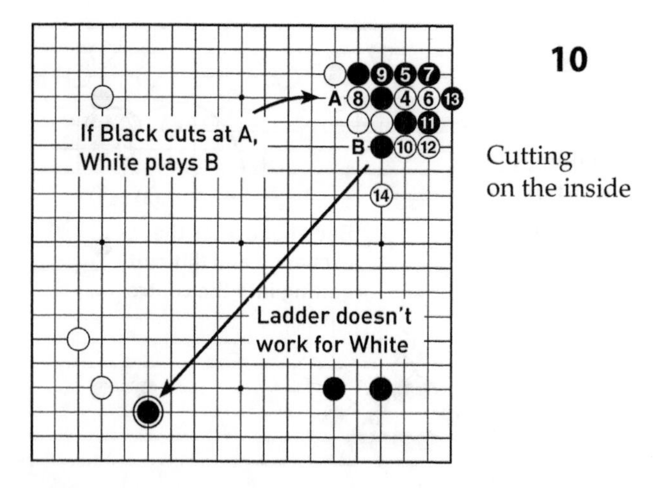

10

Cutting on the inside

If White cuts on the inside and extends at 6, then Black has a choice. Blocking at 7 is a reasonable move. White sacrifices two stones and is not dissatisfied with the sequence up to 14. But the result is even.

11

Complicated variation

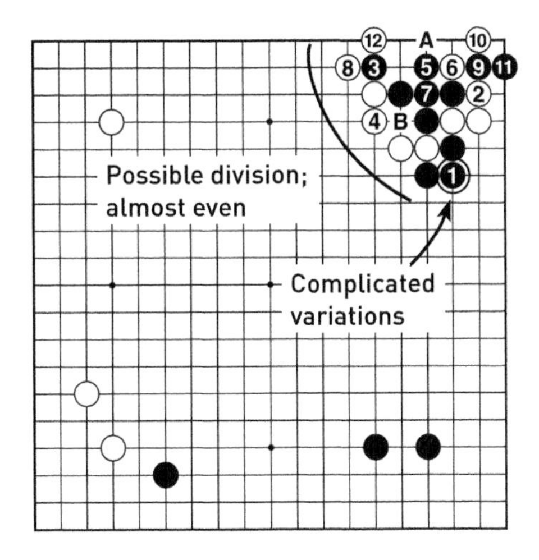

Connecting at 1 is a strong resistance. In the diagram, only one possible continuation is shown, but the atari at 10 looks good. After 12 there is the aji of a ko at A. Eliminating the aji by playing another move would be aggravating for Black. Instead of 7 he can also play B. Either way, Black 1 leads to a variety of complicated variations.

12

Cutting on the outside

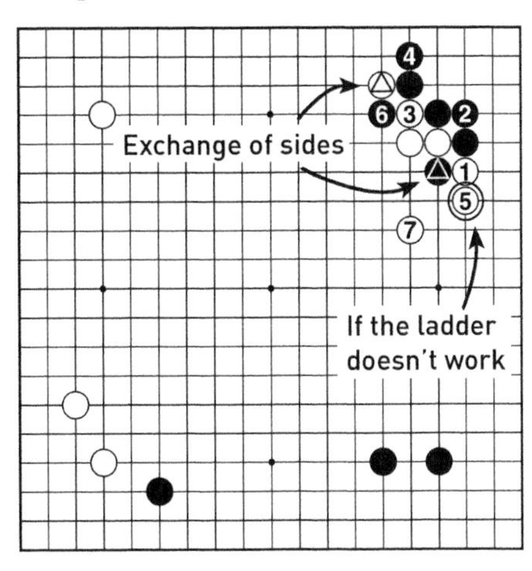

Cutting on the outside is usually the choice if the ladder works. However, this move can also be played if the ladder doesn't work. The marked stone is sacrificed and White obtains solid shape.

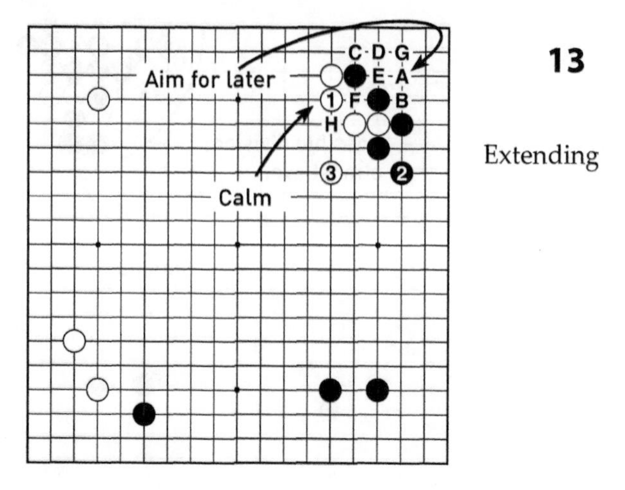

Extending with 1 is taking a safe road that will hardly lead to difficult variations. Black 2 is the bolder response, compared to B. White jumps into the centre with 3. It would be too early to move at A with White 3 and play the sequence up to H. Black would be fortified.

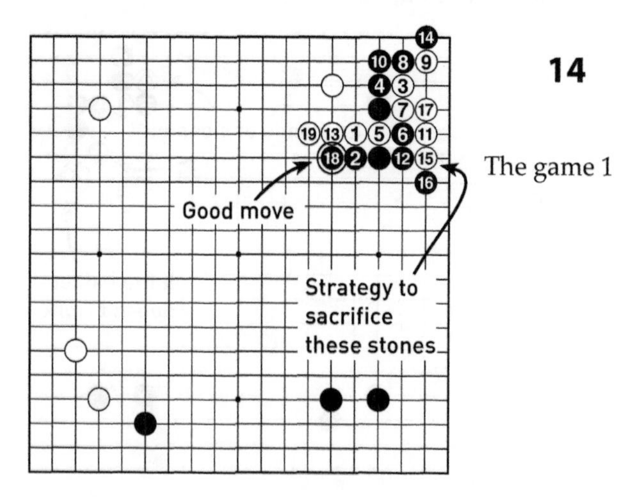

Pushing with 2 is also a strong resistance. The strategy of White 3 is to sacrifice White's stones in the corner and to get strong in the centre. Black 18 is a strong move and White 19 inevitable.

15

Opponent sacrifices

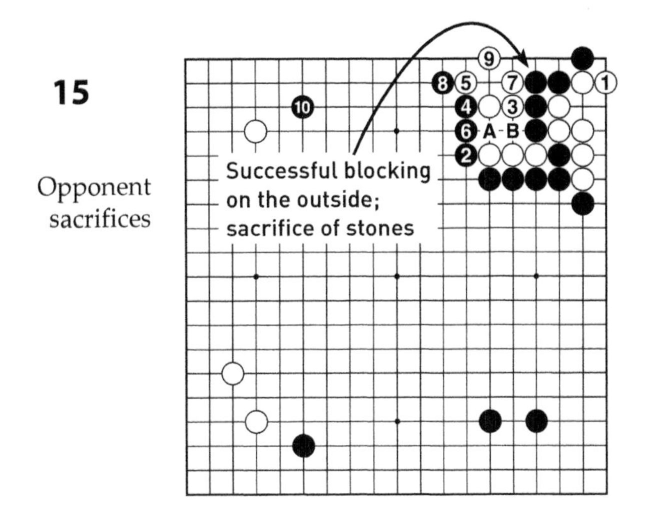

If White plays at 19 instead of 1 in the previous diagram, he will capture the corner. Black, however, now sacrifices his stones for outside influence. This doesn't look good for White. If White plays at 6 instead of 3, then Black A, White B and Black 3 follow. This is a hard fight for White.

16

The game 2

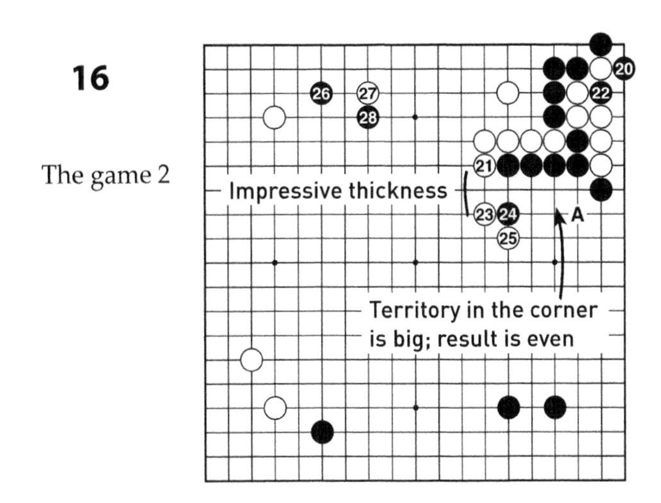

Turning at 21 is a very good move. Although Black takes the territory in the corner, White's shape after jumping to 23 is good, too. The result is even. Black 24 at A would be safer, but in the game he played the attachment and then shifted the fight to another region with 26.

The game

Moves after 53 omitted.
Black wins by 6.5 points.

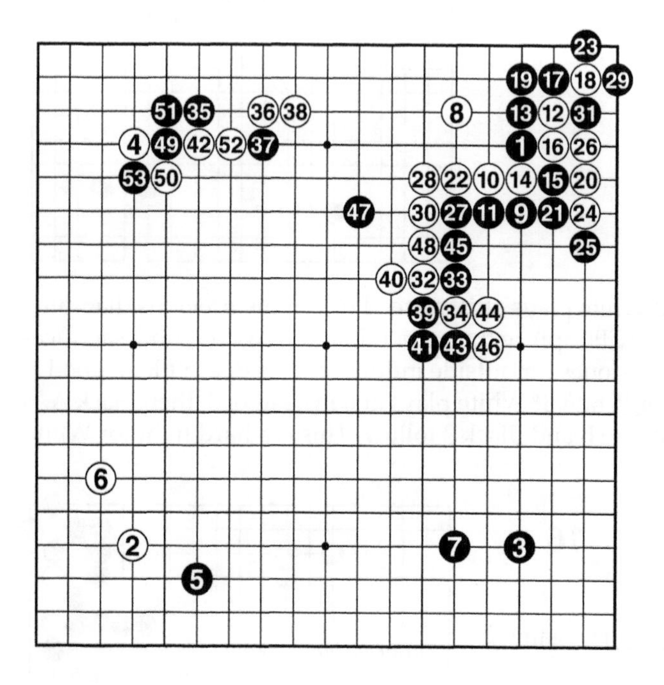

The next game shows another encounter between the two top players from China and Korea: Ke Jie 9p and Park Junghwan 9p.

Column 4
Current AI against future players

Until not too long ago people said AI would still need several decades to beat humans in go. But then AlphaGo was developed, and within a very short time human players were outplayed.

I think it is now impossible for humans to come back and again outplay AI. It takes only an instant for AI to calculate points on the board, something that ordinary people need a lot of time for.

By playing millions and millions of games against itself, an impossible amount for humans, AI keeps getting stronger and stronger. That's why I think a human player will only win against a constantly improving AI by accident.

However, in my opinion it is conceivable that future players will have the potential to beat current AI. The playing style in the opening has come under examination in recent years on the basis of AI's emergence, and it has changed enormously. It seems that humans have become quite strong in the opening stage (at least they are capable of playing in a way AI considers good).

What would happen if the future strongest player, having improved by studying with an advanced AI of the future, competed against AI from today?

Such a game should be interesting.

Strong go players don't make mistakes in the endgame, and so I think future players would stand a chance of winning against today's AI by playing the newest AI style.

What would happen, then, if a top player competed against the version of AlphaGo that played against Lee Sedol? Back then, Lee Sedol lost against AlphaGo 1–4, but the game in which Lee Sedol was able to win with a historically excellent move will continue to be talked about over the next centuries. I am convinced that this would make for an excellent game and inspire many fans and go players. I very much hope that such a game will happen.

Game 12

Again, this game began with an AI technique and developed into a large-scale battle. There seems to be an increasing tendency in current go for local fights to spread more and more across the entire board.

(1 – 9)

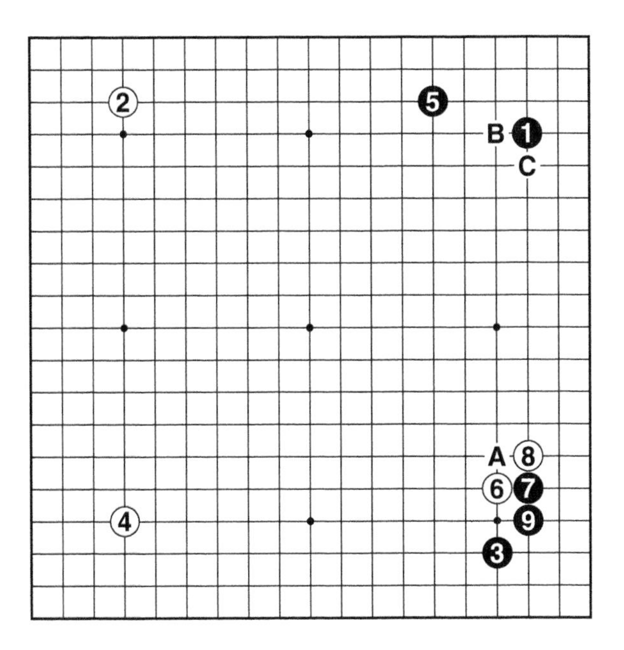

White to play

White focused on the bottom right corner first with 6 and 8. The question after that is; how should he continue on the right side? Although it is certainly an option to play a joseki move in this situation, a bit of a more efficient way of playing was chosen in the game.

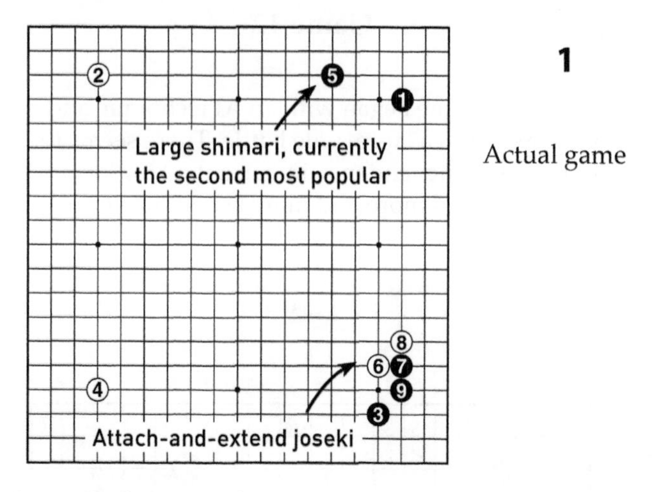

1

Actual game

Instead of Black 5, the large high shimari has often been played in recent times, but the large low shimari is also seen frequently. People still play the high shimari, but the basic shimari has sharply declined.

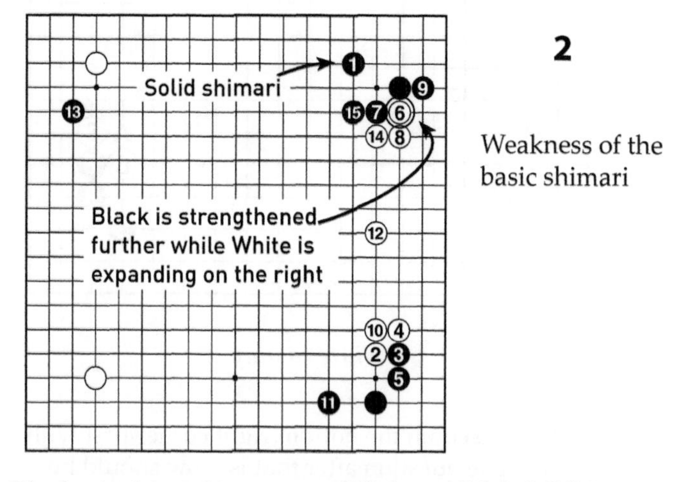

2

Weakness of the basic shimari

The basic shimari is a very solid shape. With 6, White wants to further reinforce this shape, hereby diminishing Black's efficiency. The basic shimari makes territory easily, but it also has weaknesses.

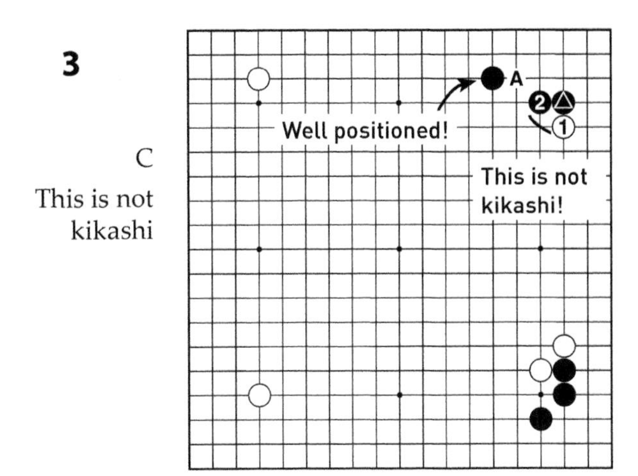

Attaching to the large shimari with 1 is clumsy, as Black answers with 2. With the basic shimari at A, the result would be a good one. If Black had a hoshi shimari and White would play at 1, then Black would answer with the marked stone, and it becomes clear how bad this exchange is.

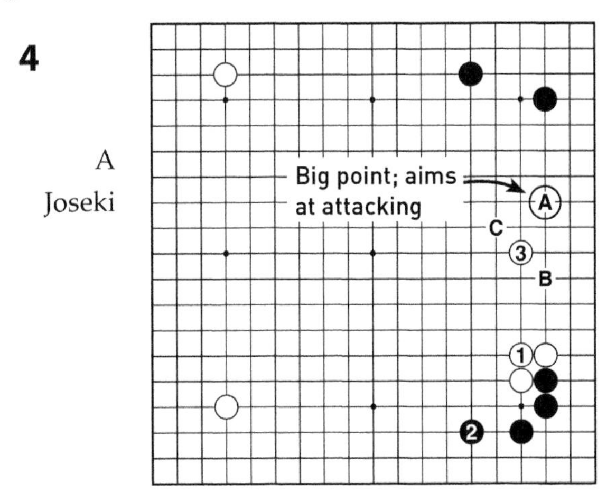

White 1 and 3 are joseki and a good development. In this shape, Black's extension to A is big, which then aims at an invasion at B or an attack with the keima at C.

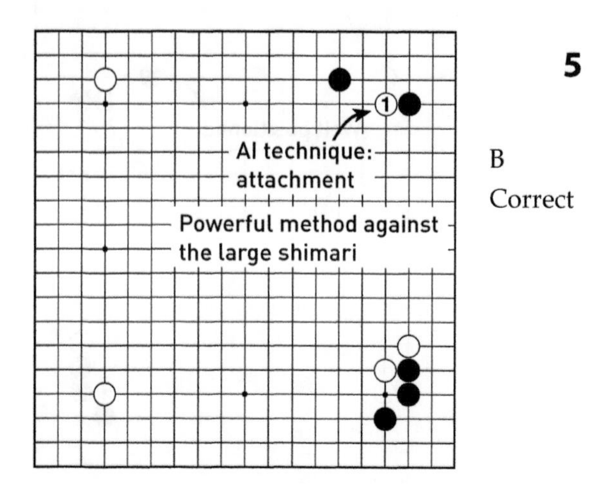

5

B

Correct

Attacking the corner with White 1 is an intriguing AI technique. Like in diagram 3, White wants to develop the right side. Black, however, has a variety of options for countermeasures. The move is complicated.

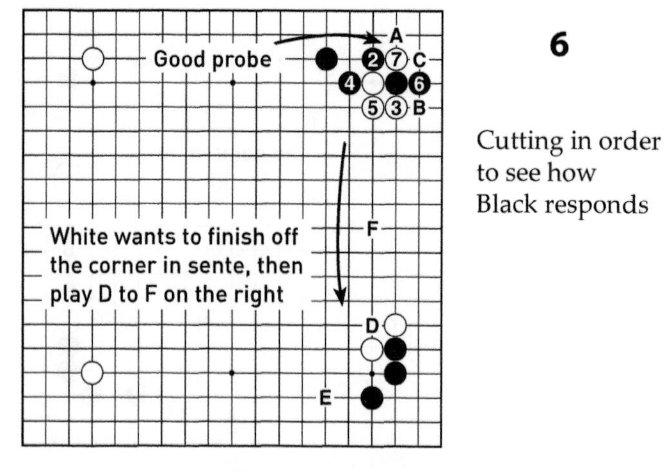

6

Cutting in order to see how Black responds

Black 2 to 6 are a calm response. Cutting at 7 is a good probe by White, as Black will hardly be able to play at A, because then B becomes sente. So B and C are reasonable choices for Black.

7

Peaceful division

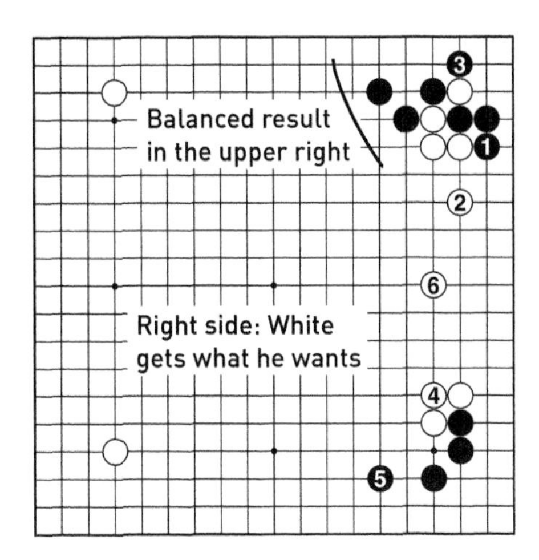

Playing the atari at 3 after turning at 1 is the most peaceful response. White expands on the right side with 4 and 6 and is not dissatisfied with this development. This is a variation frequently seen.

8

Pushing on the sixth line

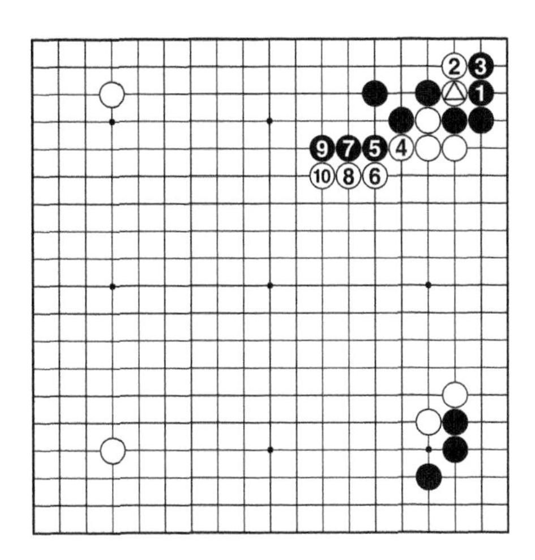

If Black plays atari with 1, White will extend at 2 and push on the sixth line with the sequence up to 10. This is a bold way of playing for White, but it is considered playable.

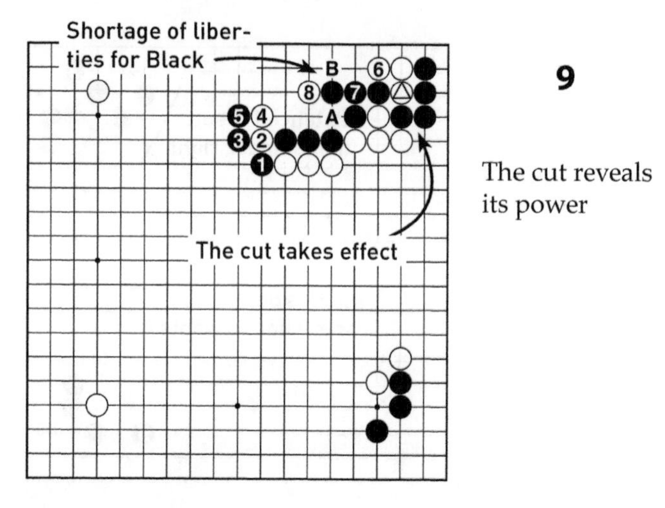

If Black wants to resist with the hane at 1, the cut comes into effect. White 8 is a good move. Things would look bad for Black if White were to play the throw-in at A or the hane at B next.

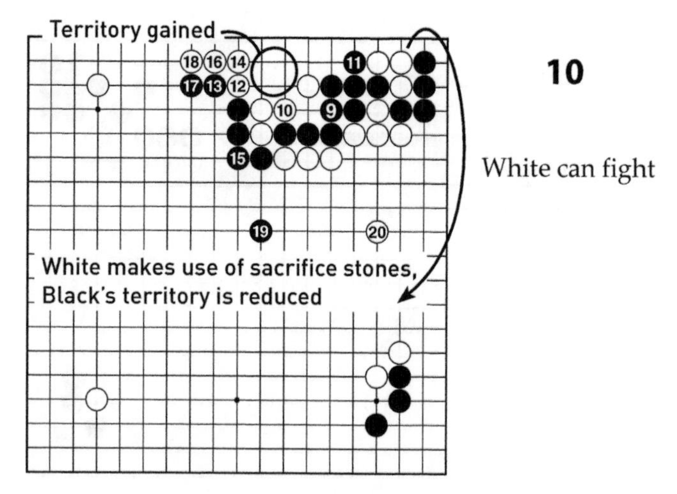

So in the end Black must connect at 9. After that, the continuation up to 20 is to be expected, which leads to a large-scale fight. In the course of this, White capitalises on his sacrifice stones in the upper right in order to gain points.

11

Variation: Hane on the outside

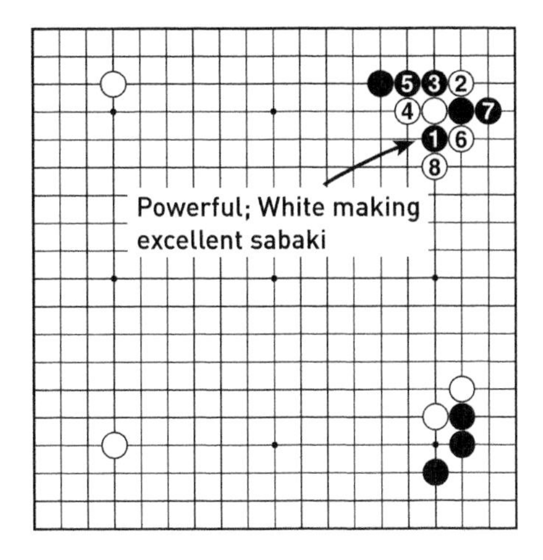

The hane on the outside is also a strong move. White's response is to make sabaki with 4 and 6. His stones seem to be separated, but the next diagram shows how White fixes his shape by sacrificing with elegance.

12

The latest joseki

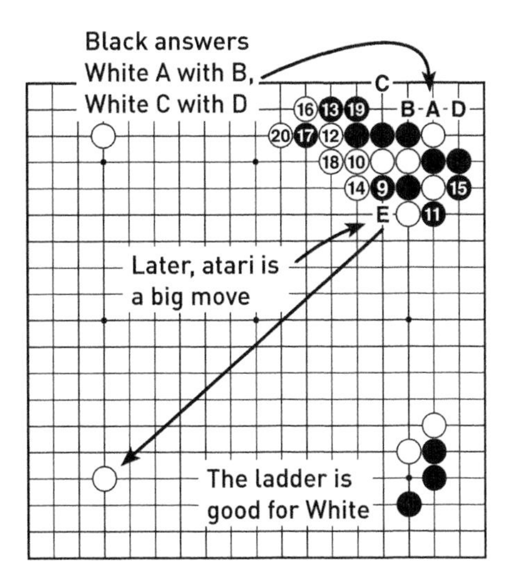

White plays atari at 14 and then the hane at 16, so he sacrifices the stone in the corner. The continuation up to 20 is often played in pro games and the result is considered even.

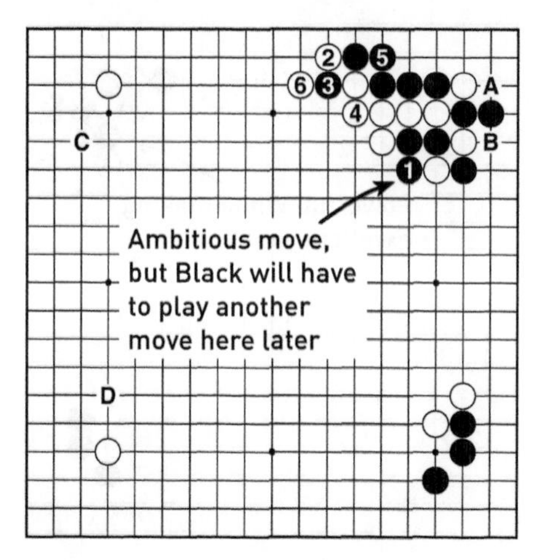

13

No advantage for Black

Black 1 seems to offer some advantage. But after the sequence up to 6, A is sente for White. This means that in the end Black has to play once more and defend. Instead of this, it would be better to play at C or D, without any of the moves in the previous diagram.

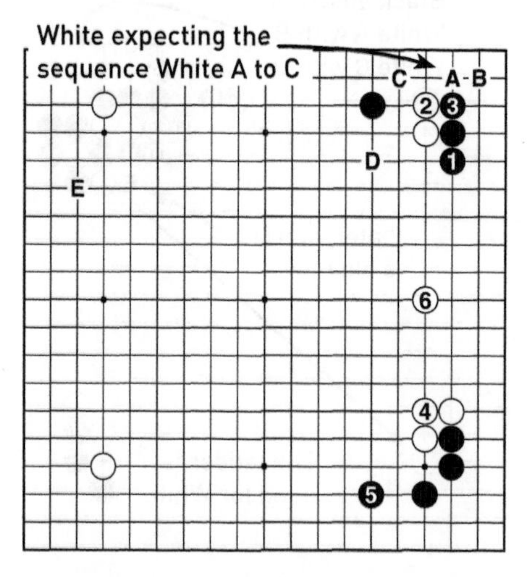

14

Variation: Extending

The extension at 1 is rarely seen. White has various options, for example 2 to 6 is playable. After that, White sets his sight at a continuation with A to C. If Black wants to settle this side quickly with D, then White will go straight to E.

15

The game 1

One more move required due to the threat of White B and C

Pushing once more before playing at A

In the game Black did not play at A, like in diagram 7, but instead boldly pushed at 10 first. White jumped to 13, forcing Black to make a move in the corner. Even at this point, it wouldn't be good for Black to defend at A right away.

16

The game 2

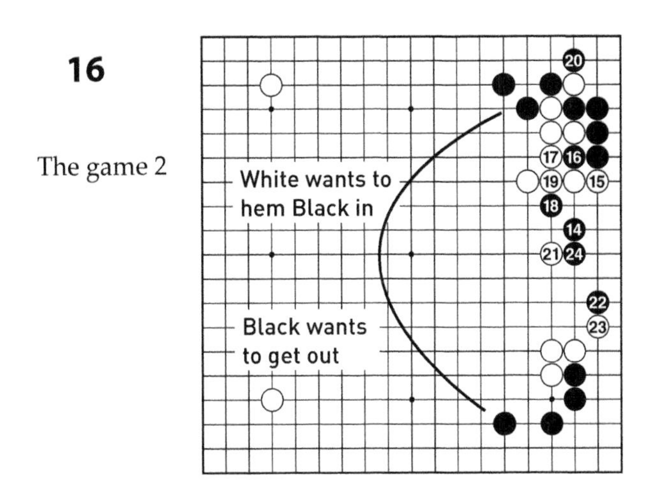

So Black turned towards the right side with 14 and 18 and then came back to 20. White 21 was a daring move that gave Black cause for concern. He attempted to destroy White's moyo with 22. White didn't want to allow himself to get separated though, and a fierce battle ensued.

The game

Moves after 57 omitted.

White wins by 2.5 points.

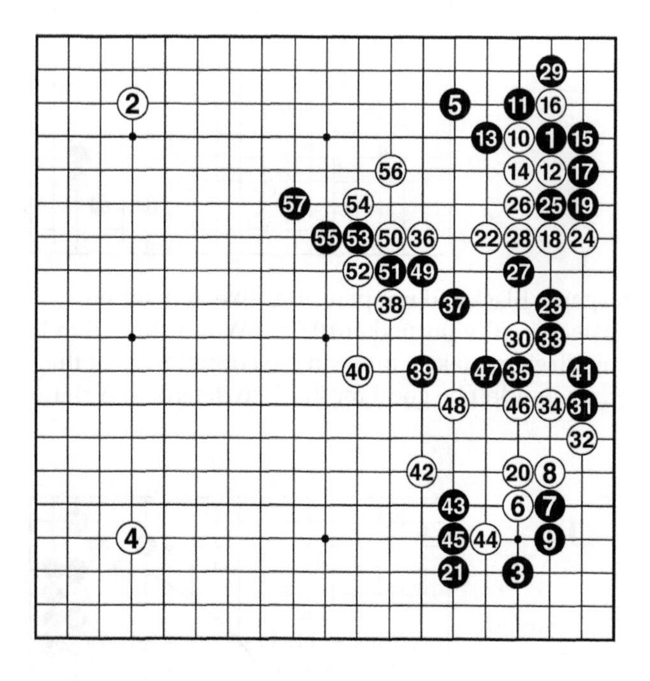

The next game is not a tournament game but a special match played on the occasion of the award ceremony for the youngest female player ever to make pro: Nakamura Sumire 1p vs Choi Jeong 9p.

Nakamura Sumire became pro at the age of ten in 2019.

Game 13

I knew about a strong schoolgirl from hearsay, but I was sceptical because of her age. Then I took a look at her games, and I was shocked: "She is strong!" I'm looking forward to following her progress.

(1 – 15)

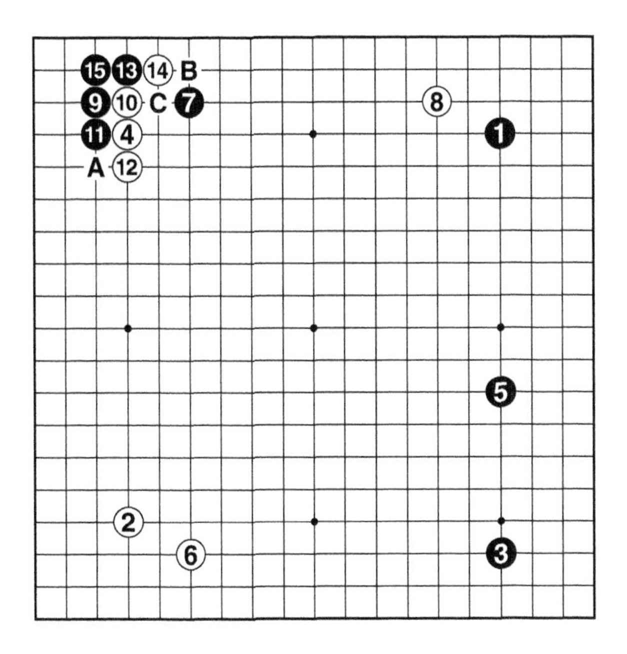

White to play

After the kakari at 7, White played tenuki and so Black invaded at the 3-3 point. After Black 15 the joseki is not yet completed. White now chose a move in AI style.

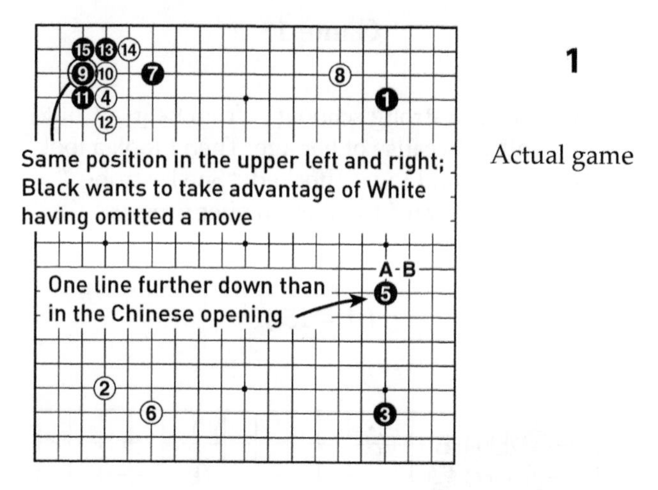

1

Actual game

Instead of A or B like in the classical Chinese opening, Black plays the powerful alternative of 5, one line further down. After the kakari at 7, White plays at 8, also kakari. Of course Black could respond to 8, but she prefers to continue in the upper left, with fighting spirit.

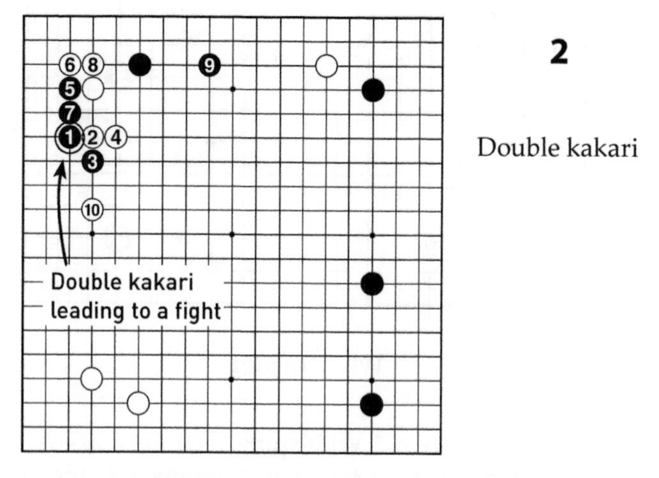

2

Double kakari

Apart from the 3-3 invasion, the double kakari is also a common play, after which the sequence up to 10 is expected. Further options instead of 1 are a move in the upper right, or a pincer.

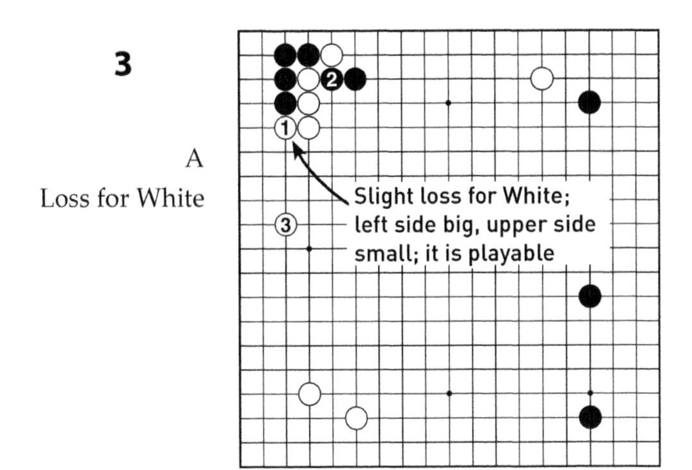

Whether blocking at 1 is good depends upon the position. After the extension to 3, White's shape looks good, but it is a small loss for White. This move should only be played if there are special reasons for it.

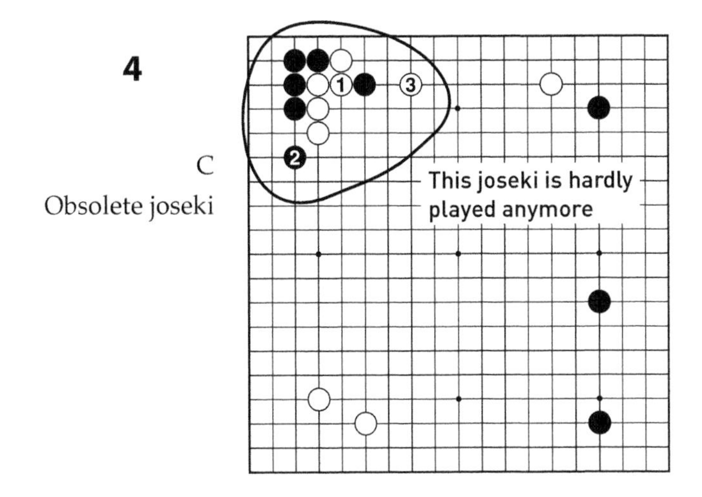

This shape is typically the result of White answering the kakari with the pincer at 3. But this joseki has seen a dramatic decline – since the emergence of AI it has been a very rare occurrence.

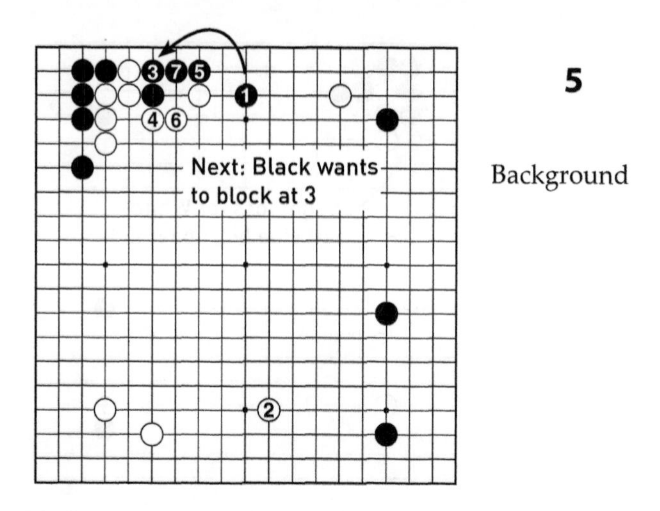

5

Background

The reason why this shape isn't played anymore is Black's attack against the group at 3. For example, if White wants to build a moyo on the upper side, then Black 1 is a good point for invasion, aiming at 3.

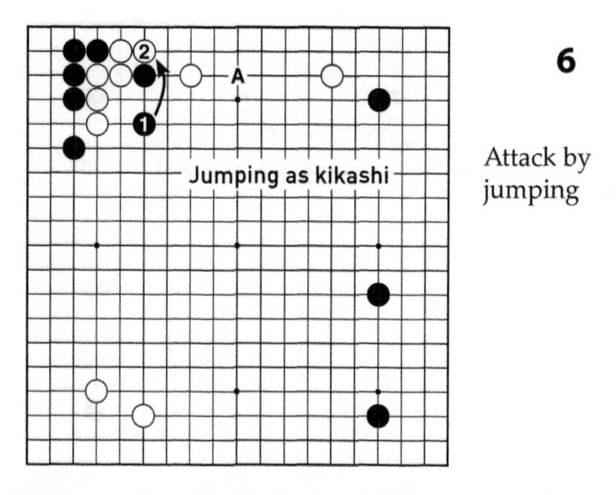

6

Attack by jumping

Black can also play the jump at 1. Because another move by Black at 2 would be very severe, White usually responds by playing at 2 directly. In that case Black 1 serves as kikashi. This is also playable for Black, instead of A.

7

Pros and cons of the hane

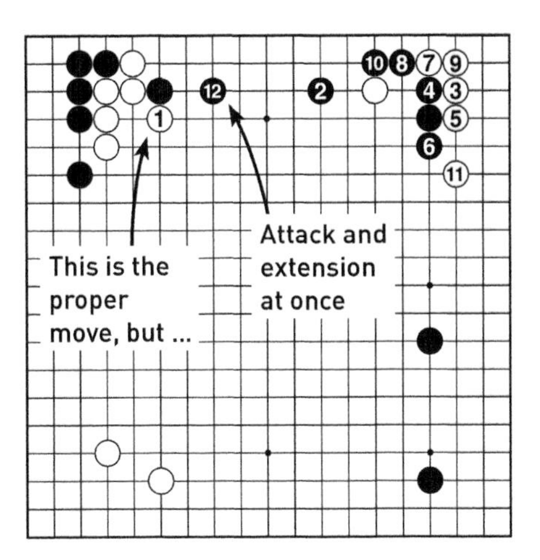

The hane at 1 is the proper move (honte). It isn't necessarily better than the pincer, as it has both pros and cons. If the continuation is played like in the diagram, then Black 12 is quite unpleasant. White 1 is solid, but also slow.

8

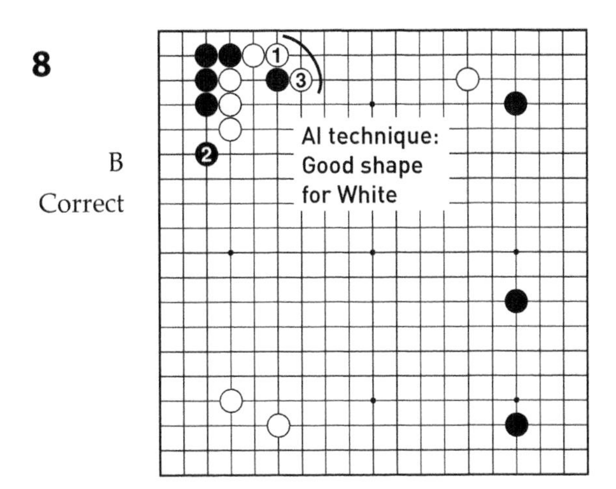

B

Correct

Crawling with 1 is the AI technique for connecting on the side. If Black now jumps out with 2, then White makes good shape with 3. The shape is similar to the one in diagram 6, but here it's better.

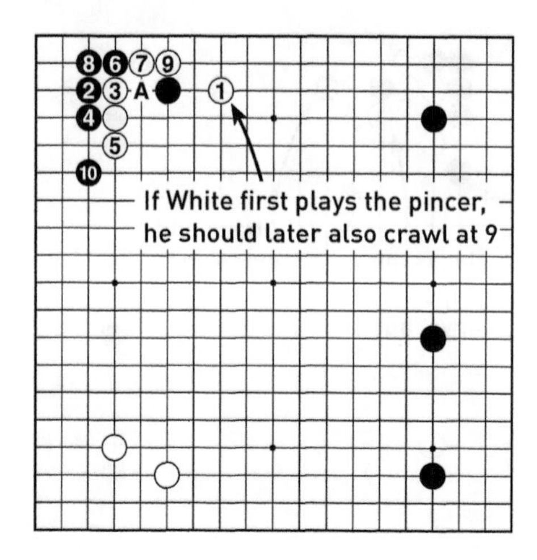

9

Crawling also after the pincer

The shape looks a little different when White first plays the pincer. In this shape, 9 is also played instead of A. It's not like this move didn't exist before, it was just played very rarely, as it was said to be disadvantageous.

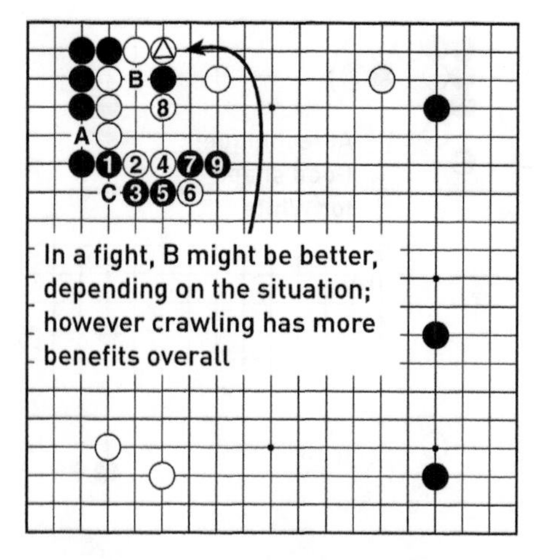

10

Why the move wasn't played

In case Black immediately pushes with 1, there is the downside that White can't aim at C, Black's box being quite safe due to the cutting point at B. Nevertheless, nowadays they say it's better to crawl on the side, because this way White forestalls blocking at the marked point.

11

Good move: White 3

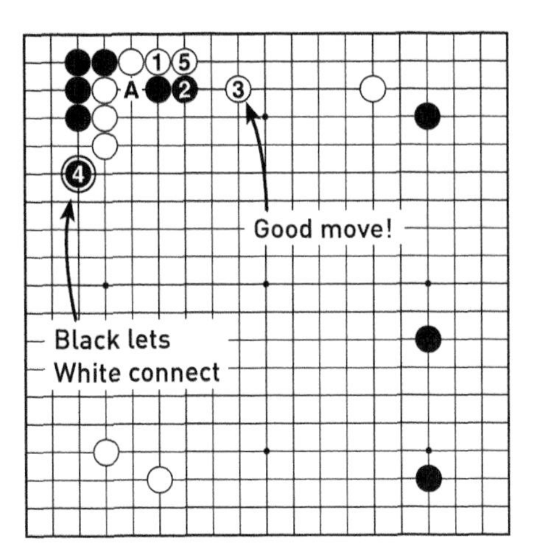

If Black extends at 2 in order to force White A, then White 3 is a good move instead of connecting. If Black now plays 4, White extends once more at 5. White is happy about not having played at A, but for Black it's also a playable variation.

12

Running impossible

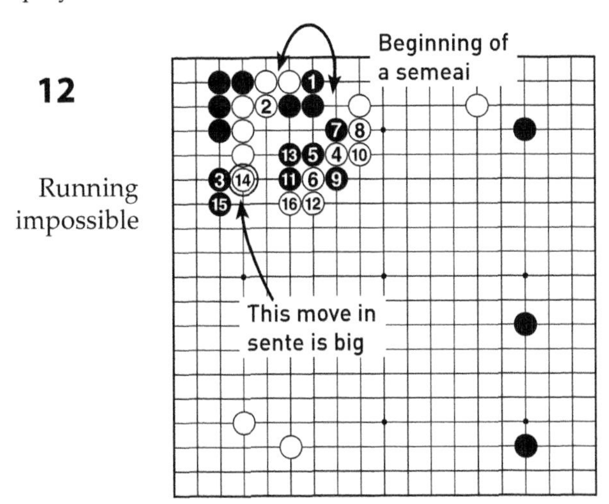

Black 1 in the game forces White to connect. Then Black jumps to 3. If White presses down with 4, Black cannot start running with 5 right away. It's not an easy fight for White either. White tries to surround Black up to 16. She can play 14 in sente.

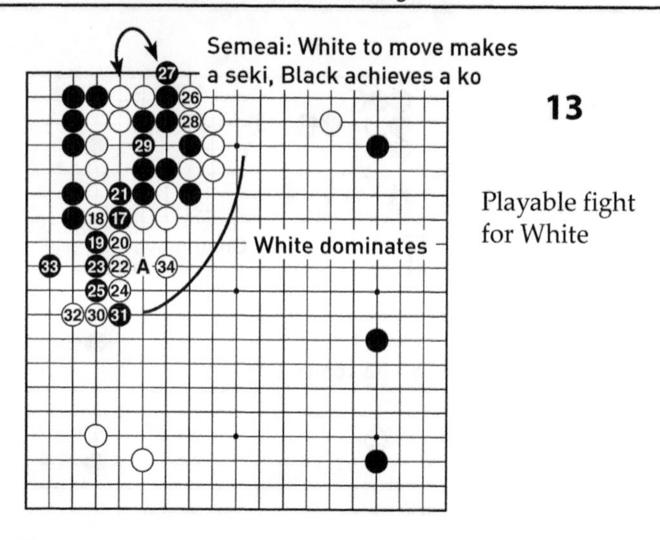

13

Playable fight for White

The sequence up to White 24 is difficult. It could be easier for White to sacrifice the stones. If a less complicated way of playing is preferred then White 23 instead of 22 is an option, followed by A. In this diagram White is superior.

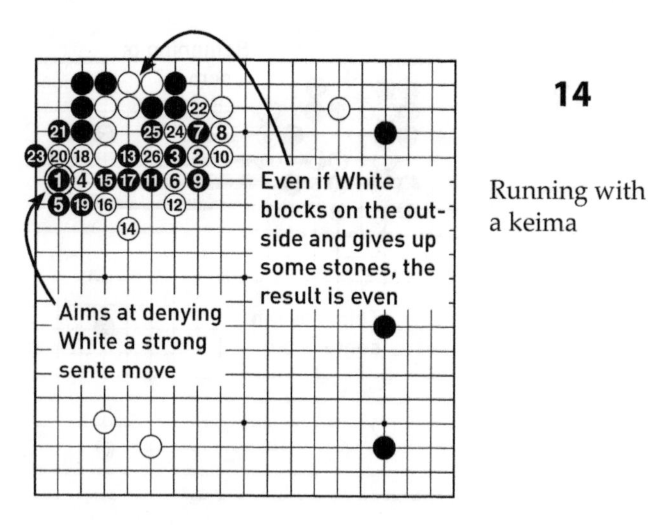

14

Running with a keima

The keima at 1 is a serious attempt at running with the Black stones. Instead of 2, White could play the attachment at 4 and then 6, or tenaciously surround Black, like in the diagram. Although White loses some stones here, she gets to set up a solid outer wall.

15

The game 1

Give up stones

Decoy

Developing the right side

After 6 it is advisable for Black to sacrifice the stones at the top. These stones are not easily captured though, and some aji remains at A. For good measure, Black also throws away the stone at 8 here, in order to further develop the right side.

16

The game 2

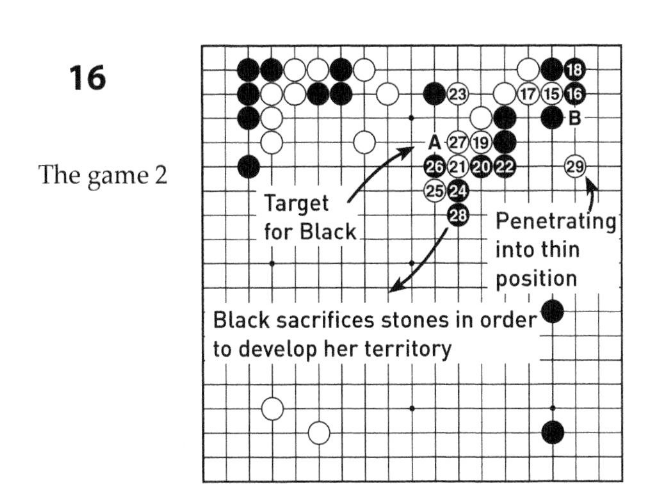

With the moves up to 28, Black conceded the upper side to White, while in exchange a large moyo emerged on the right side. Because Black connected at 18 instead of B, further blocking at A would be very severe for White. But White nonchalantly invaded at 29, since Black's position is thin.

The game

Moves after 53 omitted.
White wins by resignation.

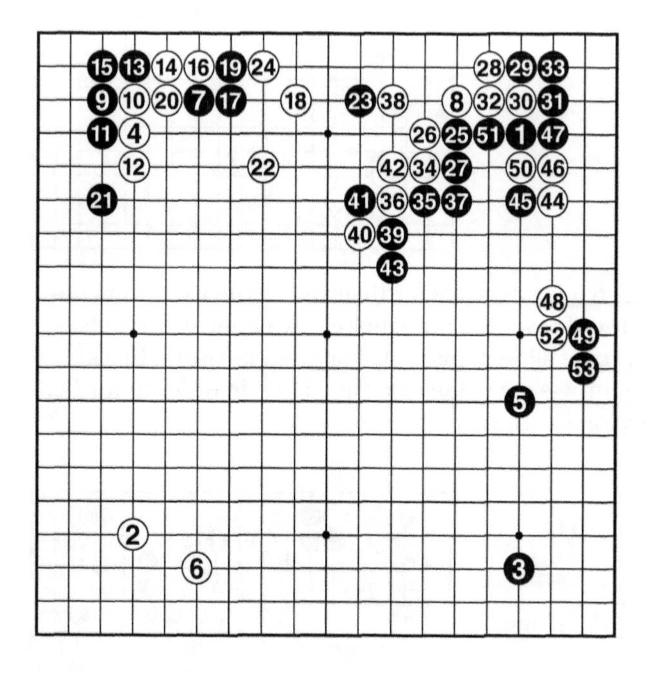

In the last game, we witness again the strongest Japanese pro player, this time in the international LG Cup: Iyama Yuta 9p vs Li Xuanhao 7p.

Game 14

After a local fight, Iyama takes the lead in this game. The answer to the problem in the diagram shows a way to respond to the keima at 11 that is currently en vogue. It's a powerful move and worth remembering.

(1 – 18)

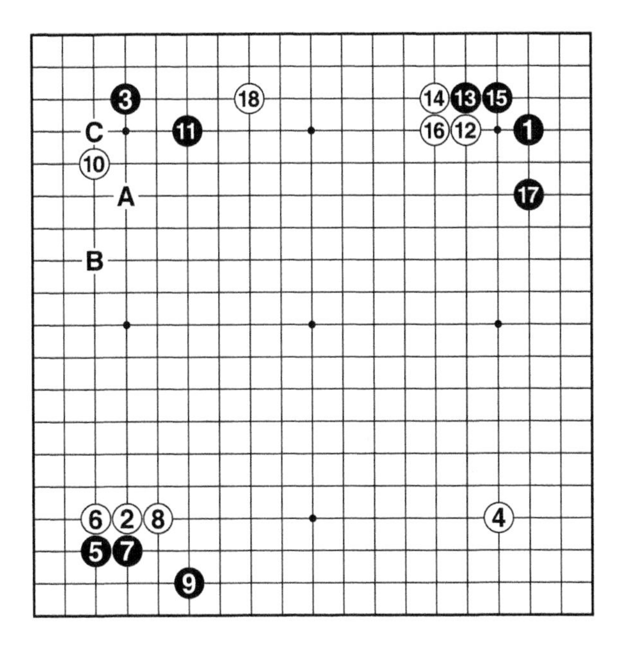

Black to play

After the approach with the low keima, AI recommends the keima at 11. The common answer used to be the kosumi, one point further left. White hits the weak point of the keima with 18, but Black has a strong answer to this.

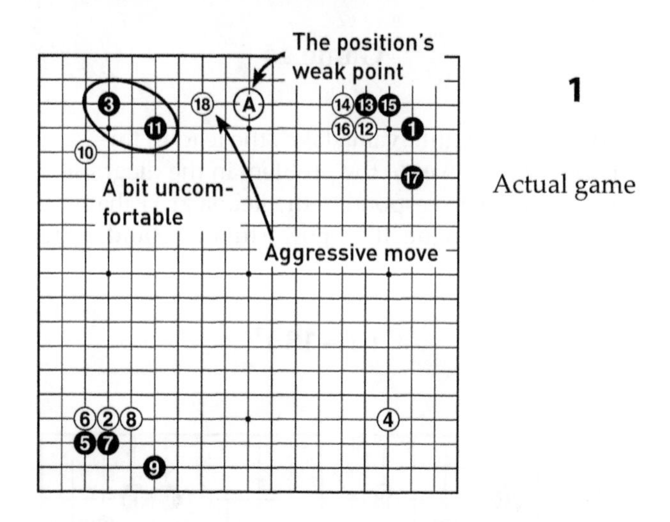

White 18 at A would not be a particularly active move. One should like to take better advantage of the opportunity. While it does leave a weakness, the intention is to exert pressure by attacking so that Black won't get into the position to throw a counterattack.

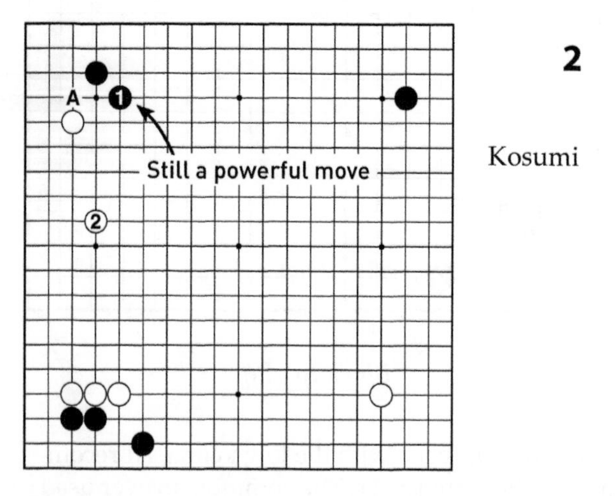

The kosumi at 1 has been played for more than a hundred years and is still considered a good move today. If Black next plays at A however, then the position of Black 1 is too close.

3

Shimari against an extension

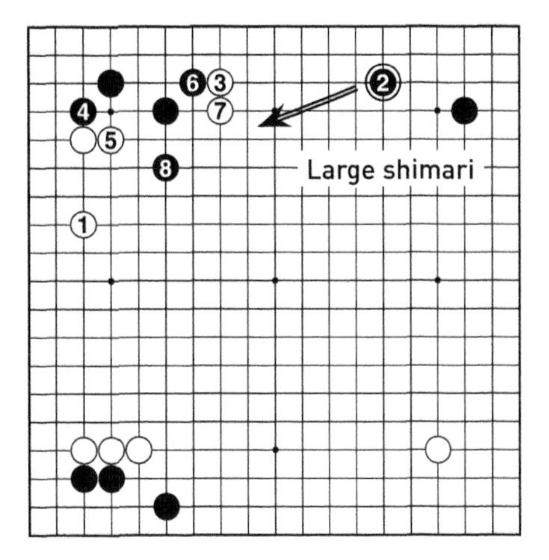

If White plays the extension to 1, then Black will take the large shimari at 2 in the upper right. Should White attack with 3, then Black needn't worry much, as he can play it safe with 4 to 8. The large shimari is well positioned in order to limit White's options for development.

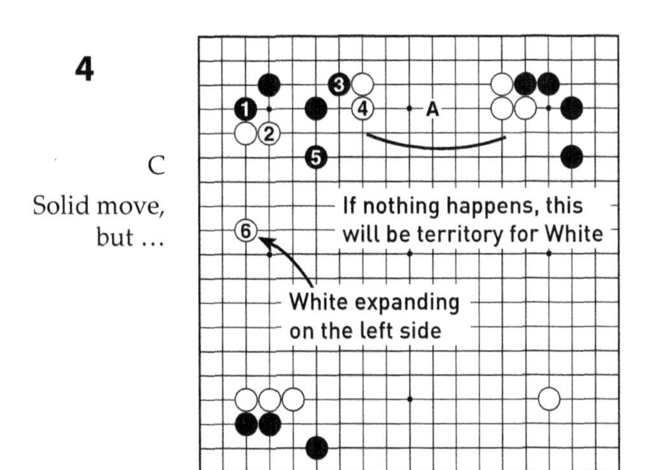

Kicking at 1 is a solid choice, but as a result White may obtain some broad territory on the upper side. Black doesn't like that, which is why he would like to invade at A. But it seems unclear how hard you can actually fight here.

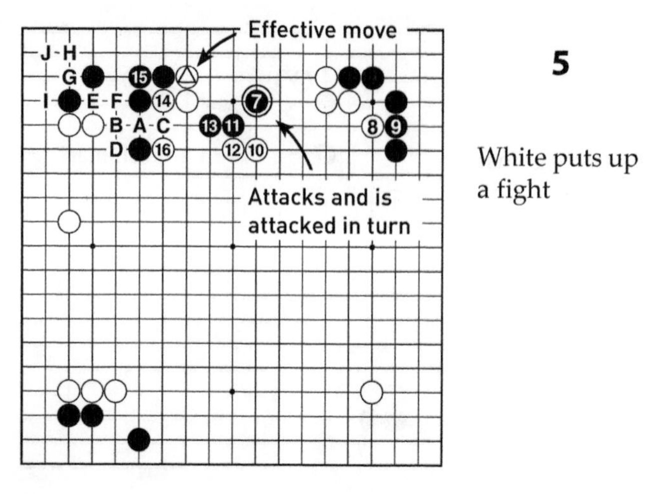

5

White puts up a fight

If Black attacks with 7, then White counters at 10. If the fight continues up to 16, then this is a good result for White. After the exchange of White 14 for Black 15, the sequence White A to Black J remains as an option.

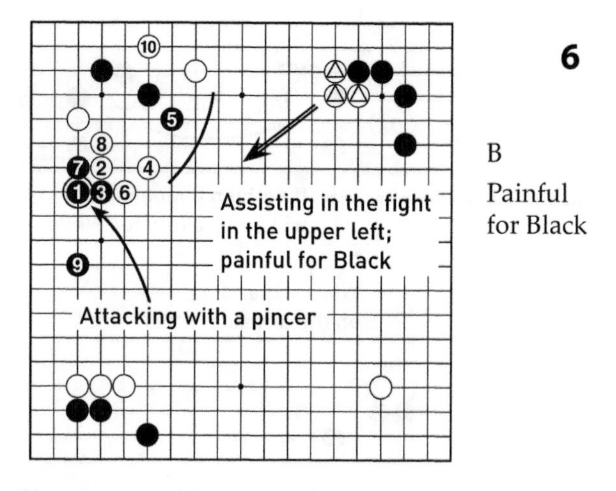

6

B

Painful for Black

The pincer at 1 is a natural move in order to punish White's tenuki. White should respond simply with 2 and 4. The sequence up to Black 9 is normal, but now Black gets attacked with the jump to 10.

7

Pressing down is perfect

Good width

Stones under attack looking connected and strong

Pressing down with 2 is the best response to the extension at 1. After this, Black would have to play once more in the corner at A to be safely alive, but that would be annoying for him. In the lower left, White has the sequence C to G in case Black approaches with B.

8

If Black plays tenuki

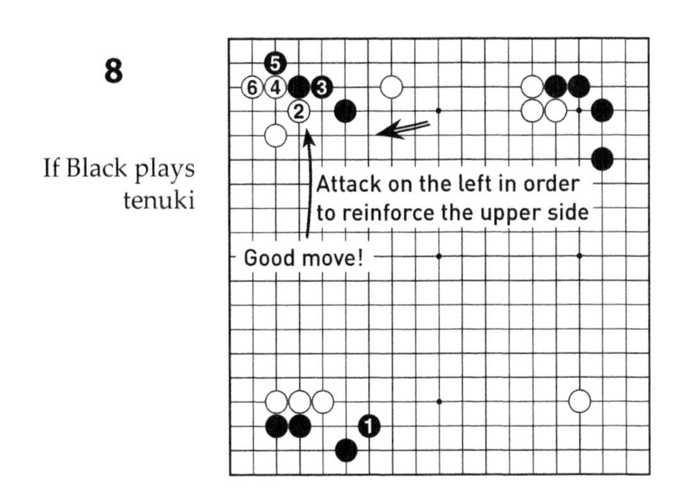

If Black plays tenuki with 1 then White should attach at 2, even if this looks a little strange. With 2 White hits the shape point. If Black stretches to 4 instead of 3, then White cuts at 3 and Black is in trouble. The sequence White 4, Black 5, White 2 would lead to Black 6.

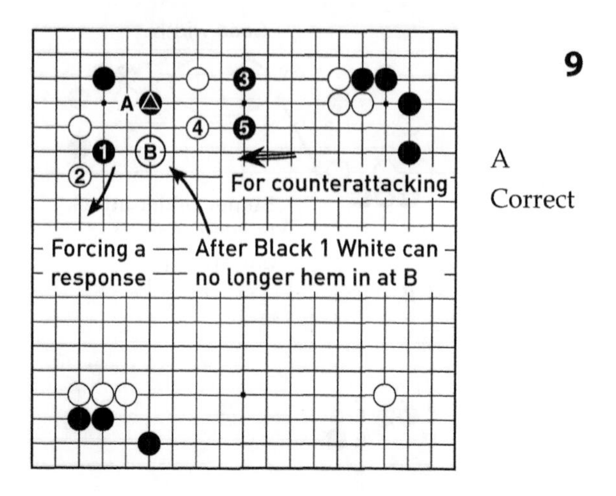

9

A
Correct

Black 1 is a move often seen when the marked stone is at A. Same as in the case of the kosumi, the intention behind Black 1 is to force White to answer at 2, while also building strength.

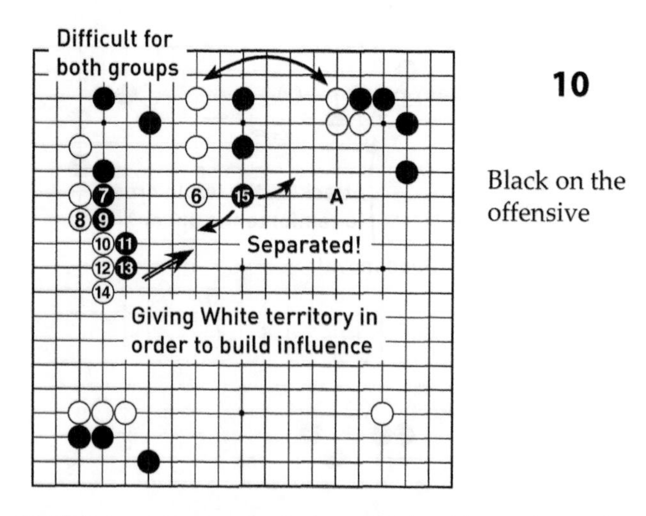

10

Black on the offensive

If White next jumps to 6, then Black will simply push with 7 and give the left side to White. Later Black can block at A. White is separated, and surviving with both of the groups is difficult.

11

Crawling

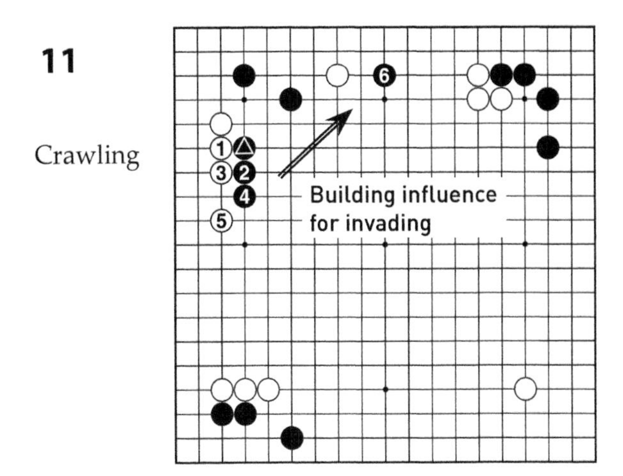

Crawling at 1 is a normal move, but the continuation is similar to the one in the previous diagram. Black invades at 6 and has a good fight.

12

Resistance

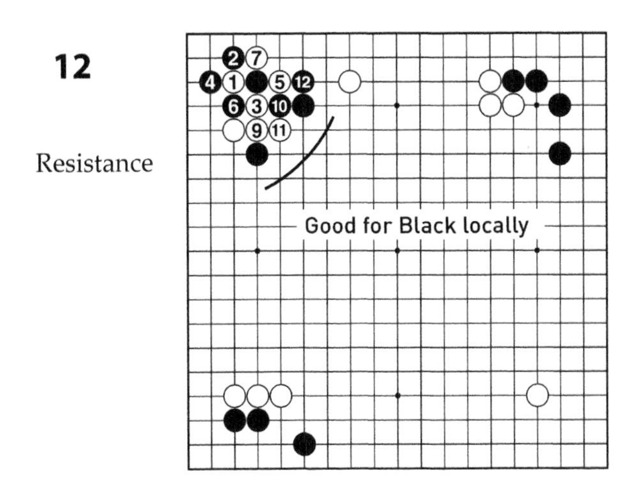

If White wants to make a base in the corner with 1 and 3, then Black wards him off with the atari at 4. The result after 12 is good for Black.

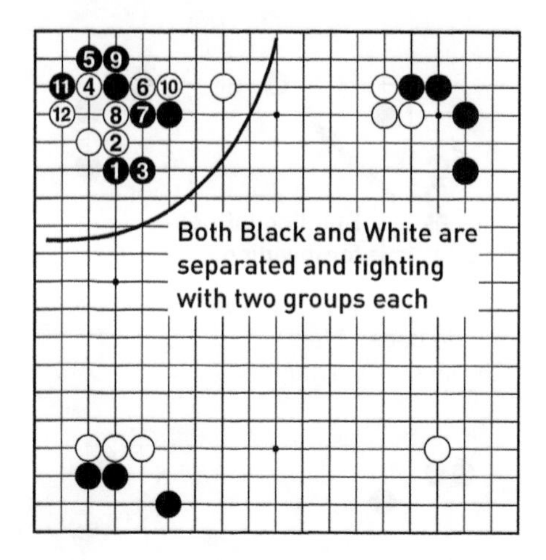

13

The game 1

White first pressed with 2 and then pushed into Black's thin position with 4 and 6. Black cut at 7 and a fight became unavoidable. With White 12 the fight lead to a ko.

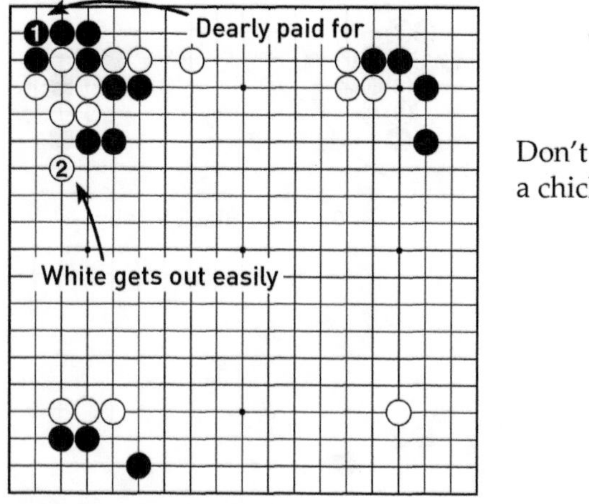

14

Don't be a chicken

If Black shuns the ko and connects at 1, things only get worse. The shape in the corner needs another move to make life. Now White simply jumps out with 2.

15

The game 2

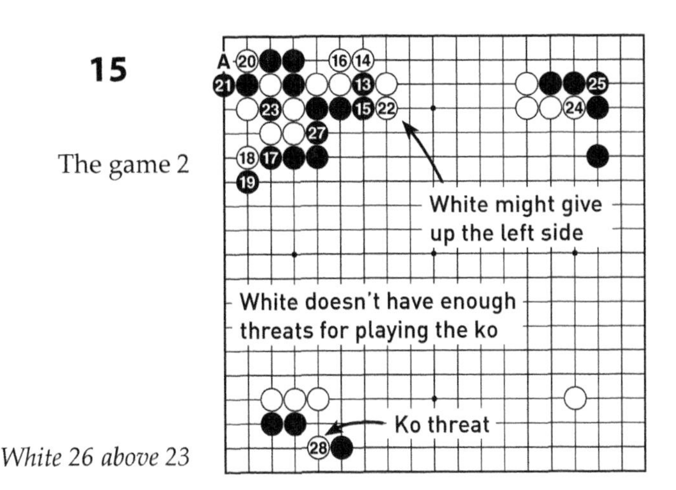

White 26 above 23

White cut at 20 in order to activate the ko (if Black plays at 23 instead of 21, White 21 follows). The ko is huge. Whether the game can be won after winning the ko still isn't sure though. Losses due to bad ko threats should be avoided. It is difficult for White to find sufficient and suitable ko threats.

16

Losses through the ko

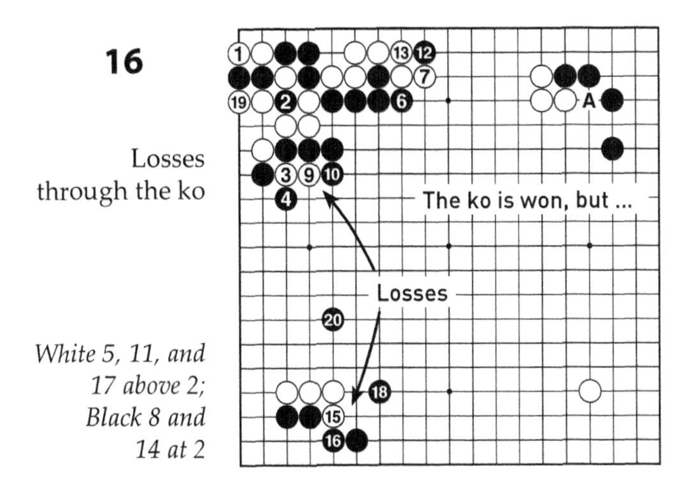

White 5, 11, and 17 above 2; Black 8 and 14 at 2

If White starts the ko with 1, the threat at A is not sufficient. There are threats such as 3, 9, and 15, but all of them come with a loss. If the price is so high, getting the corner isn't worth it.

The game

Moves after 55 omitted.
White wins by resignation.

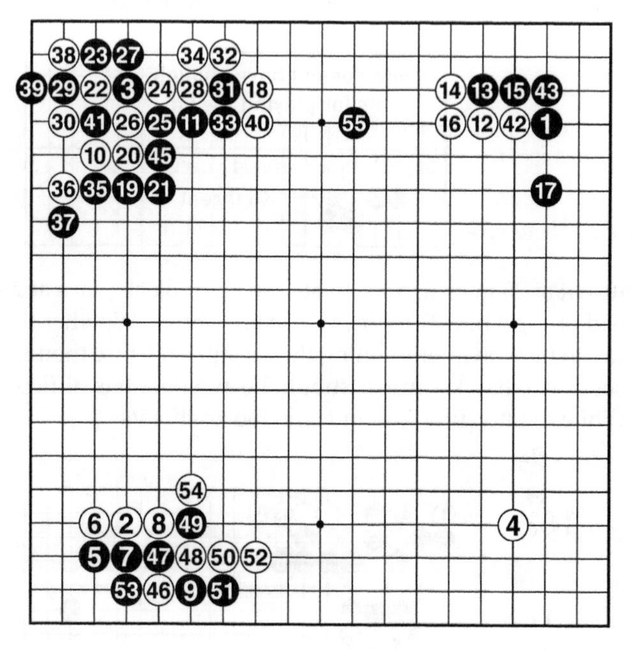

White 44 at 22

TSUMEGO IN PICTURES

THE ELEPHANT IN THE PADDY

by Izumi Hase

How do you catch an elephant? Can a question mark live? What is the relationship between go and music? And have you ever played go in a paddy field?

The Question Mark

This is one of the author's favourites. The first move is crucial. Black to live!

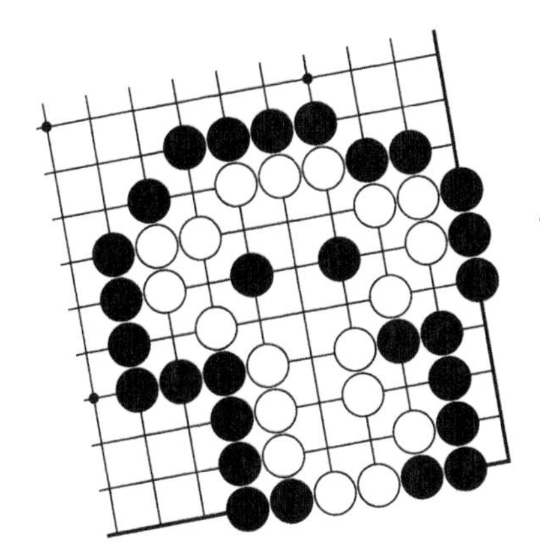

The Elephant

This is an elephant. There is a huge eye space but Black can kill the group in a beautiful way with a kind of combination that is rarely seen. Black to kill!

In this book you will experience go problems from a very different angle. The creative and amusing pictures composed of black and white stones feature amazing life-and-death exercises. Their degree of difficulty reaches from very easy to highly advanced – for beginners and dan players, for children and adults.

This book is dedicated to all those friends of go who are bored by dry exercises and endless reading. Get inspired by tsumego!

ISBN 978 3940 563 712

BLACK TO PLAY

TRAIN THE BASICS OF GO

This book series accompanies the go player from first steps until reaching shodan, the first master rank. A wide range of problems covering all fundamental topics is laid out across six books to meet the needs of any growing player.